# POTLUCK

# POTLUCK

A SPECIAL COLLECTION OF

## MORE THAN 400 RECIPES

FROM FAMILIES AND CHURCHES

ACROSS THE COUNTRY

EDITED BY DAVID JOACHIM

RODALE

© 2005 by Rodale Inc.

This 2009 edition is published for Barnes & Noble, Inc., by arrangement with Rodale Inc.

Cover photograph (family) © by Art Montes De Oca/FPG
Cover recipe photographs: Molded Beet Salad (page 144), California Oven-Fried Chicken (page 61),
Mile High Strawberry Pie (page 271), and Pennsylvania Dutch Green Beans (page 121).

Barnes & Noble, Inc.
122 Fifth Avenue
New York, NY 10011

Printed in the United States of America
Rodale Inc. makes every effort to use acid-free ∞, recycled paper ♺.

This book was originally published in 1980 as *The Yankee Church Supper Cookbook*
under the imprint Yankee Books by Rodale Inc.

Cover Design by Christina Gaugler
Interior Design by Christopher Rhoads
Interior Photography by Mitch Mandel/Rodale Images

Library of Congress Cataloging-in-Publication Data is on file with the publisher.

ISBN-13 978-1-60529-511-4
ISBN-10 1-60529-511-6

2   4   6   8   10   9   7   5   3   1   special sales hardcover

*In all Rodale cookbooks, our mission is to provide
delicious and nutritious recipes. Our recipes also
meet the standards of the Rodale Test Kitchen for
dependability, ease, practicality, and, most of all, great
taste. To give us your comments, call (800) 848-4735.*

We inspire and enable people to improve their lives and the world around them

For more of our products visit **rodalestore.com** or call 800-848-4735

*Thank you to all the wonderful cooks and recipe testers who contributed their recipes and expertise to this cookbook, and to the churches and their members who made this book possible.*

# Contents

A Word about the Recipes  ix

Conventions and Equivalents  x

Beef  1

Ham, Pork, and Lamb  34

Chicken and Turkey  55

Eggs, Cheese, Fish, and Seafood  80

Vegetable Sides and Casseroles  117

Soups and Salads  141

Breads and Breadstuffs  162

Cakes  191

Cookies and Bars  234

Pies, Pies, and More Pies  252

Puddings, Crisps, and Such  272

Recipes to Feed a Big Crowd  289

Index  310

Conversion Chart  324

# A Word about the Recipes

The idea for *Potluck* sprang from a conversation among food editors many years ago. One editor brought up the notion that some of the best food in any community was to be found at a local church supper or potluck, to which the best cooks in the area are asked to bring "your lasagna," or "that marvelous lemon pie," or whatever their specialty. Another remarked that rarely could one go home and duplicate such a local favorite from a recipe out of a standard cookbook. The only way to get such a recipe is to ask the cook.

*Potluck* has done just that. We contacted churches across the country and asked them for favorite recipes from parish members. The response was staggering—hundreds and hundreds of recipes poured in. The best ones were hand-picked on the basis of taste, originality, and accuracy. Then, we tested the best recipes and only the ones that taste-tested "delicious" made it into the book—over 400 in all. Here, you'll find recipes for all kinds of casseroles, including beef, pork, lamb, chicken, turkey, eggs and cheese, fish and seafood, and vegetables; plus all the fixin's like salads, breads, rolls, biscuits, doughnuts, cookies, cakes, pies, puddings, and other desserts. These dishes are perfect to take along to a potluck dinner or serve to family or friends. Most of the casseroles yield 6 to 8 generous servings and freeze well so that you can make them ahead of time. There is also a special section of "Recipes to Feed a Big Crowd" of anywhere from 15 to 100 in case you need to prepare food for a wedding or other large gathering.

While slick television cooking shows and high-profile celebrity cookbooks are the norm in today's high-tech world, *Potluck* harks back to a more community-oriented time in America's history. These are family recipes that have been passed down from generation to generation, evolving over decades and picking up the unique touch of every home cook or baker who has made them. Most recipes include a personal note from the cook as well as the cook's name and church. Every recipe uses easy-to-find, supermarket ingredients and simple cooking methods. Best of all, these recipes have been proven over time at countless family gatherings, church functions, and community get-togethers.

The original edition of this book was published in 1980. This revised edition has been carefully updated for the contemporary home cook. The recipes have been edited for greater clarity, and a fresh design gives them a streamlined look so that they are easier to follow, while the original voice and ingenuity of each recipe remains intact.

# Conventions and Equivalents

**Butter**—Wherever butter is called for in a recipe, either butter *or* margarine can be used with equal success. Butter is expensive, margarine more reasonable; there is a slight taste difference—no question, butter *is* better. But if you are used to margarine, use it by all means.

**Flour**—Unless otherwise specified in the recipe, flour means all-purpose white flour.

**Herbs**—These are dried unless fresh are specifically required.

**Oil, cooking or salad**—In all recipes except those for salads, cooking oil means liquid corn, safflower, or other vegetable oil, but *not* olive oil. Salad oil means your favorite kind—including olive oil.

**Shortening**—When a recipe calls for *shortening*, solid vegetable shortening such as Crisco is meant. Do not use cooking oil, lard, or bacon fat. In a pinch, margarine can be used since it is also solid vegetable shortening, but it is salted and does have a slightly different taste.

**Sour cream**—Where this is called for, the commercial product is meant, not cream soured in your refrigerator.

**Soured milk**—You can make your own by putting 2 tablespoons of lemon juice, vinegar, or other acidic liquid into a liquid measuring cup and adding milk to equal 1 cup. The thick texture is similar to buttermilk. You can also substitute buttermilk in recipes calling for soured milk.

**Spices**—These are ground unless whole cloves, crystalline ginger, or stick cinnamon is specified.

**Sugar**—Sugar is always white granulated sugar; confectioners' sugar and brown sugar are so specified. Brown sugar measurements are for packed amounts.

**Whipped salad dressing**—A Miracle Whip–type product.

**Baking, beating, or blending times**—These may vary slightly with different ovens, beaters, or blenders.

**Can sizes**—Sizes vary slightly with different brands, but similar size cans usually are similar in content. All can sizes given are based on popular brands with distribution.

**Oven heat**—Best results are always achieved by preheating the oven to the temperature required in the recipe. Please read recipe through before you begin to mix ingredients and *preheat oven* to specified temperature.

# Equivalents

Pinch or dash . . . . . . . . . . . . . . . . . . . . . . . . . . . . . . . . . . . less than ⅛ teaspoon

3 teaspoons . . . . . . . . . . . . . . . . . . . . . . . . . . . . . . . . . . . 1 tablespoon

2 tablespoons . . . . . . . . . . . . . . . . . . . . . . . . . . . . . . . . . 1 liquid ounce

4 tablespoons . . . . . . . . . . . . . . . . . . . . . . . . . . . . . . . . . ¼ cup

8 tablespoons . . . . . . . . . . . . . . . . . . . . . . . . . . . . . . . . . ½ cup

16 tablespoons . . . . . . . . . . . . . . . . . . . . . . . . . . . . . . . . 1 cup

1 cup . . . . . . . . . . . . . . . . . . . . . . . . . . . . . . . . . . . . . . . . 1 gill

2 cups . . . . . . . . . . . . . . . . . . . . . . . . . . . . . . . . . . . . . . . 1 pint

2 pints . . . . . . . . . . . . . . . . . . . . . . . . . . . . . . . . . . . . . . 1 quart

4 quarts . . . . . . . . . . . . . . . . . . . . . . . . . . . . . . . . . . . . . 1 gallon

2 cups liquid . . . . . . . . . . . . . . . . . . . . . . . . . . . . . . . . . 1 pound

2 cups butter . . . . . . . . . . . . . . . . . . . . . . . . . . . . . . . . . 1 pound

2 cups granulated sugar . . . . . . . . . . . . . . . . . . . . . . . . 1 pound

4 cups flour . . . . . . . . . . . . . . . . . . . . . . . . . . . . . . . . . . 1 pound

4 cups grated cheese . . . . . . . . . . . . . . . . . . . . . . . . . . 1 pound

Chocolate, 1 square unsweetened . . . . . . . . . . . . . . . . 1 ounce

8 egg whites . . . . . . . . . . . . . . . . . . . . . . . . . . . . . . . . . 1 cup (approximately)

16 egg yolks . . . . . . . . . . . . . . . . . . . . . . . . . . . . . . . . . . 1 cup (approximately)

Juice of 1 lemon . . . . . . . . . . . . . . . . . . . . . . . . . . . . . . 2–3 tablespoons

1 cup raw macaroni . . . . . . . . . . . . . . . . . . . . . . . . . . . . 2 cups cooked

1 cup raw rice . . . . . . . . . . . . . . . . . . . . . . . . . . . . . . . . 3–4 cups cooked

1 cup heavy cream . . . . . . . . . . . . . . . . . . . . . . . . . . . . . 2–2½ cups whipped cream

# Beef

In this chapter, you'll find all sorts of new and exciting ways to serve beef, from steaks and roasts to meat loaves and meatballs (with a wide range of savory sauces). When it comes to ground beef, the sky's the limit. Included here are ground beef pies and casseroles, a few different pasta dishes with meat sauce, and several superb beef stews.

Roast "Lion" 2

Beef Stroganoff 2

Old-Fashioned Boiled Dinner 3

Red Flannel Hash 3

Asian-Style Beef Strips 4

Beefsteak Pie 4

Chinese Pepper Steak 5

Glorified Hash 6

Beef/Ham Loaf with Mustard Sauce 6

Apple Meat Loaf 7

Barbecue Meat Loaf 8

Cheesy Meat Loaf 9

Boeuf Abdullah (Lebanese Meatballs) 9

Meatballs and Green Noodles 10

Magnificent Meatballs 11

Classic Meatballs 12

Meatball Sauces 13

Jackpot Pie 15

Italian Delight 15

Beef or Pork Chow Mein 16

Burger Bundles 16

Snowtime Beef Casserole 17

Mouthwatering Tamale Pie 18

Calorie Counter's Moussaka 18

Classic Lasagna Plus 2 19

Carry-Out Casserole 20

Quick Hamburger and Potato Casserole 20

One-Dish Ground Beef 21

Beef 'n' Bean Roll-Ups 22

Arcadian Shepherd's Pie 22

Babootie 23

Spaghetti Pie 24

Pastitsio (Greek Macaroni Pie) 25

Cannelloni 26

Company Beef Ragout 28

Boeuf Bourguignonne 29

Lazy Man's Beef Stew 30

Beef Chop Suey 30

Louisiana Beef Stew 31

Boeuf Flamande 32

Chili con Carne 33

# Roast "Lion"

The flavors of the two kinds of meat intermingle to create a delicious new taste.
Said to be Amish in origin.

Use equal portions of beef and pork roasts, any cut; total weight depends on crowd size. Allow at least ¼ pound per serving, consisting of a slice of each meat. Choose, for example, a beef rump roast and a pork shoulder of approximately the same weight. Place both meats in one roasting pan, cover the pan, and roast as for pork (35 minutes per pound; 45 minutes for rolled, boned pork roast) at 325°F until done. The beef will be well-done but not dry. Make gravy from the pan juice—the gravy is a most important part of Roast Lion—and serve with noodles or mashed potatoes.

*Gayle Flickinger, St. Mark's Episcopal Church, Canton, Ohio*

# Beef Stroganoff

Onion soup mix adds American ingenuity to this Russian classic.

| | |
|---|---|
| 2 **pounds sirloin beef steak, cut into shoestring strips ½" wide × 3" long and rolled in flour** | 1 **can (4 ounces) mushrooms** |
| | 3 **tablespoons flour** |
| | 1 **envelope onion soup mix** |
| | 2½ **cups water** |
| 2 **tablespoons butter** | ½ **cup sour cream** |

Brown beef strips in butter. Remove from skillet. Drain mushrooms, reserving liquid, and sauté in drippings in skillet. Remove from skillet. Into drippings stir flour and soup mix. Gradually add water and reserved mushroom liquid, blending well and stirring until thickened. Return meat and mushrooms to skillet, cover, and simmer, stirring from time to time, for about 20 minutes, or until meat is tender. Blend in sour cream and serve over hot egg noodles or boiled potatoes. ***Serves 6.***

*Mrs. Carlos Castro, Harwinton Congregational Church, Harwinton, Connecticut*

# Old-Fashioned Boiled Dinner

A classic dish known outside of New England as corned beef and cabbage.
Quantities as you like it; schedule given for dinner to be ready at noon.

*7:00 A.M.*    Rinse 4-pound piece of corned beef in water and place in bottom of large kettle. Cover completely with cold water. Add 2 tablespoons sugar, 1 teaspoon pickling spice, and 2 bay leaves. Bring to boiling point and boil 5 minutes. Skim scum off top, turn down heat, and simmer, covered, until tender.

*9:30 A.M.*    Scrub fresh beets within an inch of their lives and add to kettle, leaving skin and a good 4" of stem on each beet to prevent bleeding.

*10:00 A.M.*   Add peeled turnips, cut coarsely.

*11:00 A.M.*   Add peeled carrots and onions and a fair-sized cabbage cut into quarters. Add water as necessary to keep liquid level up.

*11:30 A.M.*   Add peeled, cut-up potatoes.

*12:00 noon* All should be cooked by now. Peel beets and arrange dinner on one large platter. Serve with hot cornbread or johnnycake, egg gravy (a regular white sauce with 1–2 chopped hard-boiled eggs added), horseradish, and a cruet of vinegar. Apple pie is the perfect dessert.

*P. Grimes, First Congregational Church of Pembroke, Pembroke, New Hampshire*

# Red Flannel Hash

If there is any Old-Fashioned Boiled Dinner left over, make this the next day.

Into a skilled put some bacon drippings (use bacon bits, too, if desired). Add all the Old-Fashioned Boiled Dinner leftovers to this skillet, chop, and mix together. Heat through and serve.

*P. Grimes, First Congregational Church of Pembroke, Pembroke, New Hampshire*

# Asian-Style Beef Strips

Similar to Chinese Pepper Steak (page 5) but does not need a pressure cooker.

2 pounds round steak, ¾" thick

2 tablespoons cooking oil or butter

2 cans (8 ounces each) sliced mushrooms, liquid reserved

4 tablespoons soy sauce

2 cloves garlic, minced, or ¼ teaspoon garlic powder

2 cups diced celery

4 tablespoons cornstarch

½ cup cold water

½ cup water chestnuts, sliced

Green pepper strips

Cut meat into strips ¼" wide and 3"–4" long. In large heavy saucepan, brown meat on all sides in oil or butter and drain. Add enough water to reserved mushroom liquid to equal 2 cups. Add mushroom liquid, soy sauce, and garlic. Cover and simmer 45 minutes over low heat. Add celery and mushrooms, replace cover, and continue cooking for 15–20 minutes longer. Combine cornstarch and cold water, stirring until well-blended. Gradually add to meat mixture, stirring constantly until liquid boils and thickens. Remove from heat and stir in water chestnuts. Top with pepper strips. Serve over hot rice. *Serves 6–8.*

*Ethel Innes, The Unitarian Church, Franklin, New Hampshire*

# Beefsteak Pie

A good sturdy version of an old favorite.

3 pounds lean beefsteak, cut into 1" cubes

¼ cup butter

¼ cup olive oil

3 tablespoons flour

1 can (10½ ounces) beef consommé

1 cup dry Burgundy

2 medium onions, thinly sliced

1 pound fresh mushrooms, sliced

1 cup chopped celery and leaves

1½ teaspoons dillweed

1 bay leaf

1 tablespoon Worcestershire sauce

Salt and pepper

1 unbaked 9" pie shell

1 tablespoon melted butter

Brown beef in butter and olive oil in large skillet. Sprinkle with flour. Stir in consommé, Burgundy, onions, mushrooms, celery, dillweed, bay leaf, and Worcestershire sauce. Add salt and pepper to taste. Cover and simmer for 45 minutes. Remove and discard bay leaf. Put the mixture into 2-quart casserole and cover with pie shell. Seal edges with fork, brush with melted butter, and bake at 350°F for 30 minutes, or until crust is golden brown. ***Serves 6–8.***

*Rhoda Miller, The Unitarian Church, Franklin, New Hampshire*

# Chinese Pepper Steak

If you have a pressure cooker, your church will benefit.

2 pounds boneless beef chuck
2 tablespoons fat
2 large onions, chopped
1½ cups sliced celery
2 cloves garlic, minced
1 teaspoon salt
⅛ teaspoon pepper

2 beef bouillon cubes, dissolved in 1 cup hot water
6 large green bell peppers, cut into eighths
2 tablespoons cornstarch
¼ cup cold water
1 tablespoon soy sauce

Trim fat from beef. Cut into thin strips about 1" × 2". Melt fat in pressure cooker. Add meat; cook over direct heat until browned, stirring frequently. Add onions, celery, garlic, salt, pepper, and bouillon. Close cooker, bring to 15 pounds pressure, and process for 3 minutes. Cool (letting pressure go down by itself). Add peppers. Simmer for 5 minutes. Add cornstarch blended with cold water. Cook until thickened. Add soy sauce. Serve with hot cooked rice or canned chow mein noodles. ***Serves 6–8.***

*Edie Blackstone, Concord Unitarian Church, Concord, New Hampshire*

# Glorified Hash

This versatile dish is good served for breakfast (with hot rolls and fruit),
lunch (with a salad), or supper (with a vegetable). We didn't think one can of hash
could provide 6 servings. In this recipe, it does!

1 can (15 ounces) corned beef
  hash
1 cup shredded cheese
1 tablespoon flour
¼ teaspoon salt

¼ teaspoon pepper
Pinch of nutmeg
Pinch of dry mustard
2 eggs, beaten
1¼ cups milk

Crumble hash in casserole or 9" × 9" pan and sprinkle with cheese. Combine flour, salt, pepper, nutmeg, mustard, eggs, and milk. Pour over corned beef mixture. Bake at 350°F for 35 minutes, or until custard is set. Partially cool. *Serves 6.*

*Mildred T. Melvin, Concord Unitarian Church, Concord, New Hampshire*

# Beef/Ham Loaf with Mustard Sauce

A meat loaf with a brand-new taste destined to become an old favorite.

6 slices dry bread or toast
1 pound ground beef
½ of 10¾-ounce can tomato soup
⅓ cup milk

1 egg
1 medium onion, finely chopped
1 pound cooked ham, ground

Make bread into crumbs. Combine crumbs with beef. Beat together soup, milk, egg, and onion. Combine with beef mixture. Add ham, mix well, and pack into 9" × 5" loaf pan. Bake at 350°F for 1 hour and 15 minutes. Let meat loaf stand 10 minutes after removing from oven. Serve with hot Mustard Sauce. *Serves 8–10.*

# Mustard Sauce

½ of 10¾-ounce can tomato soup
1 egg
1 tablespoon sugar

2 tablespoons prepared mustard
1 tablespoon vinegar
1 tablespoon butter

When loaf is almost done, beat soup, egg, sugar, mustard, vinegar, and butter with mixer. Mix well. Pour into saucepan and cook over medium heat, stirring constantly until mixture thickens. Keep warm in double boiler until meat loaf is done.

*Jeannette Perron, The Unitarian Church, Peterborough, New Hampshire*

# Apple Meat Loaf

An excellent loaf with a hint of apple-pie taste built right in.

1 large onion, finely chopped
2 tablespoons butter
2½ pounds ground beef
1½ cups fresh bread crumbs
2 cups finely chopped peeled and cored apples
3 eggs, beaten

1 tablespoon chopped parsley
½ teaspoon pepper
2 teaspoons salt
¼ teaspoon allspice
1 tablespoon prepared mustard or ¼ teaspoon dry mustard
¼ cup ketchup

Sauté onion in butter until soft. In a large bowl, combine onion, beef, bread crumbs, apples, eggs, parsley, pepper, salt, allspice, mustard, and ketchup. Form into loaf and place in 10" × 14" baking pan or pack into large greased loaf pan. Bake at 350°F for 1 hour. Remove from oven and let sit for 15 minutes before serving. *Serves 8–10.*

*Evelyn I. Johnson, Our Savior Lutheran Church, Hanover, New Hampshire*

# Barbecue Meat Loaf

The sauce makes the big difference here.

1 onion, minced
1½ tablespoons butter
1½ pounds ground beef
½ cup fresh bread crumbs

1 egg
½ cup tomato sauce
1½ teaspoons salt
¼ teaspoon pepper

Sauté onion in butter until soft. Combine with beef, bread crumbs, egg, tomato sauce, salt, and pepper. Mix well. Form into loaf and place in 10" × 14" baking pan. Pour ½ cup Barbecue Sauce (see below) over loaf. Bake at 350°F for 1 hour, basting from time to time with remaining sauce. *Serves 6.*

# Barbecue Sauce

1½ cups tomato sauce
½ cup water
2 tablespoons vinegar

3 tablespoons brown sugar
2 tablespoons prepared mustard
2 teaspoons Worcestershire sauce

Combine tomato sauce, water, vinegar, brown sugar, mustard, and Worcestershire sauce in saucepan, and heat until well-blended, stirring. Use as detailed above to baste meat loaf.

*Mona Winn, First Congregational Church, Littleton, New Hampshire*

# Cheesy Meat Loaf

Needs no gravy; good hot or cold.

½ cup chopped onion
¼ cup chopped green pepper
1 tablespoon butter
2 pounds ground beef
1 can (8 ounces) tomato sauce
2 eggs, beaten

4 ounces Cheddar or American cheese, grated
1 cup soft bread crumbs
¼ teaspoon thyme
1 teaspoon salt
½ teaspoon pepper

Sauté onion and green pepper in butter until onion is soft. Remove from heat and mix with beef, tomato sauce, eggs, cheese, bread crumbs, thyme, salt, and pepper. Blend well. Shape into loaf and place in 10" × 14" baking pan, or pack into large greased loaf pan. Bake at 350°F for 1 hour. *Serves 8–10.*

*Terry Lafiosca, The Unitarian Church, Franklin, New Hampshire*

# Boeuf Abdullah (Lebanese Meatballs)

With its distinctively tart yogurt sauce, this is particularly good served with wheat pilaf.

½ cup chopped onion
3 tablespoons butter
1 pound ground beef
1 egg, beaten
2 slices bread soaked in ½ cup milk

1 teaspoon salt
⅛ teaspoon pepper
1 cup dry bread crumbs
2 cups plain yogurt

Sauté onion in 1 tablespoon butter until transparent. Cool slightly. Mix with beef, egg, bread, salt, and pepper. Shape into 1¼" meatballs and roll them in dry bread crumbs. Brown slowly in remaining 2 tablespoons butter. Drain off all but 2 tablespoons fat. Gently spoon yogurt over and around meatballs. Simmer for 20 minutes. Serve hot with rice or bulgur wheat pilaf. For extra flavor, dissolve a bouillon cube in the water used to cook the rice. *Serves 6–8.*

*First Congregational Church, Littleton, New Hampshire*

# Meatballs and Green Noodles

Green noodles add their own colorful touch, but this is just as good with plain egg noodles. Meatballs and sauce can be made the day before and refrigerated, but allow 5–10 minutes longer for baking time. The recipe is easily multiplied to serve 12 or 24.

| | |
|---|---|
| 1½ cups soft bread crumbs | 1 cup milk |
| ½ cup tomato sauce | ½ cup grated Parmesan cheese |
| ¾ cup chopped onion | 2 tablespoons tomato paste |
| 4½ tablespoons shortening | ⅛ teaspoon garlic powder |
| 1¼ teaspoons salt | 4 ounces fresh mushrooms, |
| Pinch of pepper | sliced and sautéed in butter, or |
| 1 pound ground beef | 1 can (6 ounces), drained |
| ¼ cup flour | 8 ounces green (or egg) |
| 2 cans (15 ounces each) consommé | noodles |

Mix bread crumbs with tomato sauce. Sauté onion in 1½ tablespoons shortening. Combine with 1 teaspoon salt, pepper, and beef. Mix well. Shape into 2 dozen meatballs 1¼" in diameter. Sauté in remaining 3 tablespoons shortening in skillet until brown on all sides. Remove from skillet while making sauce.

Measure shortening left in skillet and add or pour off until you have ¼ cup in pan. Blend in flour smoothly over low heat. Add consommé and milk, stirring constantly until thickened. Add cheese, tomato paste, garlic powder, remaining ¼ teaspoon salt, and mushrooms.

Cook noodles according to package directions. In 3-quart greased casserole dish, place half the noodles, all the meatballs, and ⅓ of the sauce. Then put in rest of the noodles and pour remaining sauce over all. Bake at 350°F for about 20 minutes, or until bubbling. Serve with additional Parmesan cheese if you like. *Serves 6.*

*Flossie H. Ukena, Sherman Congregational Church, Sherman, Connecticut*

# Magnificent Meatballs

Good-sized meatballs wrapped in crisp bacon with a distinctive sour cream
and tomato sauce. They may be made ahead and reheated without danger of drying out.
The recipe is easily doubled or tripled for large groups.

| | |
|---|---|
| 4 pounds ground beef | 1½ teaspoons ground black pepper |
| 4 cups canned tomatoes (with juice) | 1 teaspoon oregano |
| 2 cups fine bread crumbs | 1 tablespoon finely chopped onion |
| 2 eggs | 24 slices bacon |
| 3½ teaspoons salt | 1½ cups sour cream |

Mix together beef, 2 cups tomatoes, bread crumbs, eggs, salt, pepper, oregano, and onion. Form into 24 good-sized (about 3" diameter) meatballs. Wrap each with bacon slice, overlapping bacon carefully. Place meatballs in large flat baking dish (roasting pan is handy) so that overlapped bacon is on bottom. Bake at 400°F for 45 minutes, or until bacon is crisp. Remove from oven and pour off bacon fat. Combine sour cream and remaining 2 cups tomatoes, pour over meatballs, and return to oven. Turn off heat. Serve with rice when sauce is hot. (To reheat from refrigerated state, put in 275°F oven for 30–40 minutes.) *Serves 12.*

*Elizabeth F. Bauhan, All Saints Church, Peterborough, New Hampshire*

# Classic Meatballs

This excellent recipe covers just about any need you'll ever have for meatballs!

1½ cups bread crumbs, soaked in ¾ cup milk or tomato juice, or 1½ cups dry stuffing mix, soaked in 3 cups liquid

2 eggs, beaten

1 large onion, chopped and sautéed in 2 tablespoons butter

2 pounds ground beef, or 1 pound beef, ½ pound ground pork, and ½ pound ground veal

2 teaspoons salt

¼ teaspoon pepper

Optional additions (use only 1 per batch): 4 tablespoons grated Parmesan cheese with 1 tablespoon mixed Italian seasoning; 1 cup applesauce with ½ teaspoon nutmeg, mace, or allspice; 2 tablespoons steak sauce or Worcestershire sauce

¼ cup butter

Mix soaked bread crumbs or stuffing mix, eggs, and onion in large bowl. Mixture will be runny. Mix in all the ground meat, salt, pepper, and any optional addition you choose to use. If mixture is too stiff, add a little more liquid until manageable. Roll into small meatballs, using about 1 rounded teaspoon of meat for each Swedish meatball, or 1 rounded tablespoon for Italian meatballs. Sauté meatballs in butter in large frying pan, turning frequently to brown evenly and to keep meatballs rounded. (It will probably take 3 full pans to use up all the meat. It makes a lot, but you will be amazed how fast they disappear.) Lift out meatballs carefully when done and do next panful in the same butter, especially if you are going to freeze them.

If you want to freeze raw meatballs, paper plates work well as a base, but be careful not to freeze them in a lump—they'll be almost impossible to get apart. Put raw meatballs in a bull's-eye pattern on the plate, slip into a freezer bag or cover with plastic wrap, and freeze. Makes 48 small meatballs. *Serves 6 for dinner, 8 for buffet.*

*Doris E. Berndtson, Woodmont United Church of Christ, Milford, Connecticut*

# Meatball Sauces
## Sour Cream Sauce

¼ cup flour
¼ cup melted butter or pan
   drippings
1 cup water

2 cups sour cream
1 tablespoon dillweed
Salt and pepper

Add flour to melted butter or drippings over low heat, blending well until smooth. Gradually add water, stirring, then sour cream and dill, stirring constantly until mixture bubbles and thickens. Do not boil. Season to taste with salt and pepper. Add meatballs and simmer gently until heated through. *Serves 8.*

*Kathy Paranya, The Unitarian Church, Franklin, New Hampshire*

## Brown Sauce

¼ cup butter
¼ cup flour

2 cups broth
Celery leaves or flakes

Melt butter and blend smoothly with flour. Gradually add broth, stirring constantly until smooth. Add several celery leaves or flakes. Put in meatballs and simmer gently to heat through. Remove and discard celery leaves before serving. *Serves 6.*

## Cream Gravy

3 tablespoons butter
½ cup flour
3 cups beef stock

1 cup cream
Salt and pepper

Melt butter and add flour, stirring to golden paste. Add stock gradually, stirring briskly to avoid lumps. Add cream and season to taste with salt and pepper. Simmer 4–5 minutes. Add meatballs and let cook in gravy over low heat for 40 minutes. *Serves 8–10.*

# Sweet and Sour Sauce

1 tablespoon cooking oil
¾ cup pineapple juice
2 tablespoons cornstarch
1 teaspoon soy sauce
¼ cup vinegar

½ cup water
½ cup sugar
2 slices pineapple, cut into pieces
1 large green pepper, cut into strips lengthwise

Mix oil with pineapple juice and cook over low heat for a few minutes. Mix cornstarch with soy sauce, vinegar, water, and sugar. Add to hot pineapple juice and stir until thickened. Add meatballs, pineapple pieces, and green pepper. Simmer until meatballs are hot. *Serves 6–8.*

*Mrs. Albert F. Porter, Chocorua, New Hampshire*

# Mushroom Sauce

¼ cup minced onion
3 tablespoons cooking oil
3 tablespoons flour

1½ cups chicken broth
1 can (6 ounces) mushrooms, drained

Sauté onion in oil until golden. Add flour and blend to smooth paste. Gradually add broth, stirring. Cook, stirring, until sauce thickens. Add mushrooms and meatballs and simmer gently until heated through. *Serves 6.*

*Barbara Lockhart, United Church of Christ, Keene, New Hampshire*

# Jackpot Pie

2 pounds ground beef
1 tablespoon butter
½ cup chopped onion
  Salt and pepper
2 cans (10¾ ounces each) tomato soup
3 cups water
8 ounces egg noodles
2 tablespoons Worcestershire sauce
½ cup sliced stuffed olives
2 cans (20 ounces each) cream-style corn
1 cup grated cheese (any kind)

Brown beef in butter. Remove from pan and sauté onion until tender. Add to meat along with salt and pepper to taste, soup, and water. Add uncooked noodles and simmer 10 minutes. Add Worcestershire sauce, olives, corn, and cheese. Bake at 350°F for 40 minutes. *Serves 8.*

*Ruth Higgins, Tenney United Methodist Church, Salem, New Hampshire*

# Italian Delight

1 pound ground beef
½ pound bulk sausage
1 large onion, chopped
  Pinch of garlic powder
½ teaspoon salt
⅛ teaspoon pepper
1 can (4 ounces) mushrooms
8 ounces egg noodles
1 can (10¾ ounces) tomato soup
1 can (6 ounces) tomato paste
1 can (17 ounces) tomatoes
1 cup grated Cheddar cheese

Combine beef, sausage, onion, garlic powder, salt, and pepper. Steam 3–5 minutes in covered heavy skillet, until redness disappears from beef. Do not brown. Add mushrooms (with juice). Transfer to greased 2-quart baking dish. Cook noodles and drain. Add soup, tomato paste, and tomatoes (with juice) to noodles. Stir well. Add noodles and half the cheese to meat, mixing well. Sprinkle remainder of cheese over top. Bake at 350°F for 30 minutes, or until casserole bubbles and cheese is melted. *Serves 6.*

*Marcia Fletcher, St. Anne's Episcopal Church, Calais, Maine*

# Beef or Pork Chow Mein

A Chinese delight.

1 pound ground beef
or pork
1 medium onion, chopped
2 tablespoons butter
1 teaspoon salt
2 cups diced celery
1 cup water
1 can (16 ounces) mixed Chinese
vegetables, drained

1 can (16 ounces) bean sprouts,
drained
1 can (4 ounces) sliced
mushrooms, drained
1 can (13½ ounces) pineapple
tidbits or chunks
2 tablespoons cold water
2 tablespoons cornstarch
1 tablespoon soy sauce

Cook meat and onion in butter until lightly browned. Add salt, celery, and 1 cup water. Bring to boil. Cover and simmer until celery is crisp but soft (about 10 minutes). Drain pineapple, reserving ¼ cup of juice. Add Chinese vegetables, bean sprouts, mushrooms, and pineapple, and cook until hot. Combine 2 tablespoons water and cornstarch. Stir in soy sauce and reserved pineapple juice. Add to meat mixture. Cook until slightly thickened, stirring constantly. Serve hot with cooked rice or chow mein noodles. *Serves 6.*

*Carolyn Ramsbotham, St. Thomas More Church, Durham, New Hampshire*

# Burger Bundles

One good way to make meat go further.

2 pounds ground beef
⅔ cup milk
2 cups herb-seasoned bread
stuffing
2 cans (10¾ ounces each)

condensed cream soup
(mushroom, celery, or your
choice)
4 teaspoons Worcestershire sauce
2 tablespoons ketchup

Mix beef with milk. Divide into 10 patties. On waxed paper, flatten each patty to form a 6" circle. Put equal amounts of stuffing in center of each. Draw edges over stuffing and seal. Place in 3-quart casserole. Combine soup, Worcestershire sauce, and ketchup, and heat gently until smooth and bubbly. Pour over meat. Bake uncovered at 350°F for 45–50 minutes. ***Serves 10.***

*Jill Child, The Unitarian Church, Franklin, New Hampshire*

# Snowtime Beef Casserole

This attractive dish is like a cannelloni without the pasta and the extra effort. Exceptional. This casserole will warm up even the coldest heart in wintertime.

| | |
|---|---|
| 1 **pound ground beef** | ¼ **teaspoon pepper** |
| 2 **cans (8 ounces each) tomato sauce** | 2 **packages (10 ounces each) frozen chopped spinach, cooked and drained** |
| ¼ **cup chopped onion** | 1 **pint cottage cheese** |
| 1 **teaspoon parsley flakes** | 1 **package (8 ounces) mozzarella cheese slices** |
| ½ **teaspoon oregano** | |
| 1 **teaspoon basil** | |
| ¾ **teaspoon salt** | |

Brown beef in skillet; pour off fat. Stir in tomato sauce, onion, parsley, oregano, basil, ½ teaspoon salt, and pepper. Simmer uncovered 10 minutes, stirring occasionally. Combine spinach with cottage cheese and remaining ¼ teaspoon salt. Spoon spinach mixture around edge of baking dish (9" × 13"). Pour beef mixture into center. Cut each mozzarella slice into 3 lengthwise strips. Arrange in lattice design over meat. Bake at 375°F for 20 minutes. ***Serves 8.***

*Ruth Messer, Concord Unitarian Church, Concord, New Hampshire*

# Mouthwatering Tamale Pie

A longtime Southwestern favorite.

2 pounds ground chuck
1 large onion, chopped
1 can (16 ounces) whole tomatoes
1 can (16 ounces) whole-kernel corn, drained
2 tablespoons chili powder

Salt and pepper
1 can (6 ounces) pitted black olives, drained
3 cups milk
2 cups cornmeal
2 cups shredded Cheddar cheese

Brown together chuck and onion. Add tomatoes (with juice), corn, chili powder, and salt and pepper to taste. Simmer for 30 minutes. Remove from heat and add olives. Mix milk with cornmeal and cook until thickened. Line bottom and sides of greased 3-quart casserole dish with cooked cornmeal mush. Add meat mixture and top with grated cheese. Bake at 325°F for 30 minutes. *Serves 8.*

*Phyllis Shattuck, All Saints Episcopal Church, Pasadena, California*

# Calorie Counter's Moussaka

Try this for something ethnic and different. Tastes good warmed up the next day, too.
This recipe has 378 calories per serving for 6, or 248 calories for 8.

1 pound lean ground beef
1 medium onion, chopped
5 cups peeled and cubed eggplant
1 can (8 ounces) tomatoes, cut up
1 can (16 ounces) mushrooms, drained
¼ cup chopped fresh parsley
1 clove garlic, minced

½ teaspoon oregano
½ teaspoon rosemary, crushed
¼ teaspoon cinnamon
Salt and pepper
2 eggs
8 ounces Neufchâtel cheese, cut up
1 cup plain yogurt
¼ teaspoon salt

In skillet cook beef and onion until meat is browned. Drain off fat. Stir in eggplant, tomatoes (with juice), mushrooms, parsley, garlic, oregano, rosemary, cinnamon, and salt and pepper to taste. Cook, uncovered, for 15 minutes, stirring occasionally. Turn into rectangular baking dish. Use electric mixer or blender to combine eggs, cheese, yogurt, and salt. Mix or blend until smooth. Pour over meat. Bake at 350°F for 15–20 minutes. *Serves 6–8.*

*Dorothea Ruggles, First Congregational Church, Littleton, New Hampshire*

# Classic Lasagna Plus 2

The eggs and zucchini are the two pluses—they make the "total" difference!

| | |
|---|---|
| 1 **pound ground beef** | 1 **teaspoon garlic powder** |
| ¾ **cup chopped onions** | ½ **teaspoon pepper** |
| 2 **tablespoons olive oil** | ½ **teaspoon oregano** |
| 1 **can (28 ounces) Italian tomatoes** | 8 **ounces lasagna noodles** |
| | 1 **pound cottage or ricotta cheese** |
| 2 **cans (6 ounces each) tomato paste** | 8 **ounces mozzarella cheese, shredded** |
| 2 **cups water** | 1 **cup grated Parmesan cheese** |
| 4 **tablespoons chopped parsley** | 3 **hard-boiled eggs, sliced** |
| 1 **teaspoon salt** | 2 **cups thinly sliced zucchini** |

In large heavy pan, lightly brown beef and onion in oil. Add tomatoes (with juice), tomato paste, water, parsley, salt, garlic powder, pepper, and oregano, and simmer uncovered about 30 minutes. Meanwhile, cook lasagna noodles as directed. In 9" × 13" baking pan, spread about 1 cup of sauce. Then alternate layers of noodles, sauce, cottage or ricotta cheese, mozzarella, Parmesan, hard-boiled eggs, and zucchini, ending with sauce, mozzarella, and Parmesan. Bake at 350°F for 40–50 minutes, or until lightly browned and bubbling. *Serves 6–8.*

*Sally Hale, Dublin Community Church, Dublin, New Hampshire*

# Carry-Out Casserole

A creamy, lasagna-like dish with an unusual fillip—ripe olives.

| | |
|---|---|
| 8 ounces wide egg noodles | 1 teaspoon salt |
| 2 pounds ground beef | ½ teaspoon pepper |
| 3 tablespoons butter | ¼ cup chopped black olives |
| 2 cups tomato sauce | ⅓ cup grated onion |
| 2 tablespoons flour | ½ cup chopped green pepper |
| 2 cups cottage cheese | ⅓ cup grated Parmesan cheese |
| 1 cup sour cream | (optional) |

Cook noodles according to package directions in boiling salted water. Drain. Brown beef in 2 tablespoons butter. Mix tomato sauce with flour, add to beef, and simmer for 10 minutes. Mix cottage cheese with sour cream, salt, pepper, and olives. Sauté onion and green pepper in remaining 1 tablespoon butter and add to cottage cheese mixture.

Place half the noodles in greased 3-quart casserole dish. Spread with cottage cheese mixture, top with remaining noodles, and cover all with beef mixture. Sprinkle, if desired, with grated cheese. Bake at 350°F for 30–40 minutes, or until heated through. *Serves 12.*

*Marjorie M. Stultz, Concord Unitarian Church, Concord, New Hampshire*

# Quick Hamburger and Potato Casserole

You can put this one together in a jiffy.

| | |
|---|---|
| 2⅔ cups instant mashed potato flakes | 1 can (12 ounces) corn (with sweet peppers if you can find it), *un*drained |
| 1½ cups sour cream | 1 teaspoon salt |
| 1 cup water | ¼–½ teaspoon pepper |
| 1 pound ground beef | ⅛ teaspoon oregano |
| 3 tablespoons chopped onion, or 1 tablespoon dried minced onion | ½ cup diced American or Cheddar cheese |
| 1 can (15 ounces) tomato sauce | |

In ungreased 9" × 13" baking dish, blend potato flakes with sour cream and ½ cup water. Mixture should be crumbly. If not, add more potato flakes. Pat firmly into bottom of pan. Brown beef (with onions, if using fresh). Add dried onion (if not using fresh), remaining ½ cup water, tomato sauce, corn, salt, pepper, and oregano. Spoon beef mixture over potatoes. Sprinkle with cheese. Bake at 350°F for 25–30 minutes. This recipe is easily doubled. **Serves 6.**

*Margaret Johnson, Trinity Episcopal Church, Claremont, New Hampshire*

# One-Dish Ground Beef

The title says it all.

1 **pound ground beef**
1 **cup chopped onion**
1 **can (10¾ ounces) cream of mushroom soup**
2 **cups chopped celery**
1 **cup uncooked long-grain rice**

1 **can (6 ounces) mushrooms, drained**
⅓ **cup soy sauce**
2 **cups boiling water**
½ **teaspoon salt**
¼ **teaspoon garlic powder**

**B**rown meat and drain, reserving fat in skillet. Remove meat to 2-quart baking dish. Sauté onion in reserved fat. Drain off fat and mix onion with meat. Add soup, celery, rice, mushrooms, soy sauce, water, salt, and garlic powder, and stir to combine. Bake at 350°F for 1 hour, or until celery is tender. Cover dish for last half-hour of baking. **Serves 6.**

*Bonnie Ridge, The Unitarian Church, Keene, New Hampshire*

# Beef 'n' Bean Roll-Ups

Children love these. Fun and filling.

| | |
|---|---|
| ¼ cup butter | 1½ pounds ground beef |
| 2 cups flour | 2 cans (16 ounces each) pork and |
| 2 teaspoons baking powder | beans |
| ½ teaspoon salt | ½ cup chopped onion |
| ½ cup milk | ¼ cup ketchup |
| ¾ cup molasses | Salt and pepper |

Cut butter into flour, baking powder, and salt. Add milk and ¼ cup molasses, mix well, and form into large ball. Roll out dough on floured surface to 9" × 12" rectangle. Brown meat and add to it pork and beans, onion, remaining ½ cup molasses, ketchup, and salt and pepper to taste. Bring meat mixture to boil. Spread ¾ cup of meat mixture over rolled-out dough. Starting with 12" side, roll up dough with meat inside and cut the roll into twelve 1" slices. Pour rest of meat mixture into 9" × 13" baking dish and top with dough slices. Bake at 400°F for 20–25 minutes. ***Serves 6–8.***

*Janet M. Secchiaroli, First Church of Christ, New London, Connecticut*

# Arcadian Shepherd's Pie

A "soufflé" potato topping makes something special out of this shepherd's pie.

| | |
|---|---|
| 1½ pounds ground beef | 2 eggs, separated |
| 2 onions, minced | ½ cup cream |
| 3 tablespoons + ½ cup butter | ⅛ teaspoon garlic powder |
| 1 tablespoon ketchup | 8–10 potatoes, peeled, boiled, and |
| 1 teaspoon Worcestershire sauce | mashed |
| Salt and pepper | ⅓ cup grated Parmesan cheese |
| Beef stock | |

Brown beef in 3 tablespoons butter. Add onions and sauté until golden. Mix meat and onions with ketchup and Worcestershire sauce. Season to taste with salt and pepper. Add a little beef stock and cook, covered, over low heat for 15–20 minutes. Beat egg yolks until light, whites until stiff. Beat yolks, cream, remaining ½ cup butter, and garlic powder into mashed potatoes. Gently fold in beaten egg whites. Put meat mixture into casserole and top with potatoes. Sprinkle with Parmesan cheese and bake at 350°F until puffed and browned. *Serves 6–8.*

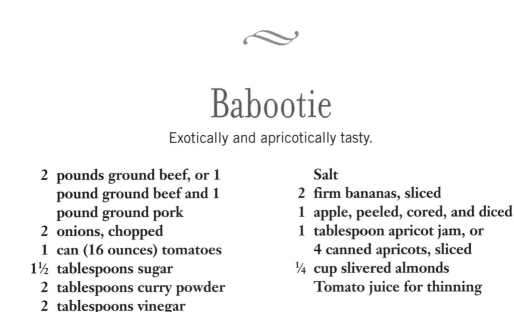

# Babootie

Exotically and apricotically tasty.

| | |
|---|---|
| 2 pounds ground beef, or 1 pound ground beef and 1 pound ground pork | Salt |
| 2 onions, chopped | 2 firm bananas, sliced |
| 1 can (16 ounces) tomatoes | 1 apple, peeled, cored, and diced |
| 1½ tablespoons sugar | 1 tablespoon apricot jam, or 4 canned apricots, sliced |
| 2 tablespoons curry powder | ¼ cup slivered almonds |
| 2 tablespoons vinegar | Tomato juice for thinning |

Brown meat and drain off fat. Add onions, tomatoes (with juice), sugar, curry powder, vinegar, salt to taste, bananas, apple, jam or apricots, and almonds. Simmer gently, stirring frequently, for 30 minutes. Add tomato juice if too thick. Serve over rice. *Serves 8.*

*Mary Nichol, First Presbyterian Church, Monroe, New York*

# Spaghetti Pie

Similar to baked lasagna but less expensive and less effort.

8 ounces spaghetti, broken into 2" pieces
2 tablespoons butter
⅓ cup grated Parmesan cheese
½ teaspoon salt
¼ teaspoon pepper
1 egg, well-beaten
1½ pounds ground chuck
1 medium onion, chopped
¼ cup chopped green pepper

2 tablespoons vegetable oil
1 jar (15½ ounces) thick spaghetti sauce
1 teaspoon sugar
½ teaspoon leaf oregano, crumbled
½ teaspoon garlic salt
1 cup cottage cheese
4 ounces mozzarella cheese, shredded

Cook spaghetti in boiling water following label directions; drain. Place in 9" × 13" baking dish. Stir in butter, Parmesan cheese, salt, pepper, and egg until thoroughly combined. Spread mixture evenly in pan.

Sauté chuck, onion, and green pepper in oil in large skillet until meat is brown; drain. Stir in spaghetti sauce, sugar, oregano, and garlic salt.

Spread cottage cheese over spaghetti layer and top with meat mixture. Bake at 350°F for 30 minutes. Sprinkle mozzarella cheese over top and bake an additional 10 minutes, or until cheese is melted and just begins to brown. Let stand 15 minutes before cutting. *Serves 6.*

*Mrs. Thomas E. Denman, Sr., The Congregational Church, East Hampton, Connecticut*

# Pastitsio (Greek Macaroni Pie)

This popular recipe happily doubles, triples, quadruples . . . or halves!

| | |
|---|---|
| 1 large onion, finely chopped | ¾ teaspoon oregano |
| 2 tablespoons butter or olive oil | 2 cups tomato puree |
| 1½ pounds ground beef | 2 tablespoons minced parsley |
| ¾ teaspoon salt | ½ pound small elbow macaroni |
| Freshly ground black pepper | 1 tablespoon cooking oil |
| ¼ teaspoon cinnamon | |

Sauté onion in butter or olive oil in large heavy pan or skillet until soft. Stir in beef and cook until lightly brown. Season with salt, pepper, cinnamon, and oregano. Stir in tomato puree and parsley. Cover and simmer gently for 20 minutes. Taste and add more salt if necessary. Cook macaroni in large kettle of well-salted boiling water until tender but still slightly firm. Drain, then rinse in lukewarm water. Mix cooking oil well through macaroni to prevent it from sticking together. Make Creamy Topping (see below).

## Creamy Topping

| | |
|---|---|
| 3 tablespoons butter | ¼ teaspoon nutmeg |
| 3 tablespoons flour | ¼ teaspoon salt |
| 3½ cups milk | ¼ teaspoon white pepper |
| 3 egg yolks, lightly beaten | ½ cup Parmesan cheese |

Melt butter and blend in flour. Stir in milk and cook about 5 minutes, stirring constantly to make a thin white sauce. Dip out 1 cup of hot sauce and pour thin stream into yolks, stirring constantly until well-blended. Pour mixture back into rest of sauce and stir for a few minutes over low heat. Do not allow to boil. Season with nutmeg, salt, and pepper.

In greased 9" × 13" Pyrex casserole, put a thin layer of macaroni, a layer of meat sauce, a second layer of macaroni, and a second layer of meat sauce. Pour Creamy Topping over all. Jiggle the dish so that some sauce runs through all layers. Sprinkle Parmesan over top. Bake at 350°F for 45 minutes. Remove from oven and let stand 15–20 minutes. Cut into large squares and serve from pan. *Serves 8.*

*Elizabeth F. Bauhan, All Saints Church, Peterborough, New Hampshire*

# Cannelloni

Pasta rolled around a filling of meat, onion, and spinach, doubly sauced red and white. Takes time but is worth it.

## Pasta

**10 lasagna noodles**          **1 tablespoon olive oil**

Add noodles and oil to boiling salted water and cook according to package directions to just al dente stage. Drain and spread noodles side by side on flat area covered with foil. (Noodles will not stick to foil.) Cover with another layer of foil until ready to use.

## Filling

**1 clove garlic, minced**
**1 large onion, finely chopped**
**2 tablespoons olive oil**
**1 package (10 ounces) frozen spinach, thawed, squeezed dry, and rechopped**
**1 pound ground beef**

**1 tablespoon butter**
**5 tablespoons Parmesan cheese**
**2 tablespoons cream**
**2 eggs, lightly beaten**
**½ teaspoon oregano**
**Salt and pepper**

Sauté garlic and onion in olive oil until onions are soft. Add spinach to pan and cook, stirring constantly, for 4–5 minutes, or until all water has boiled away and spinach shows tendency to stick to pan. Turn into large bowl. Brown beef in butter, turning and stirring to cook evenly and break up all lumps. Add to bowl with spinach, along with Parmesan, cream, eggs, and oregano. Mix well. Add salt and pepper to taste.

## Tomato Sauce

**3–4 cups tomato sauce**

# Besciamella (Cream) Sauce

6 tablespoons butter
6 tablespoons flour
1 cup milk

1 cup cream
1 teaspoon salt
⅛ teaspoon pepper

In heavy or enamel saucepan, melt butter over moderate heat. Remove from stove and stir in flour. Return to stove and add milk and cream all at once. Cook, stirring constantly, over medium heat until well-blended. Then turn up heat and bring to boil, stirring diligently to prevent sauce from scorching. Turn down heat and simmer, still stirring, for a minute or more longer until sauce is thick enough to coat spoon heavily. Remove from heat and add salt and pepper.

# Assembling Cannelloni

Pour a thin film of tomato sauce over bottom of 9" × 13" baking dish. Cut lasagna noodles exactly in half with sharp knife. Place 1 rounded tablespoon of filling at one end of each lasagna half and roll up. Place in baking dish. You will have three rows of filled halves: the rolls on the two outer rows being lengthwise with longer sides parallel to 13" side of dish; the middle row being placed crosswise, longer sides parallel to 9" side of dish. Dish will contain 16 rolls. (Two extra lasagna noodles were in case any were torn during cooking or handling.) Spread Besciamella Sauce over filled lasagna rolls. Then spoon tomato sauce *over* all; do not mix sauces. Sprinkle with Parmesan cheese and dot with butter. Bake uncovered at 375°F for 20 minutes, or until bubbling. (Cannelloni may be made ahead, covered tightly with foil or plastic wrap, and refrigerated for a day or two. It will take a little longer to bake a refrigerated cannelloni. For variation, the saucing can be reversed: place rolls on film of tomato sauce as before, but cover rolls first with tomato sauce and top with cream sauce.) *Serves 6–8.*

# Company Beef Ragout

Make sure you have some cheesecloth on hand for the herb bag (bouquet garni) called for in this succulent stew.

2 pounds stew beef, cut into 1" cubes
¼ cup flour
1 teaspoon salt
3 tablespoons fat for browning
3 cups boiling water
1 can (16 ounces) tomato sauce
4 sprigs parsley
½ teaspoon marjoram
½ teaspoon thyme
½ teaspoon rosemary

2 bay leaves
1 clove garlic
6 potatoes, cut into ½" pieces
½ cup celery, cut into 1" pieces
1 package (10 ounces) frozen peas
1 tablespoon butter
1 tablespoon sugar
4 small onions, cut in half
4 medium carrots, cut into 1" slices

Shake beef with flour and salt in paper bag. Brown meat on all sides in fat. Place in 4-quart Dutch oven and cover with water and tomato sauce. Simmer until meat is tender—about 2 hours.

Place parsley, marjoram, thyme, rosemary, bay leaves, and garlic on a square of cheesecloth and draw up edges to make a little bag. Tie tightly at neck with butcher's twine or thread. Add to Dutch oven along with potatoes, celery, and peas.

Melt butter with sugar in skillet and add onions and carrots. Cook over medium heat, stirring, until well-glazed. Add to meat mixture. Cook until vegetables are tender; check every 30 minutes, though it may take an hour or longer. Remove and discard herb bag. Refrigerate overnight and reheat in oven before serving. *Serves 10–12.*

*First Congregational Church, Littleton, New Hampshire*

# Boeuf Bourguignonne

Marinating the meat before cooking makes the difference
in this version of a favorite French stew.

3 pounds stew beef, cut into
  1½" cubes
1 medium onion, sliced
2 cups red wine
1 bay leaf
4 sprigs fresh parsley or
  2 tablespoons dried
¼ teaspoon thyme
2 tablespoons cooking oil
½ teaspoon salt

¼ teaspoon pepper
1 carrot, peeled and sliced
1 clove garlic, mashed
3 tablespoons butter
1 tablespoon flour
½ cup consommé
¼ pound salt pork, diced
24 small white onions
1 cup sliced mushrooms, fresh,
  or canned and drained

Combine beef, onion, wine, bay leaf, parsley, thyme, oil, salt, pepper, carrot, and garlic in bowl. Marinate in refrigerator for at least 4 hours, turning meat from time to time. Remove meat and pat dry with paper towels. Strain and reserve marinade. Brown meat in 2 tablespoons butter. Add flour and cook 3 minutes, stirring. Add consommé and reserved marinade and bring to boil. Cover, turn down heat, and simmer for 2 hours, stirring from time to time.

Melt remaining 1 tablespoon butter in small saucepan. Add salt pork and onions. Cook over medium heat about 10 minutes, or until golden. Transfer salt pork and onions to stew pot. Add mushrooms. Bring to boil. Cover, turn down heat, and simmer 45 minutes longer, or until meat is tender. Remove and discard bay leaf. Serve with boiled potatoes, noodles, or macaroni. *Serves 8–10.*

*Moira Burnham, Church of the Epiphany, New York, New York*

# Lazy Man's Beef Stew

One of the best and certainly the easiest. We couldn't believe that "there's no browning of the meat, yet a rich gravy and marvelous flavor develop during the long, slow cooking," and even doubted there would be enough liquid. Doubters no more—we believe!

2 pounds stew beef
4 large carrots, quartered lengthwise and cut into pieces
1 can (10¾ ounces) tomato soup
1 bay leaf
3–4 medium potatoes, cut into quarters

1 cup red cooking wine
2 onions, thinly sliced
1 package (10 ounces) frozen peas
1 cup fresh mushrooms, sautéed in butter and drained, or
1 can (6 ounces), drained (optional)

Grease large casserole dish. Add beef, carrots, soup, bay leaf, potatoes, ½ cup wine, and onions. Cover and bake at 275°F for 4 hours. Remove from oven and stir (meat will be a little dry). Add peas (still frozen), mushrooms, if using, and remaining ½ cup wine, and if necessary, a little water. Cook for 1 hour longer. Remove and discard bay leaf. *Serves 6.*

*Ethel Innes, The Unitarian Church, Franklin, New Hampshire*

# Beef Chop Suey

Like most stews, tastes best made the day before and reheated.

1 pound stew beef, cut into 1" cubes
1 tablespoon cooking oil
Water
5 medium onions, chopped
2 large stalks celery, chopped
1 can (16 ounces) bean sprouts, drained

1 can (6 ounces) mushrooms
2 tablespoons diced pimiento (optional)
2 tablespoons (or more) soy sauce
Pepper
2 tablespoons cornstarch, mixed with ¼ cup cold water

Brown beef in hot oil in large skillet or 2-quart Dutch oven. Cover with water and simmer until tender—about 2 hours, adding water as needed. Add onions, celery, bean sprouts, and mushrooms (with liquid), and continue to simmer for 30 minutes more, or until vegetables are tender. Add pimiento, if using, soy sauce, and pepper to taste. Stir in cornstarch mixture and cook, stirring, until thickened. Serve over rice or chow mein noodles—do not heat chop suey and rice or noodles together. *Serves 6–8.*

*Sharon Rivard, Woodmont United Church of Christ, Milford, Connecticut*

# Louisiana Beef Stew

An interesting stew featuring molasses, raisins, and a hint of ginger.

| | |
|---|---|
| 3 tablespoons flour | 2 tablespoons cooking oil |
| 1 teaspoon salt | 1 can (16 ounces) tomatoes |
| ½ teaspoon celery salt | 3 medium onions, sliced |
| ¼ teaspoon garlic salt | ⅓ cup red wine vinegar |
| ¼ teaspoon pepper | ½ cup molasses |
| ½ teaspoon ginger | ½ cup water |
| 3 pounds beef chuck, cut into 2" cubes | 6–8 carrots, cut on diagonal |
| | ½ cup raisins |

Combine flour, salt, celery salt, garlic salt, pepper, and ginger, and sprinkle over beef cubes. Brown beef in hot oil. Remove to Dutch oven and add tomatoes (with juice), onions, vinegar, molasses, and water. Bring to boil, cover, and simmer about 2 hours. Add carrots and raisins and simmer 30 minutes longer, or until carrots are tender. *Serves 8–10.*

*Katharine D. Foster, United Church of Christ, Keene, New Hampshire*

# Boeuf Flamande

Beef stew in a rich sauce made with beer.

½ pound salt pork, cut into
    ¼" cubes
3 pounds stew beef, cut into
    2½" cubes
1 teaspoon salt
½ teaspoon pepper
6 large onions, thinly sliced
1 teaspoon minced garlic
½ cup flour
1½ cups dark beer

2 cups beef or chicken broth, or
    2 bouillon cubes dissolved in
    2 cups boiling water
1 bay leaf
½ teaspoon thyme
2 teaspoons sugar
3 tablespoons wine vinegar
2 tablespoons chopped fresh
    parsley

Brown salt pork cubes until crisp in large skillet. Lift out to small bowl and reserve. Sprinkle beef with salt and pepper and brown in hot fat over medium heat. Transfer browned beef to 2-quart baking dish or casserole. To fat remaining in skillet, add 3 tablespoons butter if necessary. Add onions and cook gently until golden. Add garlic and cook for 2–3 more minutes. Stir in flour, blending well with onions and garlic, and cook for 2–3 minutes. Gradually stir in beer, then broth or bouillon, stirring constantly over medium heat. Add bay leaf, thyme, and sugar, turn heat to high, and bring to boil. Then turn down heat immediately and simmer sauce for 5 minutes. Pour sauce over meat in casserole, cover casserole, and bake at 375°F for 1½ hours, or until meat is tender. Stir in vinegar and sprinkle stew with parsley and browned salt pork. Remove and discard bay leaf. Serve over noodles, rice, or boiled potatoes. *Serves 8–10.*

# Chili con Carne

This recipe tastes even better after freezing.

2 pounds stew beef, cut into ¾" cubes
¼ cup cooking oil
1 cup minced onion
2 cloves garlic, mashed
2 tablespoons chili powder
1 tablespoon paprika
2 teaspoons oregano
1 teaspoon ground cumin
1 teaspoon salt
¼ teaspoon pepper
1 cup water, or 2½ cups canned tomatoes

Brown beef in oil on all sides. Add onion and garlic and cook 5 minutes, stirring constantly. Stir in chili powder, paprika, oregano, cumin, salt, pepper, and water or tomatoes (with juice). Simmer until meat is tender, from 3 hours to all day (improves with length of cooking time). Stir and add water from time to time to keep liquid at original level. Serve with rice or kidney beans. *Serves 8.*

*Mary Nichol, First Presbyterian Church, Monroe, New York*

# Ham, Pork, and Lamb

Ham is a perennial favorite at church suppers. It's easy to fix, popular with crowds, and delicious! Here you'll find new twists on ham and cheese, ham loaf, and ham casserole. The recipes for pork chops, pork loin, and sausage are winners, too. One stand-out is the richly-flavored Cassoulet, made with both sausage and lamb cubes. It'll make any crowd happy. There are also two other fragrant lamb stews and a pair of blue-ribbon lamb casseroles.

Ham and Chicken Luncheon Dish  35

Ham in Cream Sauce  35

Ham and Cheese Almost Soufflé  36

Ham and Rice Dinner  36

Governor's Casserole  37

Crêpes Fasnacloich  38

Pineapple Upside-Down Ham Loaf  39

Ham Pancake Pie  40

Sausage and Rice Casserole  40

Sweet Ham and Pork Loaf  41

Ham Loaf with Cranberry Sauce  42

Cajun Pork Meatloaf  43

French Pork Pie (Tourtière)  44

Pork Tenderloin with
Granny Smith Apples  45

Pork Chop Roast with Honeyed
Sweet Potatoes  46

Teriyaki Pork Loin  46

Sausages Cooked in White Wine  47

Wagon-Wheel Sausage-Bean Casserole  48

Cowboy Bob Beans  48

Lamb-Rice Casserole  49

Slow Cooker Middle-Eastern
Lamb Shanks  50

Cassoulet  51

Mediterranean Lamb & Eggplant Bake  52

Swedish Lamb and Lentil Stew  53

Rosemary Lamb Stew  53

Lamb Poulette  54

# Ham and Chicken Luncheon Dish

The naturally delicious combination of ham and chicken is enhanced by just a touch of curry.

¼ cup butter
¼ cup flour
1¼ cups milk
½ cup chicken broth
¼ cup white wine
½ teaspoon curry powder
   Salt and pepper

1 cup diced cooked chicken
1 cup diced cooked ham
¼ pound sliced fresh mushrooms,
   or 1 can (4 ounces), drained
2 tablespoons diced pimiento
   (optional)

Melt butter and blend in flour. Add milk and broth gradually, stirring constantly. Bring to boil, still stirring, and cook until thickened. Lower heat and stir in one at a time wine, curry powder, salt and pepper to taste, chicken, ham, mushrooms, and pimiento, if using. Simmer 10 minutes, stirring occasionally, until heated through. Serve in pastry shells or toast cups or over rice. *Serves 6.*

# Ham in Cream Sauce

This versatile recipe can be ladled over English muffins or toast for brunch, served with noodles or rice, or served as a side dish with a cheese soufflé.

4 tablespoons + 2 teaspoons
   butter
4 tablespoons flour
2 cups milk
¼ teaspoon nutmeg

Salt and pepper
1 pound cooked ham, diced
2 tablespoons chopped chives
6 tablespoons sherry

Melt 4 tablespoons butter in saucepan and add flour, blending well. Add milk, stirring well and cooking over medium heat until thickened. Add nutmeg and salt and pepper to taste. Remove from heat. Cook ham in 2 teaspoons butter for about 10 minutes, stirring, and add chives. Cook gently 3–4 more minutes. Add sherry and heat through. Combine ham with cream sauce and serve. *Serves 6–8.*

# Ham and Cheese Almost Soufflé

Also referred to as a mock soufflé or strata casserole, this puffy delight can be made with diced chicken, shrimp, or tuna instead of ham. If you are planning to take one to a potluck supper, bake it at the church because it will fall slightly as it cools.

| | |
|---|---|
| 8 slices white bread | 3½ cups milk |
| ¾ pound Cheddar cheese, cubed | 2 teaspoons Worcestershire sauce |
| 3 cups diced cooked ham | 1 teaspoon dry mustard |
| 1 can (4 ounces) sliced mushrooms, drained (optional) | ½ teaspoon paprika |
| | 1 teaspoon salt |
| 6 large or 8 small eggs | ⅛ teaspoon pepper |

In buttered 3-quart casserole dish, alternately layer bread, cheese, ham, and mushrooms, if using, until casserole is full, ending with layer of cheese. Beat together eggs, milk, Worcestershire sauce, mustard, paprika, salt, and pepper, and pour over casserole. If liquid does not show two-thirds of way up in dish, add more milk. Bake at 350°F for 1 hour. Serve immediately. *Serves 6–8.*

*Women's Association of The Congregational Church, Amherst, New Hampshire*

# Ham and Rice Dinner

Ham and rice are the only ingredients you are sure of in this beguilingly different dish. The rest is a guessing game.

| | |
|---|---|
| 3 cups hot cooked rice | 2 tablespoons dry white wine (optional) |
| 2½ cups cooked ham, cut into julienne strips | 1½ teaspoons prepared mustard |
| 1½ tablespoons butter | ¼ teaspoon dillweed |
| ½ cup chopped onion | ¾ cup sour cream |
| 2 cups thinly sliced celery | ⅓ cup sliced pimiento |
| 1 can (10¾ ounces) cream of chicken soup | |

While rice is cooking, sauté ham in butter for 2 minutes. Add onion and celery, and cook over medium heat until tender crisp. Stir in soup, wine, if using, mustard, and dillweed, and heat thoroughly. Add sour cream and pimiento. Heat but do not boil. Serve over rice. ***Serves 6.***

*Diane Gularneau, The Unitarian Church, Franklin, New Hampshire*

# Governor's Casserole

The Governor of New Hampshire dropped by for lunch the day this was being tested and gave it his enthusiastic endorsement.

1 package (20 ounces) frozen cauliflower florets

1 package (20 ounces) frozen broccoli florets

4 tablespoons butter

3 tablespoons flour

3 cups milk

6 ounces (or 1½ cups) shredded Cheddar cheese

4 ounces (or 1 cup) grated Parmesan cheese

½ teaspoon salt

3 cups chopped ham

3 cups fresh bread crumbs, tossed with 4 tablespoons melted butter

Cook cauliflower and broccoli in boiling salted water until slightly underdone. Drain and set aside. Melt butter in 1-quart saucepan. Stir in flour and blend well. Gradually add milk, stirring constantly until thickened. Add Cheddar, Parmesan, and salt, and stir over low heat until cheese melts. Place vegetables in ungreased 4-quart casserole dish and sprinkle with chopped ham. Pour cheese sauce over all. Make a border of buttered crumbs around edge of casserole. Bake uncovered at 350°F for 20–30 minutes, or until crumbs are lightly browned. ***Serves 10–12.***

*Mrs. Daniel Burnham, Community Church, Dublin, New Hampshire*

# Crêpes Fasnacloich

Crêpes stuffed with ham and chicken and baked in a sherried cream sauce.
Easy to make and fabulous to eat. Serve with green salad.

## Crêpes

2 eggs, beaten
1 cup flour
1 cup milk

1 tablespoon cooking oil
½ teaspoon salt

**P**ut eggs in bowl and beat in flour. Add milk, oil, and salt, beating batter until smooth. Refrigerate to allow ingredients to blend while you make sauce.

## Sauce

4 tablespoons butter
4 tablespoons flour
3 cups milk
Scant ½ teaspoon salt (if you

don't use salted cooking sherry,
use 1 teaspoon salt)
⅓ cup cooking sherry
Pinch of tarragon (optional)

**M**elt butter in top of double boiler and blend in flour. Add milk, 1 cup at a time, cooking over medium heat and stirring constantly until sauce thickens. Stir in salt, sherry, and tarragon, if using. Cover sauce and keep warm over hot water while you cook the crêpes.

Place 1 tablespoon butter and 1 tablespoon cooking oil on griddle or skillet over high heat until butter is melted and dash of cold water thrown onto griddle bounces in drops rather than sits and boils. Pour off excess fat into measuring cup to leave thin coating on skillet. Turn heat down to medium and ladle batter, a scant ¼ cup at a time, onto griddle. As soon as batter is on griddle, pick up griddle and rotate slowly and smoothly, tilting so that batter spreads evenly to form thin, round pancake 6"–7" in diameter. Return to heat and cook until top side of pancake is just set. Turn (loosen by sliding pancake flipper under, pick up edges of pancake with fingers, and flip). Cook a minute or so on other side (crêpe should be just golden on each side) and stack on plate. Add more of butter-oil mixture if crêpes start to stick. You should have 7–8 crêpes. (This step can be done ahead, as crêpes can be frozen and kept for up to a week.)

# Meat Filling

1 cup diced cooked ham
2 cups diced cooked chicken or
turkey

Parsley for final garnish

$M$ix ham and chicken or turkey together and add ¾ cup sauce, mixing well with meat. Grease 9" × 13" baking dish. Place about 2 rounded tablespoons of meat mixture on each crêpe and roll up. Arrange rolled-up crêpes in dish. Pour rest of sauce over filled crêpes and bake at 350°F for 20–25 minutes (longer if elements of dish are cold to start with), or until sauce is bubbling and filling is heated through. Sprinkle with parsley. *Serves 8.*

*O. P. Valhalla, St. Matthew's Church, Bedford, New York*

# Pineapple Upside-Down Ham Loaf

3 tablespoons butter
⅓ cup light brown sugar
 Canned pineapple slices
 Maraschino cherries (optional)
1 pound (4 cups) ground cooked
 ham
⅔ pound freshly ground raw pork

2 cups bread crumbs
2 eggs, beaten
1 cup milk
1 teaspoon salt
⅛ teaspoon pepper
½ teaspoon dry mustard

$M$elt butter with brown sugar and place in bottom of 8" × 8" × 2" pan. Place layer of pineapple slices (with a cherry in the middle of each if desired) on top of sugar mixture. Mix together ham, pork, bread crumbs, eggs, milk, salt, pepper, and mustard, and spread evenly on top of fruit. Bake at 350°F for 1½ hours. Turn out onto platter and cut into squares. *Serves 6.*

*Gladys Delay, Harwinton Congregational Church, Harwinton, Connecticut*

# Ham Pancake Pie

Sweet potatoes, apples, and ham under an unusual roof.

2 medium sweet potatoes, peeled
   and sliced thinly
3 cups (about ¾ pound) diced
   cooked ham
3 medium apples, peeled, cored,
   and sliced
½ teaspoon salt
¼ teaspoon pepper

3 tablespoons brown sugar
¼ teaspoon curry powder
⅓ cup water or apple juice
1 cup pancake mix
1 cup milk
½ teaspoon dry mustard
2 tablespoons melted butter

In 2-quart greased baking dish, layer half the potatoes, half the ham, and half the apples. Combine salt, pepper, brown sugar, and curry powder, and sprinkle half the mixture over layers in dish. Repeat the process with remaining potatoes, ham, apples, and brown sugar mixture. Pour water or apple juice over all. Cover dish and bake at 375°F until sweet potatoes are tender—about 40 minutes. Beat together pancake mix, milk, mustard, and butter. Take casserole from oven when potatoes are done and pour pancake batter over top. Bake 20 minutes more, uncovered, or until pancake is puffed and golden. *Serves 6.*

# Sausage and Rice Casserole

Simple, inexpensive, and nourishing.

2 large onions, sliced
2 tablespoons cooking oil
1 pound sausage links
1 can (16 ounces) tomatoes

3 cups cooked rice
½ cup grated Cheddar or
   American cheese

Sauté onions in oil. Remove to bowl. Brown sausages in oil and cut each link into thirds. Mix onion and sausage with tomatoes (with juice) and rice. Pour into buttered casserole. Bake at 350°F for 1 hour. Fifteen minutes before hour ends, sprinkle with grated cheese. *Serves 8.*

*Mary Wakefield, First Congregational Church, Rindge, New Hampshire*

# Sweet Ham and Pork Loaf

1 pound (4 cups) ground cooked ham
⅔–¾ pound freshly ground raw pork
2 eggs, beaten
1 cup milk

1 cup dry bread or cracker crumbs
1½ teaspoons dry mustard
½ teaspoon salt
¼ teaspoon pepper

Combine meats and add eggs. Stir in milk, crumbs, mustard, salt, and pepper, and mix well. Form into loaf and place on rack in baking dish, or pack into greased 9" × 5" loaf pan. Bake at 400°F until slightly browned (15–20 minutes). Meanwhile, prepare sauce.

## Sauce

¼ cup vinegar
¼ cup water
¾ cup brown sugar

1 teaspoon prepared mustard or ½ teaspoon dry mustard

Combine vinegar, water, brown sugar, and mustard in saucepan and bring to gentle boil. Cook for 5 minutes.

Remove loaf from oven and pour half the sauce over it. Return to oven for 30 minutes. At end of this time, pour over rest of sauce. Place loaf pan on cookie sheet to catch any sauce that might boil over, and bake for 15 more minutes. When loaf is done, invert pan and remove loaf at once to prevent sticking. *Serves 6–8.*

*Shirley T. Oladell, Harwinton Congregational Church, Harwinton, Connecticut*

# Ham Loaf with Cranberry Sauce

1 cup milk
1 cup soft bread crumbs (white)
1½ pounds cured ham, ground

1 pound freshly ground lean pork
2 eggs, beaten

Scald the milk and pour it over bread crumbs. Add to ham and pork and mix thoroughly until no bread crumbs show. Add eggs and mix again. Put into 9" × 5" loaf pan, then set loaf pan into shallow pan containing hot water at least 1" deep. Bake at 375°F for 2 hours. If loaf browns too much, cover meat with foil. Pour off fat and excess juice; serve plain or with Cranberry Sauce (see below). *Serves 8.*

## Cranberry Sauce

1 cup canned jellied cranberry
   sauce
¼ cup light corn syrup

¼ cup water
   Whole-berry cranberry sauce
   for garnish

Boil jellied cranberry sauce, corn syrup, and water until thick. Cool; do not chill. Pour over loaf before serving and put under broiler a few minutes. Garnish platter with whole-berry cranberry sauce. Drain the berries if too juicy.

*Nellie H. Crane, The United Church, Northfield, Vermont*

# Cajun Pork Meatloaf

Dishes from Louisiana's Cajun country are often very spicy, but the heat level in this main dish is moderate. For more heat, double or even triple the amount of cayenne and Tabasco sauce called for here.

2 tablespoons butter
½ cup finely chopped green bell pepper
⅓ cup finely chopped celery
2 green onions, finely chopped
3 tablespoons minced garlic
1 teaspoon cumin
½ teaspoon black pepper
¼ teaspoon cayenne pepper
⅛ teaspoon nutmeg

1½ teaspoons salt
2 bay leaves
½ cup half-and-half
½ cup ketchup
2 teaspoons Worcestershire sauce
1½ teaspoons Tabasco sauce
1½ pounds ground pork
8 ounces ground turkey
2 eggs, beaten

Melt butter in skillet over medium heat. Add green bell pepper, celery, green onions, and garlic. Sauté for 5 minutes or until golden. Reduce heat if vegetables brown too fast. Stir in cumin, black pepper, cayenne, nutmeg, salt, and bay leaves. Cook for 1 minute or until fragrant. Add half-and-half, ketchup, Worcestershire sauce, and Tabasco sauce; simmer, stirring to combine, for 2 minutes. Remove from heat to cool; remove and discard bay leaves.

Place pork and turkey in bowl. Add eggs and reserved vegetables. Mix until completely blended (mixture will be very moist). Spoon into greased 9" × 5" loaf pan and bake at 350°F for about 70 minutes or until an instant-read thermometer inserted in center registers 160°F. Cool for 10 minutes. Carefully pour off any liquid in pan. Turn loaf onto serving platter. *Serves 6–8.*

*Melinda Ingalls, Gay Street United Methodist Church, Mount Vernon, Ohio*

# French Pork Pie (Tourtière)

Make this rich and savory Canadian specialty as one 10" pie
or as individual meat "pasties" or turnovers.

## Crust

3  cups flour
1  teaspoon salt

1  cup shortening
⅔  cup water

Combine flour and salt. Cut in ½ cup shortening, then add remaining ½ cup shortening. Mix well and stir in water. Roll out. Makes enough pastry for one 10" two-crust pie.

## Filling

2  pounds pork, trimmed of fat
   and ground or cut into ½" cubes
1  pound ground beef
1  cup hot water
¼  teaspoon nutmeg

¼  teaspoon allspice
2  teaspoons salt
½  cup chopped onion
¼  teaspoon pepper
3  cups bread crumbs

Mix together pork, beef, water, nutmeg, allspice, salt, onion, pepper, and bread crumbs. Place in pastry-lined 10" pie plate and top with remaining pastry. Cut a few slits in top crust to allow steam to escape. Bake at 325°F for 1½ hours, or until pie is nicely browned. **Serves 6–8.**

*Diane Gularneau, The Unitarian Church, Franklin, New Hampshire*

# Pork Tenderloin with Granny Smith Apples

Warm spices and crispy apples make this pork main dish especially popular for autumn gatherings.

½ cup olive oil
1 tablespoon minced garlic
3 teaspoons cinnamon
1 teaspoon nutmeg
1 teaspoon cumin
3 pounds pork tenderloins, trimmed of fat

Salt and pepper
¼ cup butter
4 Granny Smith apples, unpeeled, cored, sliced ½" thick
3 tablespoons sugar

In large zipper-lock bag or bowl, combine oil, garlic, 1½ teaspoons cinnamon, ½ teaspoon nutmeg, and cumin. Add pork; rub to coat with marinade. Seal bag or cover dish. Refrigerate, turning occasionally, up to 8 hours.

Heat large non-stick skillet over medium-high heat. Remove pork and place in skillet; discard marinade. Brown on all sides, about 2–3 minutes per side. Season to taste with salt and pepper. Transfer to rectangular baking pan large enough to allow 2" between each tenderloin. (Do not wash skillet.) Roast at 400°F for 18–20 minutes or until an instant read thermometer inserted in thickest part of tenderloin registers 160°F. Remove and allow to rest 5 minutes.

Melt butter in same skillet over medium-high heat. Add apples and sauté for 5 minutes or until tender and browned. With spatula, scrape any browned bits on skillet bottom. Reduce heat if apples are browning too quickly. In small dish, combine sugar, remaining 1½ teaspoons cinnamon, and remaining ½ teaspoon nutmeg; add to skillet. Cook, stirring, about 2 minutes or until sugar melts. Slice pork at an angle into ½" thick slices. Arrange on large platter; spoon apples in center. *Serves 6–8.*

*Bonnie Williams, New World United Methodist Church, Arlington, Texas*

# Pork Chop Roast
# with Honeyed Sweet Potatoes

An enchanting blend of Hawaiian fruitiness and New England heartiness.

3 large sweet potatoes
6 pork chops, cut ¾" thick
¼ cup sifted flour
2 teaspoons salt
⅛ teaspoon pepper
Melted fat
1 tablespoon prepared mustard

1 tablespoon brown sugar
6 pineapple slices
6 green pepper rings, ¼" thick
6 onion slices, ¼" thick
1 cup pineapple juice
1 cup honey
3 tablespoons melted butter

Boil potatoes until soft, then cut in half and peel. Meanwhile, coat chops with mixture of flour, salt, and pepper. Brown in melted fat. Arrange chops in shallow baking dish. Spread with mustard and brown sugar. Top each chop with pineapple, green pepper, and onion. Pour pineapple juice over chops. Coat sweet potatoes with honey and melted butter and arrange around chops. Bake covered at 350°F for 30 minutes; then remove cover and bake 30 minutes longer, or until chops are tender. *Serves 6.*

*Woodmont United Church of Christ, Milford, Connecticut*

# Teriyaki Pork Loin

Good served with rice, peas combined with celery and water chestnuts, hot mustard, or horseradish applesauce.

1 4-pound pork loin (3 pounds if
  boned)
1 can (6 ounces) frozen
  pineapple or orange juice
⅓ cup soy sauce
3–4 cloves garlic, crushed

1 tablespoon cornstarch, mixed
  with 2 tablespoons water
½ cup drained pineapple chunks
  or diced fresh orange (optional)
Pineapple or orange slices
Parsley or watercress

Marinate loin 8 hours, turning from time to time, in mixture of fruit juice, soy sauce, and garlic. When ready to cook, preheat oven to 375°F. Drain pork, reserving marinade, and place in open roasting pan on rack. After 10 minutes, turn oven down to 325°F. Roast 35 minutes per pound (45 minutes per pound for boned roast), or until done—internal temperature should read 185°F—and pork is richly glazed. During last half-hour, brush several times with marinade.

Heat remaining marinade in saucepan and adjust seasonings. Add cornstarch and water mixture and cook, stirring, until thickened. Add pineapple chunks or diced orange if desired. Pour a little sauce over roast and garnish meat with fruit slices and a little parsley or watercress. Serve rest of sauce in gravy boat. *Serves 8–10.*

*Evelyn H. Chase, Concord Unitarian Church, Concord, New Hampshire*

# Sausages Cooked in White Wine
This exquisite sauce is not hard to make, but what it does
to the lowly sausage link is hard to believe.

| | |
|---|---|
| 2 **pounds link sausage** | ¼ **teaspoon thyme** |
| 2 **tablespoons butter** | 1 **bay leaf** |
| 2 **tablespoons chives** | ¼ **teaspoon marjoram** |
| 1 **tablespoon flour** | 3 **cups white wine, unsalted** |

Brown sausages slowly in skillet, pricking skins first to prevent bursting. Remove and drain on paper. Discard fat in pan. Melt butter and add chives and flour. Cook over low heat for 2–3 minutes. Add thyme, bay leaf, marjoram, and wine, stirring to blend well, and simmer sauce for 20 minutes. Return sausages to skillet and heat in sauce until sauce thickens. Remove and discard bay leaf. Serve with mashed potatoes, omelet, or popovers. *Serves 6–8.*

# Wagon-Wheel Sausage-Bean Casserole

Handsome and hearty fare with a Western flair.

1 pound dry lima beans
6 cups water
2 teaspoons salt
1 clove garlic
1 pound fresh link sausages
4 medium onions, sliced and broken into rings
1 medium green pepper, chopped (optional)

1 can (10¾ ounces) tomato soup
2 tablespoons brown sugar
¼ teaspoon pepper
½ teaspoon dry mustard
¼ teaspoon ground thyme
1 tablespoon celery flakes
⅓ cup white wine
½ cup grated Cheddar cheese

Bring beans and water to boil and boil for 3 minutes. Turn off heat and let stand 1 hour. Add 1 teaspoon salt and garlic and simmer until tender, or until bean skins wrinkle when you blow on beans gently—about 1 hour. Drain beans and remove garlic. Brown sausages lightly and remove from pan, along with all but 2 tablespoons fat. Drain sausage and set aside. In fat remaining in pan, sauté onion rings and green pepper (if using) until tender. In 2-quart casserole, mix well together the beans, onions, green pepper, if using, remaining 1 teaspoon salt, soup, brown sugar, pepper, mustard, thyme, celery flakes, and wine. Arrange sausages like wagon-wheel spokes on top of bean mixture. Cover and bake at 350°F for 1 hour. Remove cover and top with grated cheese. Melt cheese under broiler. *Serves 6–8.*

# Cowboy Bob Beans

A tasty dish that's easy on both cook and pocketbook. Serve with salad and garlic bread.

1 can (28 ounces) yellow-eye beans
1 can (15 ounces) kidney beans
1 onion, chopped
1 green pepper, chopped

1 clove garlic, minced
1 pound frankfurters, sliced
3–4 tablespoons butter
1 can (20 ounces) chunk-style pineapple, drained, reserving juice

Combine beans. Sauté onion, green pepper, garlic, and frankfurters in butter and add the beans. Stir in pineapple chunks and half the juice from can. Bake at 350°F for 30 minutes. *Serves 6.*

*Harriet E. Oinonen, The Congregational Church, New Ipswich, New Hampshire*

# Lamb-Rice Casserole

A traditional pilaf recipe—better than most.

3 pounds lamb—shoulder, loin, or leg
3 cups water
1 clove garlic, mashed
1 onion, halved
1 stalk celery with leaves, cut into large pieces

½ cup chopped onion
1 cup uncooked rice
2 tablespoons shortening or oil
1 teaspoon salt
½ teaspoon pepper

Place lamb, water, garlic, onion, and celery in heavy saucepan and bring to boil. Simmer 1 hour. Skim fat. Remove lamb from bones and cut into 1" cubes. Strain broth and reserve.

In large saucepan or flame-proof casserole, brown onion and rice in shortening or oil. Add lamb, 2½ cups reserved broth, salt, and pepper. Bring to boil and cook, covered, 30 minutes, or until rice is done and most liquid is absorbed. Serve immediately, or cool and store 1 or 2 days. To reheat, add a little lamb broth or water, and cook slowly over medium heat, stirring occasionally, until dish is hot. *Serves 8–10.*

*Alice Halliday, St. Thomas's Episcopal Church, Hanover, New Hampshire*

# Slow-Cooker Middle-Eastern Lamb Shanks

Low, steady cooking makes lamb shanks as tender as butter. Serve cooked rice or orzo pasta with this richly flavored dish.

4½–5 **pounds lamb shanks**
1 **carrot, thinly sliced**
1 **onion, quartered and sliced**
¼ **cup chopped parsley**
2 **large cloves garlic, minced**
½ **teaspoon oregano**
½ **teaspoon salt**

½ **teaspoon pepper**
1 **can (14 ounces) diced tomatoes with juice**
1 **cup dry red wine**
1 **cup beef broth**
2 **tablespoons fresh lemon juice**

Place lamb, carrot, onion, parsley, garlic, oregano, salt, and pepper in 6-quart slow cooker. With hands or tongs, toss ingredients to coat evenly with seasonings. Add tomatoes with juice, wine, broth, and lemon juice. Set cooker to high. Cook for 30 minutes. Reduce setting to low and cook for 7 hours. ***Serves 6–8.***

*Rebecca Gale, Franklin Community Church, Franklin, Michigan*

# Cassoulet

You can make this French provincial classic in many variations on the same basic theme, depending on the kind of meats you add. Always a showstopper, though it does take time.

2 cups dry white beans, pea or great Northern
4 cups chicken or beef broth
2 carrots, diced
1 large onion, stuck with cloves
1 stalk celery with leaves, sliced
1 teaspoon salt
1 teaspoon sugar
2 bay leaves
2 tablespoons parsley flakes, or 3 sprigs fresh
5 peppercorns
½ teaspoon thyme
1 large onion, sliced

1 clove garlic, mashed
1 pound sausage (kielbasa, knockwurst, or salami), pork, or ham cut into 1" pieces
1 pound lean stewing lamb, cut into 1" cubes, or leftover roast lamb or other meat
4 tablespoons butter or fat
2 cups tomatoes, drained
  Large piece of bacon rind, slice of lean salt pork, ham bone, or ham hock
  Sliced cooked duck, goose or chicken meat (optional)

Soak beans overnight; drain. Simmer in broth with carrots, cloved onion, celery, salt, and sugar. At start of cooking, add to broth, bay leaves, parsley, peppercorns, and thyme tied up in cheesecloth bag. Cook beans until just tender—when skins wrinkle if blown upon. Sauté sliced onion; garlic; sausage, pork, or ham; and uncooked lamb in butter or fat. When meat is lightly browned, add tomatoes and simmer for 10 minutes. (If using *cooked* leftover meat, add now.) Place bacon rind, salt pork, or ham bone or hock in bottom of large casserole dish. Remove cloved onion and herb bag from bean pot. Drain beans, reserving broth. Layer casserole dish alternately with beans and mixed meats, ending with meat layer. Place sliced poultry meat, if using, on top. Pour bean broth over to just cover. Bake uncovered at 300°F for 2 hours. At the end of 2 hours, check liquid level; add more broth if necessary, replace cover, and return to oven for 1 more hour. (Good reheated, too.) *Serves 8–10.*

# Mediterranean Lamb and Eggplant Bake

Earthy Mediterranean flavors meld in this easy-to-tote dish.
For a variation, ground beef may replace the lamb.

Salt
4 medium (3 pounds) unpeeled eggplants, sliced lengthwise into ¼"-thick slabs
2 cups chopped onion
2 tablespoons olive oil
2 teaspoons oregano
1½ teaspoons cinnamon
1½ teaspoons cumin
1 teaspoon black pepper
1 teaspoon cayenne pepper
2½ pounds ground lamb
1 can (28-ounces) crushed tomatoes in puree
½ cup chopped parsley or cilantro
12 tablespoons plain dry bread crumbs
½ cup grated Pecorino Romano cheese

Sprinkle salt generously over both sides of eggplant. Arrange in single layer on several thicknesses of paper toweling. Cover with paper toweling. Repeat layering. Set weighted tray atop paper towels. After 30 minutes, remove tray and press gently to squeeze any remaining bitter juices from eggplant. Rinse slices under cold water; pat dry.

Meanwhile, sauté onion in oil in large skillet over medium-high heat for 5 minutes. Add oregano, cinnamon, cumin, black pepper, cayenne, and 1½ teaspoons salt. Sauté for 3 minutes or until onions are soft. Crumble lamb into pan. Cook for about 5 minutes or until only traces of pink remain. Tilt pan and skim off and discard excess fat. Add tomatoes. Cook for 3 minutes or until heated. Stir in parsley or cilantro.

Mix 3 tablespoons breadcrumbs with cheese; set aside. Scatter 3 tablespoons breadcrumbs over bottom of greased 11" × 15" (5-quart) lasagna dish. Cover with one-third of eggplant slices topped with one-third of lamb mixture. Repeat two times with breadcrumbs, eggplant, and lamb mixture. Cover with aluminum foil. Bake at 375°F for 1 hour. Remove foil. Sprinkle with reserved cheese and breadcrumbs. Bake 10 minutes or until cheese bubbles. Allow to sit 15 minutes before serving. *Serves 8–10.*

*Bonnie Beck, First United Church of Oak Park, Oak Park, Illinois*

# Swedish Lamb and Lentil Stew

1½ medium onions, sliced
1½ tablespoons butter or oil
1½ pounds lean lamb, cubed
3 cups beef stock
   Salt and pepper

1½ cups red or brown lentils, soaked
   in water to cover for 3 hours
1 bay leaf
1 teaspoon marjoram
   Parsley

Sauté onions in butter or oil until tender. Remove and set aside. Turn up heat and brown lamb on all sides, stirring to prevent sticking. Return onions, add stock to cover and salt and pepper to taste, and simmer for 30 minutes. Drain lentils and add to pot with bay leaf and marjoram. Simmer 45 minutes longer, adding water or stock as necessary and stirring from time to time. Remove and discard bay leaf and bring slowly to boil. Sprinkle with parsley and serve hot. *Serves 6–8.*

# Rosemary Lamb Stew

Serve with Lemon-Spinach Rice (page 117) for a gourmet meal.

3 pounds lamb, fat removed and
   cut into 1½" cubes
1½ tablespoons cooking oil
1½ tablespoons butter
½ teaspoon rosemary
2 cloves garlic, mashed
   Pinch of sage

½ teaspoon pepper
1 tablespoon flour
¾ cup red wine
1 cup chicken stock
4 anchovy fillets, mashed
   Parsley

In Dutch oven, brown lamb in oil and butter. Add rosemary, garlic, sage, and pepper. Blend flour with a little wine to form a paste, then add rest of wine to paste and add to lamb. Add stock and cook, stirring, until slightly thickened. Cover and simmer for an hour or so, stirring from time to time, or until meat is tender. Dip out ½ cup sauce, combine with anchovies, then pour back into stew and blend. Simmer 5 minutes longer, garnish with parsley, and serve with rice, new potatoes, or noodles. *Serves 6.*

# Lamb Poulette

The piquant, lemon-flavored sauce complements the lamb beautifully. Be sure you remove the stew from the heat before adding the egg yolks.

2 pounds lamb, shoulder or loin, trimmed and cut into 1½" pieces
Salt
3 cups boiling water
2 tablespoons butter
1½ tablespoons flour
2 cups boiling water, or 1 cup beef stock and 1 cup boiling water
1 teaspoon salt
¼ teaspoon pepper

Bouquet garni made up of 1 sprig parsley, 1 teaspoon thyme leaves, and 1 bay leaf tied into small square of cheesecloth
6–8 small white onions
10–12 fresh mushrooms, or 1 can (6 ounces), drained
Juice of ½ lemon
2 egg yolks

Sprinkle meat with salt and cover with 3 cups boiling water. Let stand 10 minutes and drain. Place meat in heavy saucepan with butter. Melt butter and stir in flour—do not let meat brown. Stir flour in well, then gradually add 2 cups boiling water, or beef stock and water, stirring constantly. Meat should be barely covered. Stir in salt and pepper, and add bouquet garni and onions. Simmer, covered, for 1 hour over low heat. Add mushrooms and simmer 30 minutes longer, or until meat is tender. Add more liquid if meat becomes dry.

When meat is tender, remove pan from heat and stir in lemon juice. Beat egg yolks in separate bowl and stir ½ cup hot sauce into them. Add yolks and sauce to meat, stirring in thoroughly. Sample sauce and add salt and pepper to taste. Place on serving dish and serve over rice or noodles. *Serves 6–8.*

# Chicken and Turkey

Where *would* we all be without these two marvelous birds? Truly they are among the most versatile of all meats—*and* the least expensive. Talented cooks from across the country have provided here a marvelous array of classics and creations for just about every occasion. None are difficult, all are delicious, and all are different. Three remarkable stuffings are included at the end of the chapter.

Manicotti with Creamed Chicken and Almonds  56

The Sultan's Favorite Chicken  57

Asian-Style Chicken  58

Layered Chicken  58

Chicken Piquant  59

Lazy Chicken in Herbed Sauce  60

Hot Chicken Salad  60

Chicken Sour Cream Bake  61

California Oven-Fried Chicken  61

Spring Chicken Maryland  62

Chicken Pie with Crust  63

Chicken Pie with Biscuit Topping  64

Chicken Loaf or Ring  65

Nutty Chicken Pie  66

Chicken Spaghetti Dinner  66

Chicken Rice Casserole  66

Rich Chicken Noodle Casserole  67

Peachy Chicken  68

Chicken à la King  68

Chicken Soufflé  69

Chicken Potato Casserole  70

Chicken and Corn Pudding  70

Chicken Enchiladas  71

Guisado de Pollo  72

Never-fail Chicken Delicious  72

Chicken Marengo  73

Coq au Vin  74

Easy Chicken Cacciatore  74

Paella Valenciana  75

Turkey Curry  76

Italian Turkey Casserole  76

Turkey Terrapin  77

Turkey Florentine  78

Special Stuffing  78

Parsley-Lemon Stuffing  79

Turkey Dressing  79

# Manicotti with Creamed Chicken and Almonds

Easier to make than it appears and very elegant.

1 chicken, cooked, skinned, boned, and cut into ½" cubes
1 tablespoon dry white vermouth
½ lemon
Salt and freshly ground pepper
2 tablespoons + 1 teaspoon butter
¼ cup finely chopped onion
3 tablespoons flour
1½ cups chicken broth
¾ cup heavy cream
½ cup grated Gruyère or Swiss cheese
3 tablespoons blanched almonds
1 small egg, lightly beaten
1 cup ricotta cheese
6 tablespoons Parmesan cheese
3 tablespoons chopped parsley
12 oven-ready manicotti shells*
½ teaspoon grated lemon rind

Place chicken in bowl with vermouth and squeeze lemon over meat. Sprinkle with salt and pepper to taste and set aside.

Melt 2 tablespoons butter in saucepan and add onion. Cook, stirring, until onion is wilted. Sprinkle with flour and cook, stirring with wire whisk or fork. Add broth, stirring rapidly with whisk. When thickened and smooth, add ½ cup cream. Simmer about 10 minutes, stirring occasionally; then add Gruyère or Swiss and salt and pepper to taste. Stir to blend and set aside.

Meanwhile, melt remaining 1 teaspoon butter in small ovenproof skillet and add almonds in one layer. Bake at 350°F until golden brown, shaking skillet and stirring almonds from time to time so they won't burn. Remove and let cool.

Mix chicken with almonds, egg, ricotta, 4 tablespoons Parmesan, and parsley, then add enough cheese sauce to bind chicken mixture.

To assemble, spoon equal amounts of chicken mixture inside each manicotti. In baking dish large enough to hold manicotti in one layer, spoon enough sauce into dish to cover bottom. Arrange filled manicotti over sauce. Mix remaining ¼ cup cream with cheese sauce and pour over manicotti. Bake, covered, at 350°F for 30–40 minutes until piping hot and bubbling. Sprinkle with remaining 2 tablespoons Parmesan and run briefly under broiler to glaze. Sprinkle with grated lemon rind and serve hot. ***Serves 10–12.***

*Helen D. Tawse, St. James' Episcopal Church, Keene, New Hampshire*

*Regular lasagna noodles may be substituted for manicotti. Cook and fill as described in Cannelloni (see page 26). Crêpes (see Crêpes Fasnacloich on page 38) can also be used.

# The Sultan's Favorite Chicken

An especially nice chicken divan. Goes well with fluffy, hot buttered rice.

2 broiler-fryers, or a 5-pound fowl
2 stalks celery
1 medium onion
2½ cups lightly salted water
6 tablespoons butter
½ cup flour
1 cup milk

2 cups strained chicken stock
1 teaspoon curry powder
1 teaspoon lemon juice
1 cup mayonnaise
2 packages (10 ounces each) frozen broccoli
Pimiento strips

Simmer chicken with celery and onion in water until tender. Remove meat from bones in large pieces. Strain and reserve stock. Melt butter in saucepan, blend in flour, and gradually add milk and stock. Cook over low heat until thick and smooth, stirring constantly. Remove from heat and add curry powder, lemon juice, and mayonnaise. Beat with rotary beater until very smooth. Cook and drain broccoli. Arrange in bottom of greased 3-quart casserole. Place pieces of chicken on top and pour sauce over all. Garnish with pimiento strips and bake at 400°F for 20 minutes, or until heated through. *Serves 8.*

*Baptist Women's Fellowship, New London, New Hampshire*

# Asian-Style Chicken

An interesting combination of tastes and textures. Serve with extra soy sauce on the side.

1 package (10 ounces) frozen
  peas
1 cup diced cabbage
1 can (5 ounces) water chestnuts,
  drained
¼ cup cooking oil
6 tablespoons flour
½ teaspoon ground ginger
2½ cups chicken stock

1 tablespoon soy sauce
2 cups cooked, diced chicken
1 can (4 ounces) sliced
  mushrooms, drained
1 can (5 ounces) bamboo shoots,
  drained
1 can (16 ounces) mixed Chinese
  vegetables, or 2 cups fresh
  bean sprouts

Boil peas and cabbage together 2 or 3 minutes until crisp. Slice water chestnuts. In large skillet, heat oil, blend in flour and ginger, and stir until smooth. Add chicken stock slowly, stirring constantly until sauce thickens and bubbles. Add soy sauce, chicken, peas and cabbage, mushrooms, bamboo shoots, and Chinese vegetables or bean sprouts. Stir thoroughly until hot. Serve over hot rice or noodles. *Serves 6–8.*

*Betty W. Doyle, United Church of Christ, Keene, New Hampshire*

# Layered Chicken

If you freeze this casserole, do not add the Chinese noodles until ready to bake.

3 chicken legs, cooked
1 can (10¾ ounces) cream of
  mushroom soup
1½ cups cooked rice
2 cans (4 ounces each) mushroom
  pieces, or ½ pound fresh, sliced

1 pint sour cream
½ package dry onion soup mix,
  crushed
1 can (5 ounces) chow mein
  noodles

Cut chicken meat from bones into large pieces. Place in bottom of greased 2-quart baking dish. Pour mushroom soup over chicken. Add layer of rice and layer of mushrooms. Pour sour cream over all and sprinkle with onion soup mix. Cover with noodles and bake at 350°F until hot and bubbly. **_Serves 6._**

*Charlotte Stone, First Congregational Church, Portland, Connecticut*

# Chicken Piquant

Chicken pieces cooked in spicy white wine sauce.

| | |
|---|---|
| 1 **broiler-fryer, cut into 6–8 pieces** | 2 **teaspoons ground ginger** |
| ¾ **cup white wine** | ¼ **teaspoon oregano** |
| ¼ **teaspoon salt** | ¼ **cup soy sauce** |
| ¼ **cup cooking oil** | 1 **cup chicken broth** |
| | 2 **tablespoons brown sugar** |

Place chicken pieces in Dutch oven. Combine wine, salt, oil, ginger, oregano, soy sauce, broth, and brown sugar, and pour over chicken. Cover and bake at 375°F for 1 hour. Then uncover and bake at 400°F for 15 minutes more to brown and thicken sauce. Serve with rice. **_Serves 6._**

*Jill Child, The Unitarian Church, Franklin, New Hampshire*

# Lazy Chicken in Herbed Sauce

A Hollandaise-like sauce that makes itself. Cook a package of frozen broccoli right along with 1 cup raw rice, and serve chicken and sauce with or over this Broccoli-Rice.

1 broiler-fryer, cut into 6–8 pieces
2 tablespoons butter
2 tablespoons cooking oil
1 teaspoon grated lemon rind
¼ teaspoon basil

¼ teaspoon oregano
2 tablespoons lemon juice
1 can (10¾ ounces) cream of chicken or cream of mushroom soup

Skin chicken and brown lightly in hot butter and oil. Drain off fat and place chicken in baking dish. Mix together lemon rind, basil, oregano, lemon juice, and soup and spoon over top of chicken. Cover and bake at 325°F for 1–1¼ hours. Can be made the night before and reheated. *Serves 6.*

*Evelyn H. Chase, Concord Unitarian Church, Concord, New Hampshire*

# Hot Chicken Salad

Crunchy and flavorful chicken dish. For variety, substitute ½ cup diced onion and ½ cup diced green pepper for 1 of the 2 cups of celery.

2 cups cubed cooked chicken
2 cups thinly sliced celery
1 cup mayonnaise
½ cup toasted slivered almonds
2 teaspoons lemon juice

½ teaspoon salt
½ cup grated cheese
1 cup toasted bread cubes or croutons

Combine chicken, celery, mayonnaise, almonds, lemon juice, and salt. Pile lightly into greased baking dish. Sprinkle with cheese and bread cubes or croutons. Bake at 450°F for 20 minutes, or until bubbly. *Serves 6.*

*Shirley T. Oladell, Harwinton Congregational Church, Harwinton, Connecticut*

# Chicken Sour Cream Bake

Rich, different, and distinguished—but oh, so easy to do.
The chipped beef ends up tasting like Italian prosciutto ham.

6 chicken breast halves, skinned,
boned, and halved again if too
large to be wrapped in beef slice

1 jar (4 ounces) chipped beef,
rinsed in boiling water and
drained

12 slices bacon

2 cups sour cream

1 can (10¾ ounces) cream of
asparagus or cream of
mushroom soup

Paprika

Wrap each breast section in slice of chipped beef, then wrap with bacon. Mix sour cream and soup. Place chicken in greased casserole dish and pour soup mixture over it. Sprinkle with paprika to taste. Bake uncovered at 325°F for 2 hours. *Serves 6–8.*

*Catherine B. Anderson, United Methodist Church of the Hamptons, Hampton, New Hampshire*

# California Oven-Fried Chicken

Moist, tender, and habit-forming!

1 frying chicken, cut into 8 pieces

¼ pound melted butter

⅛ teaspoon garlic powder

⅛ teaspoon paprika

⅛ teaspoon thyme

1 teaspoon salt

1½ cups dry bread crumbs or
finely crushed cornflakes

Dip chicken pieces in butter, then shake in paper bag containing garlic powder, paprika, thyme, salt, and crumbs or cornflakes. Place skin side up in lightly greased 9" × 13" baking dish, and bake at 350°F for 50 minutes or until done. *Serves 6–8.*

*Mary Wakefield, First Congregational Church, Rindge, New Hampshire*

# Spring Chicken Maryland

A specialty of dining-car chefs during the Golden Age of Pullman travel
that well deserves its fame. Easily divided.

3 broiler-fryers, cut up
6 tablespoons cooking oil
¼ cup flour
½ teaspoon salt
⅛ teaspoon pepper
3 slices (½" thick) salt pork, cut into square dice

3 pinches of nutmeg
¾ cup melted butter
3 cups cream or evaporated milk
Paprika
Parsley sprigs

Cut chickens into quarters. Brush with oil and dredge with flour, salt, and pepper. Fry salt pork in large skillet until brown. Add nutmeg. Place chicken on top of pork (without draining off fat) and baste with melted butter. Cover skillet and cook about 30 minutes over medium-low heat until tender. Turn chicken pieces over. Add 1 cup cream or evaporated milk, turn heat up to medium, and cook uncovered to let cream cook down. When sauce is fairly thick, add another cup of cream or milk, cook as before until thickened, and add the last cup of cream or milk. Cook until thick. To serve, spoon cream gravy over chicken pieces, sprinkle with paprika to taste, and garnish with parsley sprigs. *Serves 12.*

# Chicken Pie with Crust

2 cut-up broiler-fryers
1 large onion, quartered
4 carrots, peeled and cut into pieces
2–3 cups water
¼ teaspoon rosemary
½ teaspoon thyme
¼ teaspoon marjoram

2 teaspoons salt
1 teaspoon pepper
1 package (10 ounces) frozen peas
⅓ cup butter
⅓ cup flour
1 cup cream

Put chicken into pot with onion and carrots. Add water to cover, rosemary, thyme, marjoram, 1 teaspoon salt, and ½ teaspoon pepper. Bring to boil and simmer, covered, for about 45 minutes, or until chicken is cooked. Drain chicken and reserve broth. Remove bones and skin from chicken pieces and cut meat into bite-sized chunks. Return chicken to vegetables and add frozen peas. Remove 1½ cups broth from pot. Melt butter in saucepan and blend in flour. Gradually add hot broth and cream, stirring constantly until thickened and smooth. Add remaining 1 teaspoon salt and ½ teaspoon pepper. Pour sauce over chicken and vegetables, adding more broth if necessary.

## Pastry

1 cup shortening
3 cups flour

½ teaspoon salt
½–¾ cup cold water

Cut shortening into flour mixed with salt. Add water. Mix well to form ball. Roll out top and bottom crusts.

Place bottom crust in 9" deep-dish pie plate. Pour in chicken mixture and cover with top crust. Brush with milk. Pierce three small holes in top crust to let steam escape and put ring of foil around edge to prevent overbrowning. Bake at 350°F for 35–40 minutes, or until brown, removing foil after about 10 minutes. *Serves 6–8.*

*Crust: Evelyn Shaw, Pilgrim Congregational Church, New Haven, Connecticut*

# Chicken Pie with Biscuit Topping

Use the recipe on page 58 for chicken, vegetables, and sauce.
Place in 9" × 13" baking dish and top with Baking Powder Biscuits.

## Baking Powder Biscuits

2 cups flour
4 teaspoons baking powder
1 teaspoon salt

⅓ cup shortening
¾ cup milk

Sift together flour, baking powder, and salt, and cut in shortening. Add milk to make soft dough. Knead a few times on floured board. Lightly roll out to ½" thickness and cut with 2" cutter. Bake at 450°F for 10–15 minutes, or until chicken mixture is hot and biscuits are well-browned. *Serves 6–8.*

*Biscuits: Susie Cleveland, The United Church, Northfield, Vermont*

# Chicken Loaf or Ring

Like its first cousin, meat loaf, good cold or hot.
Fill a hot chicken ring with rice or macaroni, a cold ring with fresh salad.

2 cups scalded milk
2 eggs, lightly beaten
1 cup soft bread crumbs
½ teaspoon salt
¼ teaspoon paprika

1 teaspoon Worcestershire sauce
3 cups diced cooked chicken
½ cup chopped celery
1 green pepper, chopped
1½ tablespoons lemon juice

Pour hot milk slowly in a thin stream onto eggs, stirring constantly. Add bread crumbs, salt, paprika, Worcestershire sauce, chicken, celery, pepper, and lemon juice. Mix well, and pour into buttered loaf pan or ring mold. Bake at 300°F until knife inserted in center comes out clean—45–60 minutes, approximately. The ring will cook in less time than the loaf. Do not overbake. Remove from oven and let stand 10 minutes before unmolding. *Serves 6–8.*

# Nutty Chicken Pie

Chicken, mushrooms, and almonds in a velvety cream sauce under a pastry cover.

¼ cup butter
¼ cup flour
1 cup light cream
½ teaspoon salt (omit if you use bouillon cube to make broth)
¼ teaspoon pepper
1 cup chicken broth

¼ teaspoon dillweed
1 teaspoon chopped parsley
2 cups cooked diced chicken
1 can (4 ounces) sliced mushrooms, drained
½ cup toasted slivered almonds
Pastry for single-crust 9" pie

Melt butter and blend in flour. Gradually stir in cream and cook, stirring, until smooth and thick. Add salt, pepper, chicken broth, dillweed, and parsley, and cook until smooth and thick once more. Stir in chicken, mushrooms, and almonds. Pour into 9" deep-dish pie plate and cover with pastry. Slash top and bake on cookie sheet in oven preheated to 450°F for 10 minutes. Reduce heat to 350°F and bake 15 minutes more. *Serves 6.*

# Chicken Spaghetti Dinner

Spaghetti with a difference. The secret is the long simmer.

1 green pepper, chopped
1 cup diced celery
2 large onions, chopped
3 cloves garlic, chopped
½ cup cooking oil
1 can (16 ounces) tomato puree
2 cans (6 ounces each) tomato paste

2 puree cans water (32 ounces)
1 cup-up broiler-fryer, or 3 large chicken breasts, halved
1 teaspoon cinnamon
1 teaspoon salt
½ teaspoon pepper
½ teaspoon allspice
8 ounces spaghetti

Sauté green pepper, celery, onions, and garlic in ¼ cup cooking oil. Add tomato puree, paste, and water. Simmer 1½ hours, uncovered, stirring from time to time. Brown chicken pieces in remaining ¼ cup oil. Add with cinnamon, salt, pepper, and allspice to simmering sauce and continue to simmer, covered, for 1½ hours longer, or until chicken is tender. Cook spaghetti as directed and drain. Place in serving dish. Pour chicken and sauce over spaghetti. *Serves 6.*

*Virginia Colivos, Greek Orthodox Church of the Annunciation, Dover, New Hampshire*

# Chicken Rice Casserole

An elegant version of a hot chicken salad.

2 cups diced cooked chicken
1 cup sliced celery
2 teaspoons finely chopped onion
½ cup chopped walnut meats
2 cups cooked rice
1 can (10¾ ounces) cream of chicken soup

½ teaspoon salt
¼ teaspoon pepper
1 tablespoon lemon juice
½ cup mayonnaise
½ cup water
3 hard-boiled eggs, sliced
2 cups crushed potato chips

In large bowl, combine chicken, celery, onion, walnuts, rice, soup, salt, pepper, and lemon juice. Mix mayonnaise with water until smooth and add to chicken mixture. Gently fold in egg slices. Turn mixture into greased 9" × 9" pan. Bake at 450°F for 25 minutes. Remove and top with potato chips. Return to oven for another 5 minutes. **Serves 6–8.**

*Emilie C. Bugbee, The Congregational Church, Somers, Connecticut*

# Rich Chicken Noodle Casserole

Tabasco lends a special touch to this creamy invention.

| | |
|---|---|
| 3 cups uncooked medium egg noodles | 1½ teaspoons salt |
| 1 cup cottage cheese | ¼ teaspoon Tabasco Sauce |
| 1 cup sour cream | ¼ cup sliced pitted ripe olives |
| 6 tablespoons grated Parmesan cheese | 2½ cups diced cooked chicken |

Cook noodles according to package directions. Combine cottage cheese, sour cream, 4 tablespoons Parmesan, salt, and Tabasco. Stir in olives, noodles, and chicken. Turn into greased 2-quart casserole and sprinkle with remaining 2 tablespoons Parmesan cheese. Cover and refrigerate. One hour before serving, bake, covered, at 350°F for 35 minutes. Uncover and bake for 25 minutes longer. **Serves 6.**

*Woodmont United Church of Christ, Milford, Connecticut*

# Peachy Chicken

A fruitful combination of flavors; good served over rice.

3 chicken breasts, halved
½ cup flour
Salt and pepper
2 tablespoons butter
2 tablespoons cooking oil
1½ cups orange juice

2 tablespoons vinegar
2 tablespoons brown sugar
1 teaspoon basil
½ teaspoon nutmeg
1 can (16 ounces) peach (or apricot) halves, drained

Shake chicken pieces in bag with flour and salt and pepper to taste; brown in butter and oil. Place browned chicken in greased 3-quart casserole dish. Combine orange juice with vinegar, sugar, basil, and nutmeg, and pour mixture over chicken. Cover and bake at 375°F for 1 hour and 15 minutes, or until tender. Baste often. Then place peach or apricot halves between chicken pieces, baste well, and bake uncovered for 15 minutes longer. *Serves 6.*

*Barbara Pasichuke, First Congregational Church, Littleton, New Hampshire*

# Chicken à la King

This used to be *the* dish for special occasions, but somehow you don't run into it as often these days. Still good, though.

1 cup sliced mushrooms
4 tablespoons butter
4 tablespoons flour
½ teaspoon salt
¼ teaspoon pepper

2 cups milk or chicken stock
2½ cups cooked diced chicken
1 cup cooked peas
3 tablespoons diced pimiento

Sauté mushrooms in butter. Blend in flour, salt, and pepper. Gradually stir in milk or stock. Cook over medium heat, stirring, until thickened. Add chicken, peas, and pimiento. Heat well and serve in pastry shells or Toast Cups. *Serves 8.*

# Toast Cups

Cut crusts from bread slices. Press slices into muffin tins so 4 points of bread stick up. Bake at 400°F about 10 minutes, or until toasted and brown. Allow to cool a few minutes in pan so cups will hold their shape. If making these ahead, warm them for a few minutes on a cookie sheet before using.

# Chicken Soufflé

This recipe has been multiplied to serve over a hundred for a church luncheon or dinner. Just as good warmed up.

16 slices white bread, buttered on one side, with crusts removed
3–4 whole chicken breasts, cooked, boned, skinned, and sliced
½ cup mayonnaise
1 cup grated Cheddar cheese

5 eggs
2 cups milk
1 teaspoon salt
1 can (10¾ ounces) cream of mushroom or cream of chicken soup

Butter a 9" × 13" baking dish. Line bottom with 8 slices bread. Cover with sliced chicken meat, spread slices with mayonnaise, and sprinkle with ½ cup Cheddar cheese. Top with remaining 8 slices bread. Beat together eggs, milk, and salt, and pour over entire casserole. Refrigerate overnight or all day. When ready to bake, spread soup over top. Bake at 350°F for 45 minutes. Sprinkle with remaining ½ cup Cheddar cheese, return to oven, and bake for 15 minutes longer. *Serves 10.*

*Joan Dean, Grace Congregational Church, Rutland, Vermont*

# Chicken Potato Casserole

Thyme-touched scalloped potatoes topped and cooked with chicken.

4 cups thinly sliced peeled
  potatoes
4–5 medium onions, sliced
  Salt and pepper
  Ground thyme
½ cup hot water

1 can (13 ounces) evaporated milk
2 slices bacon
2 tablespoons butter
2 broiler-fryers, about 3 pounds
  each, cut up
  Paprika

Put potatoes and onions in large roasting pan and sprinkle with salt, pepper, and thyme to taste. Add water. Reserve ¼ cup milk and pour remainder over vegetables. Put in 400°F oven while preparing chicken.

In large skillet, cook bacon until browned; remove and drain. Add butter to skillet, then chicken, and brown on all sides, removing pieces as they brown. Put chicken in pan with potatoes and sprinkle lightly with more salt, pepper, and thyme. Crumble bacon and sprinkle over top. Cover tightly with foil and bake at 400°F for 1 hour. Uncover, pour reserved milk over top, and sprinkle with paprika to taste. Bake 30 minutes longer. *Serves 8.*

*Don Wyant, Woodmont United Church of Christ, Milford, Connecticut*

# Chicken and Corn Pudding

A smooth taste that goes well with other casseroles and with salads.

2 cups diced cooked chicken
3 eggs, well-beaten
3 cups milk
2 tablespoons flour
1½ teaspoons salt

⅛ teaspoon pepper
¼ cup minced onion
¼ cup minced green pepper
1¾ cups canned whole-kernel
  corn, drained

Place chicken in greased casserole dish. Beat eggs, milk, and flour together in bowl, and add salt, pepper, onion, green pepper, and corn. Pour over chicken. Bake at 325°F for 1 hour or longer—until custard is set and knife inserted in center comes out clean. *Serves 6–8.*

*Alma L. Hedrick, Harwinton Congregational Church, Harwinton, Connecticut*

# Chicken Enchiladas

3 tablespoons olive oil

3 stalks celery, chopped

1 large onion, chopped

3 large cloves garlic, minced

2 jalapeños, minced (optional)

3 cups (1 pound) coarsely chopped cooked chicken

1 can (8¾ ounces) corn kernels, drained, or 1 cup frozen corn kernels

2 teaspoons chili powder

½ teaspoon salt

½ teaspoon pepper

6 cups canned red or green enchilada sauce

1 can (14 ounces) black olives, drained and chopped

2 tablespoons minced fresh parsley

2 tablespoons minced fresh cilantro + ½ cup cilantro leaves for garnish

2 dozen flour tortillas (8" in diameter)

2 bags (8 ounces each) shredded Cheddar-Jack cheese mix

1 carton (16 ounces) sour cream

6–8 cups chopped lettuce

Heat oil in 6-quart pot over medium-high heat. Add celery, onion, garlic, and half the jalapeños, if using. Sauté for 10 minutes or until browned. Reduce heat if mixture is browning too quickly. Add chicken, corn, chili powder, salt, pepper, 1½ cups enchilada sauce, and all but ½ cup olives. Stir and reduce the heat to low. Simmer, stirring occasionally, for about 1 hour or until chicken is in shreds and sauce is thickened. Stir in parsley and 2 tablespoons minced cilantro.

Divide 1 cup of remaining enchilada sauce among two greased 11" × 15" (5-quart) lasagna pans, spreading sauce to cover bottom. Pour remaining 3½ cups sauce in shallow container wide enough to hold a tortilla. One at a time, dip both sides of a tortilla in sauce; shake off excess. (Canned sauces vary in thickness; if sauce is thick, use a pastry brush to lightly coat both sides.) Place tortilla in one lasagna pan. Place 2 tablespoons chicken mixture and 2 tablespoons cheese in center. Roll, then tuck in ends and place seam-side down at end of pan. Continue until all filled tortillas are placed, two per row, divided equally between the pans. Cover with sauce remaining in shallow container. Sprinkle with reserved olives and cheese. Bake at 350°F for about 20 minutes or until sauce bubbles and cheese melts. Allow to cool for 10 minutes. Garnish with sour cream, lettuce, and cilantro leaves. Pass remaining jalapeños, if using, at the table. ***Serves 12–16.***

*Taunya L. DeLuca, St. Daniel the Prophet Catholic Community, Scottsdale, Arizona*

# Guisado de Pollo

This hearty Mexican-style chicken stew is subtly and intriguingly spiced.

4 tablespoons cooking oil
2 broiler-fryers, cut into serving pieces
2 chorizos (Spanish sausages), or 2 hot Italian sausages
½ pound cooked ham, diced
2 cups tomatoes, or 1 can (16 ounces)
1 clove garlic, finely minced
½ cup chopped onion

¼ cup finely chopped parsley
¼ pound almonds, roasted and ground
¼ teaspoon cloves
¼ teaspoon cinnamon
Salt and pepper
¾ cup dry white wine
¼ cup capers
3 yellow wax peppers, cut into strips (optional)

Heat oil and brown chicken on all sides. Transfer browned pieces to large Dutch oven or casserole dish. Remove sausage meat from casing and sauté with ham in oil until lightly browned. Pour off most of oil and add tomatoes (with juice), garlic, onion, parsley, almonds, cloves, and cinnamon. Add salt and pepper to taste. Bring to boil and pour over chicken. Cover and simmer about 15 minutes. Add wine, replace cover, and simmer 45–60 minutes longer, or until chicken is thoroughly cooked. Serve garnished with capers and wax peppers (if using) over cornbread or rice. *Serves 8–10.*

*Helen D. Tawse, St. James Episcopal Church, Keene, New Hampshire*

# Never-fail Chicken Delicious

An unusual combination of potatoes, chicken, and sausage.
Our recipe tester reported, "Makes the potatoes taste fabulous."

6 medium potatoes, peeled and quartered
1 teaspoon oregano
1 teaspoon paprika
½ teaspoon garlic powder
1 teaspoon salt

½ teaspoon pepper
1 frying chicken, cut up
1 pound sweet Italian sausage links, cut up
¼ cup vegetable oil

Arrange potatoes in large, shallow 3-quart casserole. Mix oregano, paprika, garlic powder, salt, and pepper, and sprinkle half the mixture over potatoes. Arrange chicken and sausage on top. Pour oil over and sprinkle with remaining seasonings. Cover and bake at 425°F for 1 hour. Uncover, and bake at 375°F for 30 minutes, or until a nice brown. *Serves 6.*

*Joanna Miller, Dublin Community Church, Dublin, New Hampshire*

# Chicken Marengo

Marengo is the name of a small Piedmontese village where Napoleon's chef, on the eve of the battle of Marengo, purportedly invented this famous dish to tempt his general's lagging appetite.

| | |
|---|---|
| 1 cup sliced fresh mushrooms | 1 clove garlic, minced |
| 2 tablespoons butter | ½ cup consommé or dry white wine |
| 1 broiler-fryer (3–4 pounds), cut into 6 serving pieces Salt and pepper | 2 tomatoes, cut into wedges and seeded |
| 2–3 tablespoons cooking oil | ¼ teaspoon thyme |
| 4 green onions, with tops removed, sliced | 1 tablespoon chopped parsley |

Sauté mushrooms in butter for 2 minutes; set aside. Sprinkle chicken pieces with salt and pepper to taste, and sauté in hot oil until brown. Remove chicken from skillet and set aside. Reserve drippings. Sauté onions and garlic in drippings until onions are soft. Stir in consommé or wine, tomatoes, and thyme, scraping bottom of skillet well. Add chicken to skillet. Cover and simmer 30 minutes, or until chicken is tender. Add sautéed mushrooms. Sprinkle with parsley and serve. *Serves 6.*

*Joan Young, The Unitarian Church, Franklin, New Hampshire*

# Coq au Vin

Chicken in a rich red wine sauce.

1 tablespoon flour
Salt and pepper
3 chicken breasts, halved
1 tablespoon minced onion
2 tablespoons cooking oil
12 small white onions

1 cup sliced mushrooms
½ cup red wine
½ cup chicken broth
1 clove garlic, minced
1 bay leaf
½ teaspoon thyme

Mix flour with salt and pepper to taste. Dredge chicken in flour mixture. In large skillet, brown chicken and minced onion in oil. Place chicken in 4-quart casserole. Sauté small white onions and mushrooms in skillet until lightly browned. Add wine, broth, garlic, bay leaf, and thyme. When liquid starts to boil, stir well, pour into casserole, cover, and bake at 350°F for about 40 minutes. Before serving, remove and discard bay leaf. *Serves 6.*

*Joan Young, The Unitarian Church, Franklin, New Hampshire*

# Easy Chicken Cacciatore

A bachelor's delight!

1 chicken (3 pounds), or the equivalent in parts
1 jar (15½ ounces) spaghetti sauce

½ package Good Seasons Garlic Mix

Cut up chicken into 6 serving portions. Combine spaghetti sauce with garlic mix. Dip each piece in sauce. Place in baking pan, and pour remaining sauce over all. Cover with aluminum foil and bake at 350°F for about 1 hour, or until tender. After removing chicken, use sauce in pan to pour over cooked noodles to accompany chicken. *Serves 6.*

*Rev. Eugene B. Navias, Concord Unitarian Church (1957–1963), Concord, New Hampshire*

# Paella Valenciana

As the French do with cassoulet, the Spanish make their justly famed paella in all sorts of different ways, depending on the meat or seafood locally available.

1 pound chorizo or Italian sweet or hot sausage
½ cup diced cooked ham
1 onion, chopped
1 clove garlic, minced
4 tablespoons cooking oil
1 can (4 ounces) mushrooms, liquid reserved
1 can (8 ounces) minced clams, liquid reserved
1 package (10 ounces) frozen peas, cooked with liquid reserved
1 can (6 ounces) tomato paste

2 bay leaves
¼ teaspoon pepper
½ teaspoon sugar
1½ cups white wine
¾ teaspoon salt
2 cups chicken stock
1½ cups uncooked long-grain rice
½ teaspoon ground saffron or yellow food coloring (optional)
2 cups cooked chicken, cut into julienne strips
1 tablespoon chopped parsley

Cut sausage in ½" slices and sauté along with ham, onion, and garlic in 2 tablespoons oil. Drain mushrooms, clams, and peas and reserve liquid. If necessary, add enough water to liquid to equal 1½ cups. Set aside mushrooms, clams, and peas. Add tomato paste, bay leaves, pepper, sugar, wine, reserved liquid, and salt. Simmer for 30 minutes. Heat chicken stock to boiling. In large casserole or Dutch oven, brown rice in remaining 2 tablespoons oil, stirring. Add hot stock and saffron or food coloring, if using, to rice. Add ham and sausage mixture and chicken and stir. Cover tightly and bake at 375°F for 30 minutes, or until rice is cooked. Check at end of 30 minutes and add more liquid if necessary. When rice is done, stir in mushrooms, clams, parsley, shrimp, and peas. Bake uncovered at 375°F for 15–20 minutes to fluff rice and heat through. *Serves 8–10.*

# Turkey Curry

This is a wonderful way to re-present the Thanksgiving turkey!

1 cup sliced sautéed fresh (or canned and drained) mushrooms
⅓ cup minced onion
1 large apple, peeled, cored, and diced
3 cups diced cooked turkey

6 tablespoons butter
3 tablespoons flour
½ teaspoon salt
1–1½ teaspoons curry powder
1½ cups turkey stock, mixed with a little cream

Sauté mushrooms, onion, apple, and turkey in butter until apple and onion are tender. Remove from heat and stir in flour, salt, and curry powder. Blend in ½ cup liquid and return to stove. Cook, stirring and gradually adding remaining 1 cup liquid, over medium heat until sauce has thickened. Put in top of double boiler and cook over boiling water 15 minutes longer. Taste to adjust seasoning. Serve with hot rice. *Serves 6.*

# Italian Turkey Casserole

A different way to use turkey or chicken—with Italian cornmeal mush, or polenta.

1½ quarts water
1 teaspoon salt
½ cup yellow cornmeal
2 Italian hot sausages, cooked and sliced (optional)
3 cups diced cooked turkey or chicken

1 pound sliced mushrooms
3 tablespoons butter
2–2½ cups meatless tomato sauce
¾ cup grated Parmesan cheese
Pepper

Place water and salt in large saucepan. Bring to boil and gradually add cornmeal, stirring constantly with wooden spoon. Cook over medium heat until consistency of mashed potatoes (about 30 minutes). Put into 10" × 10" buttered baking dish and level off with spoon. Spoon sausage, if using, and turkey or chicken over polenta layer. Sauté mushrooms in butter and lay on top of turkey or chicken. Spread tomato sauce over all. Sprinkle with Parmesan and a little pepper to taste. Bake at 350°F for 45 minutes. *Serves 6–8.*

*Clorinda C. Duke, United Church, East Calais, Vermont*

# Turkey Terrapin

For luxurious leftovers.

| | |
|---|---|
| 4 tablespoons butter | mushrooms (or use canned and drained) |
| 2 cups minced cooked turkey or chicken | 2 hard-boiled eggs |
| ½ cup flour | Salt and pepper |
| Chicken stock | Paprika |
| 1½ cups thin cream | ½ cup sherry |
| 1 cup sliced sautéed fresh | Parsley |

Melt butter in frying pan. Dredge turkey or chicken well with flour and add to butter along with enough stock to blend well, stirring to keep mixture smooth. Add cream, mushrooms, and eggs with whites cut into strips and yolks sieved. Season to taste with salt, pepper, and paprika. Cook slowly until thick and creamy, and just before serving stir in sherry. Spoon over toasted and buttered English muffins, and garnish with chopped parsley. *Serves 6.*

# Turkey Florentine

Turkey, spinach, and mushrooms in a smoothly delicious sauce.

8 tablespoons butter
1 chicken bouillon cube
3 cups diced cooked turkey
1 cup canned, drained mushrooms
¼ cup flour
2 cups milk
1 cup grated Colby or Cheddar
cheese

1 teaspoon salt
3 tablespoons sherry
Dash of nutmeg
2 packages (10 ounces each)
frozen chopped spinach,
cooked and drained

Melt 4 tablespoons butter and crush bouillon cube into hot butter. Sauté turkey in butter for 2–3 minutes, stirring to heat evenly. Remove turkey and add mushrooms to butter. Sauté for 2–3 minutes and add to turkey. Keep turkey and mushrooms hot. In same pan used to sauté, melt remaining 4 tablespoons butter and blend in flour. Gradually add milk, stirring until sauce is smooth and thick. Add cheese, salt, sherry, and nutmeg, stirring until cheese is melted. Butter a 9" × 13" baking dish. Spread spinach over bottom. Cover with turkey and mushroom mixture. Pour sauce over all and bake at 350°F for 30 minutes, or until heated through and bubbly. *Serves 8.*

# Special Stuffing

The blue cheese in this elegant stuffing enhances the flavor of almost any poultry.

¼ cup butter
½ cup chopped celery
1 cup sliced mushrooms
½ cup chopped onion
4 cups croutons
¼ cup chopped parsley
½ cup sliced water chestnuts

½ cup crumbled American blue
cheese
1 tablespoon poultry seasoning
¾ teaspoon sugar
Dash of pepper
Broth from giblets

In butter, sauté celery, mushrooms, and onion. In large bowl, combine croutons, parsley, water chestnuts, blue cheese, poultry seasoning, sugar, and pepper. Add celery and onion mixture. Blend well, tossing lightly. Add enough broth to dampen ingredients. Mix well. *Makes 8 cups.*

# Parsley-Lemon Stuffing

The lemon rind and parsley endow this stuffing with a clean, light flavor all its own.

| | |
|---|---|
| 6 tablespoons butter + ¾ cup melted butter | Grated rind of 3 lemons |
| 1 medium onion, chopped fine | 1½ cups chopped parsley |
| 3 cups fresh bread crumbs | 3 eggs, well-beaten |
| | Salt and pepper |

Melt 6 tablespoons butter and sauté onion until tender and golden. In mixing bowl, combine bread crumbs, lemon rind, parsley, and onion. Add eggs and ¾ cup melted butter, and mix well. Season with salt and pepper to taste. ***Enough to stuff 1 large or 2 small chickens.***

# Turkey Dressing

A really imaginative stuffing—enough to stuff into a 21-pound holiday turkey.

| | |
|---|---|
| 1 pound bulk pork sausage | ¼ cup chopped green pepper |
| 8 cups bread cubes | ½ cup sliced almonds |
| ½ cup butter | 2 teaspoons salt |
| 2 cloves garlic, minced | ½ teaspoon pepper |
| 2 cups chopped celery and leaves | ¼ teaspoon nutmeg |
| 1 cup chopped onion | 1 teaspoon poultry seasoning |
| 1 cup coarsely chopped mushrooms | Pinch of cayenne pepper |
| ¼ cup chopped parsley | ½ of 10½-ounce can consommé |
| | ½ cup dry sherry |

Sauté sausage until light brown. Drain, reserving fat, and remove to large bowl. To pork fat, add bread cubes and stir. Remove to bowl with pork. In butter, sauté garlic, celery, onion, mushrooms, parsley, green pepper, and almonds until tender. Season with salt, pepper, nutmeg, poultry seasoning, and cayenne. Add consommé and sherry. Heat through. Add to bread cubes and pork mixture. Toss thoroughly.

*Marcia Gehrke, United Methodist Church of the Hamptons, Hampton, New Hampshire*

# Eggs, Cheese, Fish, and Seafood

Egg-and-cheese casseroles are some of the best loved. And they can be served at any meal—from breakfast to a midnight supper. From omelettes to quiches, these dishes are sure to please family and friends.

Despite the sometimes-high price of fish and seafood, the importance of this food to our diet has not changed. The seafood recipes here range from the delicious to the absolutely extraordinary, including several inventive fish casseroles and tasty shrimp dishes.

Baked Omelet  81

Easy Eggs and Tomato Benedict  81

Scrambled Eggs in Mushroom
and Cheese Sauce  82

Three-Cheese Deviled Eggs  83

Brunch Eggs  83

Deviled Egg and Spinach Casserole  84

Ham and Eggs Brunch Casserole  84

Mushroom Business  85

Spaghetti Carbonara  86

Quiche Lorraine  86

Spinach Quiche  87

Mushroom Quiche  87

Corn Flan  88

Clam Casserole  88

Crab and Corn Bake  89

Scalloped Clams  89

Mock Lobster Casserole  90

Kedgeree  90

Marit's Fish Casserole  91

Salmon Pudding  92

Flounder Crowns with Florentine Stuffing  92

Fish Casserole  93

Fabulous Flounder Fillets  94

Shrimp and Rice Casserole  95

Gourmet Shrimp  95

Spicy Shrimp with Mango-Fennel Salsa  96

Deviled Eggs, Shrimp, and Mushrooms in
Cheese Sauce  96

Shrimp and Blue Cheese Casserole  97

Sesame Scallops and Salmon with Cucumber  98

Salmon Mousse with Cucumber Sauce  99

Crisp Tuna Balls with Spicy Cheddar Dip  100

# Baked Omelet

The North Madison Congregational Church has served this omelet to 100 people at Easter sunrise breakfasts. Multiply recipe given below by number of persons to be served. Rises high in oven but will fall when taken out. Don't worry—it is supposed to.

1½ tablespoons butter
1 tablespoon cream
⅛ teaspoon dry mustard
1 tablespoon grated cheese
Dash of onion powder

⅛ teaspoon salt
Dash of pepper
¼ teaspoon sweet basil
1 egg

In pan, melt ½ tablespoon butter. In bowl, combine cream, mustard, cheese, onion powder, salt, pepper, basil, remaining 1 tablespoon butter, and egg. Beat until frothy and pour into 6" ovenproof skillet or 1-quart casserole (mixture should be ¼" deep in pan). Bake at 350°F for 20–25 minutes, or until firm and beginning to brown. Cut into squares and serve.

*Sonja Gibbs and Jan Woerheide, North Madison Congregational Church, North Madison, Connecticut*

# Easy Eggs and Tomato Benedict

The sauce—mayonnaise, milk, lemon juice, basil, and pepper— is a very acceptable substitute for hollandaise and easily made.

2 medium tomatoes
½ cup mayonnaise
¼ cup milk
½ teaspoon lemon juice
¼ teaspoon dry basil

Dash of pepper
4 English muffins, split and toasted
Salt
8 eggs, poached and drained

Cut each tomato into 4 slices and set aside. In small saucepan, combine mayonnaise, milk, lemon juice, basil, and pepper. Heat. Keep warm. Cover each muffin half with a tomato slice. Sprinkle lightly with salt. Top with poached egg and pour sauce on top. *Serves 4 or 8.*

*Mrs. Henry Johnson, Swanzey Congregational Church, Swanzey, New Hampshire*

# Scrambled Eggs in Mushroom and Cheese Sauce

The richest scrambled eggs in the world! May be prepared up to the broiling point and kept at room temperature for an hour ahead of time.

¾ **cup butter**
1 **pound fresh mushrooms, quartered**
2 **tablespoons minced scallions or shallots**
6 **tablespoons flour**
2 **cups milk, scalded**

1 **cup heavy cream**
**Salt and pepper (season both sauce and eggs separately; use in all about ½ teaspoon salt and ⅛ teaspoon pepper)**
16 **eggs**
½ **cup grated Parmesan cheese**

Melt 3 tablespoons butter in large frying pan and sauté mushrooms until just beginning to brown. Add scallions or shallots and cook for 2 minutes. Drain and set aside.

Make sauce by melting 3 tablespoons butter in 2-quart saucepan over medium heat. Blend in flour, and add milk gradually, stirring until smooth and thickened. Add ½ cup cream and let simmer, stirring, for about 5 minutes. Stir in remaining ½ cup cream to thin sauce so that it definitely coats a spoon but is not too thick. Add salt and pepper to taste. Set aside.

Scramble eggs in 4 tablespoons butter until just set. Add salt and pepper to taste.

Pour thin layer of sauce over bottom of buttered 9" × 13" baking dish. Sprinkle with 2 tablespoons cheese. Cover with half the scrambled eggs, then the mushrooms. Pour 1 cup sauce on top. Sprinkle 3 tablespoons more cheese over sauce and remaining eggs. Pour rest of sauce over all, sprinkle with remaining cheese, and dot with remaining butter. Brown lightly under *preheated* broiler for 1–2 minutes. ***Serves 12.***

*Moira Burnham, Church of the Epiphany, New York, New York*

# Three-Cheese Deviled Eggs

This recipe can easily be doubled. For a flavor variation, replace the mustard with curry powder.

6 hard-boiled eggs, cooled, shells removed
½–¾ cup mayonnaise
2 tablespoons grated Cheddar cheese
2 tablespoons grated Swiss cheese

2 tablespoons minced chives
¼ teaspoon stone-ground prepared mustard
⅛ teaspoon pepper
¼ cup (2 ounces) cubed Velveeta cheese

Cut eggs in half lengthwise. Remove yolks and place in bowl; set whites aside. Mash yolks with ½ cup mayonnaise, Cheddar, Swiss, 1 tablespoon chives, mustard, and pepper. In microwaveable bowl, cook Velveeta on high for 1 minute, until melted; stir until smooth. Stir into yolk mixture. For creamier texture, add up to ¼ cup more mayonnaise. Pipe yolk mixture through pastry bag fitted with large decorative tip or spoon into egg-white halves. Sprinkle with remaining 1 tablespoon chives. Refrigerate until serving. *Makes 12.*

*Lynne S. Froning, Saint Paul United Methodist Church, Lincoln, Nebraska*

# Brunch Eggs

A delicious Mediterranean version of poached eggs—similar to pipérade.
Double the recipe to serve 6 for supper.

2 medium onions, sliced
3 tablespoons butter
3 green peppers, thinly sliced
½ cup chopped parsley
½ cup water
½ teaspoon salt

¼ teaspoon pepper
3 medium tomatoes, skinned and cut into wedges
6 eggs
½ cup shredded Muenster or mozzarella cheese

Sauté onions in butter for 5 minutes. Add green peppers and parsley and sauté, stirring. Add water, salt, and pepper. Cover pan and cook, stirring occasionally, for about 10 minutes, or until liquid evaporates. Reduce heat. Add tomato wedges. With back of tablespoon, make 6 depressions in vegetables. Break 1 egg in each depression. Cook, covered, for about 4 minutes. Uncover, sprinkle with cheese, and cook another 1–2 minutes longer until set. *Serves 6.*

*Mrs. Henry Johnson, Swanzey Congregational Church, Swanzey, New Hampshire*

# Deviled Egg and Spinach Casserole

Easily divided or multiplied. *The* answer to all those leftover Easter eggs!

12 hard-boiled eggs
6 tablespoons mayonnaise
¼ teaspoon dry mustard
⅛ teaspoon pepper
4 packages (10 ounces each) frozen chopped spinach
½ cup butter

¼ cup flour
4 cups milk
2 cups grated sharp cheese
1 teaspoon Worcestershire sauce
1 teaspoon salt
¼ teaspoon Tabasco Sauce

Cut eggs in half lengthwise and remove yolks. Mash yolks with mayonnaise, mustard, and pepper. Blend until smooth and fill egg whites with mixture. Cook spinach, drain, and squeeze out all moisture. Melt butter in saucepan and blend in flour. Add milk gradually to flour and butter paste, stirring constantly while cooking over medium heat until sauce thickens. Reserve ¼ cup grated cheese, and stir remaining cheese into sauce until cheese melts. Add Worcestershire sauce, salt, and Tabasco Sauce. Place spinach in greased 3-quart baking dish or casserole dish with half the cheese sauce. Mix spinach and sauce together with fork. Place deviled egg halves on top of spinach and cover with remaining cheese sauce. Sprinkle reserved grated cheese over all. Bake at 375°F for 20–25 minutes, or until bubbly and lightly browned. (Can be reheated at 325°F in covered dish.) *Serves 8–10.*

# Ham and Eggs Brunch Casserole

This comforting dish can be assembled the night before serving. Cool the potatoes, onions, and peppers before adding the egg mixture, then refrigerate and bake the next morning.

2 cups (8 ounces) frozen hash brown potatoes
1½ cups chopped onions
1½ cups chopped green or red bell peppers
1 tablespoon vegetable or olive oil
1 pound ham steak, cut into small cubes

1 cup shredded Cheddar cheese
12 eggs
1 cup milk
1 teaspoon salt
1 teaspoon pepper
1 teaspoon dry mustard
½ teaspoon thyme (optional)

Press potatoes into 9" × 13" greased baking dish; place in oven broiler 6" from heat source, stirring occasionally, for about 8 minutes to brown. Remove.

Sauté onions and peppers in oil in large skillet over medium-high heat for 5 minutes or until golden. Spread onions, peppers, and ham evenly over potatoes. Sprinkle with cheese. In bowl, beat eggs, milk, salt, pepper, mustard, and thyme (if using). Pour into baking dish. Bake at 350°F for about 45 minutes or until eggs are cooked in center. *Serves 6–8.*

*Lynne S. Froning, Saint Paul United Methodist Church, Lincoln, Nebraska*

# Mushroom Business

An interesting version of the ever-popular strata that vegetarians and mushroom fans will love.

| | |
|---|---|
| 1 **pound fresh mushrooms, coarsely sliced** | ¾ **teaspoon salt** |
| 3 **tablespoons butter** | ⅛ **teaspoon pepper** |
| 8 **slices buttered white bread** | 2 **eggs** |
| ½ **cup chopped onion** | ⅓ **cup milk** |
| ½ **cup chopped celery** | 1 **can (10¾ ounces) cream of mushroom soup** |
| ½ **cup chopped green pepper** | 1 **cup shredded Cheddar cheese** |
| ½ **cup mayonnaise** | |

Sauté mushrooms in butter until aroma is released. Cut 3 of the bread slices into cubes and place in buttered 2-quart casserole dish. Combine onion, celery, green pepper, and mayonnaise. Add salt and pepper and spread over bread cubes. Add mushrooms. Top with 3 more cubed bread slices. Beat eggs slightly with milk and pour over. Refrigerate for at least 1 hour or overnight. Before baking, spread soup over top and sprinkle with last 2 cubed bread slices. Bake at 300°F for 60–70 minutes or at 350°F for 50–60 minutes. About 10 minutes before end of baking time, sprinkle with cheese. *Serves 8.*

*Elizabeth K. Macrum, St. Stephen's Episcopal Church, Bucksport, Maine*

# Spaghetti Carbonara

This marvelous dish has been described as "Italian scrambled eggs and bacon."
If so, it is scrambled eggs and bacon taken to the nth power. Easily multiplied
or divided for breakfast, brunch, lunch, or dinner.

1 pound thin bacon slices
2 large onions, chopped fine
1 cup dry white wine
6 large or 8 medium eggs
¼ pound butter, softened

1 cup heavy or sour cream, warmed slightly
2 cups grated Parmesan cheese
½ cup chopped parsley
2 pounds spaghetti or linguine
Black pepper

Cook bacon slices until crisp. Drain on paper towels. Leave 3 tablespoons bacon fat in skillet. Sauté onions in bacon fat until golden and soft. Add wine and cook until it evaporates. Beat together eggs, butter, cream, Parmesan, and parsley. Add onions. Cook spaghetti in boiling salted water as directed on package. Transfer with slotted spoon to large warmed bowl. Add egg and cheese mixture and toss. Crumble bacon and sprinkle over top. Grind black pepper liberally over all and serve. *Serves 8.*

*Adele Mac Veagh, Emmanuel Church, Webster Groves, Missouri*

Quiche, that delectable French invention, is a treat at any meal, hot or cold, can be sold at bazaars by the slice, served in bite-size pieces as an hors d'oeuvre, or taken in a brown bag to work. Quiche can be made in a number of ways. Here are several.

# Quiche Lorraine

¼ pound bacon strips
1 baked 9" pastry shell
½ cup chopped onion (optional)
3 eggs
1½ cups cream

½ teaspoon salt
Pinch of pepper
¾ cup grated Gruyère or Swiss cheese
2 tablespoons butter

Cook bacon until crisp. Drain and break up into small pieces. Scatter pieces evenly on bottom of pastry shell. Sauté onion, if using, in bacon fat until soft, then distribute evenly in bottom of pastry shell with bacon. Beat eggs, cream, salt, and pepper together. Add cheese. Pour egg mixture into shell on top of bacon pieces. Cut butter into tiny dots and scatter over top of custard. Set pie plate on cookie sheet and place in 375°F oven. Bake for 40–50 minutes, checking after 25 minutes and thereafter every 10 minutes or so. Quiche is done when a silver knife inserted into center comes out clean. Cool on cake rack and serve warm. Reheats well. *Serves 6.*

# Spinach Quiche

½ cup finely diced cooked ham
1 baked 9" pastry shell
1 package (10 ounces) frozen chopped spinach, cooked, drained, and rechopped
2 tablespoons chopped onion
3 tablespoons butter

3 eggs
1½ cups heavy cream
½ teaspoon salt
½ teaspoon pepper
½ teaspoon nutmeg
¼ cup grated Gruyère or Swiss cheese

Scatter ham evenly over bottom of pastry shell. Cook spinach and onion in 2 tablespoons butter, stirring from time to time, until *all* liquid has evaporated and spinach begins to stick to pan. Remove from heat. Beat eggs with cream, salt, pepper, and nutmeg. Add spinach and cheese and blend well. Pour into pastry shell. Cut the remaining 1 tablespoon butter into dots and sprinkle over top. Bake at 375°F for 40 minutes, or until set. Quiche is done when a silver knife inserted into center comes out clean. Cool slightly and serve. Reheats well. *Serves 6.*

# Mushroom Quiche

Follow the preceding recipe for Spinach Quiche, substituting 1 cup cooked sliced mushrooms (drained, if you use canned) for spinach. Cook with onion in butter until onion is golden.

# Corn Flan

Like a crustless corn quiche.

3 eggs
1 cup whole milk or half-and-half
4 tablespoons melted butter
1 package (16 ounces) frozen
corn niblets, thawed
½ teaspoon salt
¼ teaspoon pepper

Pinch of cayenne pepper
¼ teaspoon nutmeg
½ pound Vermont Cheddar
cheese, thinly sliced
2 tablespoons grated Parmesan
cheese

Beat together eggs, milk or half-and-half, and butter. Stir in corn, salt, pepper, cayenne pepper, and nutmeg. Place half of mixture in buttered pie pan or 1½-quart baking dish. Spread with Cheddar cheese, top with remaining corn mixture, and sprinkle with Parmesan cheese. Bake at 325°F for approximately 45 minutes, or until set. Let stand a few minutes before cutting. *Serves 6.*

*Margaret Michaelsen, North Bennington Congregational Church, North Bennington, Vermont*

# Clam Casserole

Easy to make and good to eat.

2 cans (8 ounces each) minced
clams
24 crushed saltines

2 eggs, beaten
1½ cups milk
¼ cup melted butter

Combine clams (with juice), saltines, eggs, milk, and butter. Season to taste with salt, pepper, and/or herbs. Pour into 1½-quart casserole. Bake at 400°F for about 45 minutes. *Serves 6.*

*Catherine B. Anderson, United Methodist Church of the Hamptons, Hampton, New Hampshire*

# Crab and Corn Bake

Delicious and rich. May be prepared ahead.

¼ cup butter
2 tablespoons flour
½ cup milk
½ teaspoon salt
   Dash of pepper
1 tablespoon lemon juice
1 teaspoon prepared mustard
½ teaspoon horseradish
½ teaspoon Worcestershire sauce

1 can (6½–7½ ounces) crabmeat, flaked
2 hard-boiled eggs, chopped
1 can (16 ounces) whole-kernel corn, drained
1 can (16 ounces) cream-style corn
½ cup grated Parmesan cheese
½ cup buttered bread crumbs

Melt butter in saucepan and blend with flour. Gradually add milk and cook over medium heat, stirring, until white sauce thickens. Stir in salt, pepper, lemon juice, mustard, horseradish, and Worcestershire sauce. Mix together crabmeat, eggs, and corn. Add sauce and turn into greased 1½-quart casserole. Top with cheese and crumbs. Bake at 400°F for 15 minutes, or until heated through and bubbly. *Serves 6.*

*Shirley Doherty, The Unitarian Church, Franklin, New Hampshire*

# Scalloped Clams

A quick and tasty seafood supper.

32 Ritz crackers, crushed
1 can (6½ ounces) minced clams
1 can (10 ounces) baby clams
¼ teaspoon thyme
2 eggs

1 cup milk
1 can (10¾ ounces) cream of mushroom soup
2 tablespoons melted butter

Cover bottom of greased 9" × 13" baking dish with some cracker crumbs. Mix together minced and baby clams and thyme and spoon some over layer of crumbs. Repeat layers of crumbs and clams and top with layer of crumbs. Beat eggs and combine with milk, soup, and butter. Pour over crumbs and clams. Bake at 350°F for 1 hour. *Serves 8.*

*Rachel Seaward, The Unitarian Church, Franklin, New Hampshire*

# Mock Lobster Casserole

Marvelous way to make the relatively inexpensive haddock
into something much fancier. It works!

2 pounds haddock fillets
¼ teaspoon salt
1 cup canned (or frozen and
   thawed) cream of shrimp soup
1 tablespoon lemon juice or
   sherry

½ teaspoon minced onion
⅛ teaspoon garlic powder
¼ cup melted butter
½ teaspoon Worcestershire sauce
¾ cup bread crumbs or crushed
   Ritz crackers

Place fish in greased 2-quart casserole. Sprinkle with salt. Mix soup with lemon juice or sherry. Pour over fish. Bake uncovered at 375°F for 20 minutes. While baking, sauté onion and garlic in butter. Remove from heat and add Worcestershire sauce. Then blend with crumbs or crackers. Sprinkle over fish and bake 10 minutes more. *Serves 6.*

*Cheryl Tutt, Ascutney Union Church, Ascutney, Vermont*

# Kedgeree

The English eat kedgeree for breakfast, but it's good for supper, too.
Spinach—salad, creamed, or soufflé—is a natural with kedgeree.

6 tablespoons butter
1 teaspoon curry powder
1½ cups raw rice
2 pounds white fish fillets (such
   as cod or haddock)
2 cups water
1 teaspoon salt

4 hard-boiled eggs
Juice of ½ lemon
½ cup chopped fresh parsley
Pepper
Dash of Worcestershire sauce
¼ cup milk (optional)

Melt butter in saucepan; add curry powder and blend well. Add rice, stirring to coat well. Set aside. Poach fish in water for 10 minutes, or until done. Reserving broth, remove fish and set aside. To fish broth, add enough water to bring liquid up to 3 cups. Add with salt to rice in saucepan and bring to boil. Simmer, covered, until rice is tender and liquid is absorbed. Flake fish and chop eggs finely. In large mixing bowl, toss rice with fish. Add chopped egg, lemon juice, parsley, pepper to taste, and Worcestershire sauce. Toss well. If mixture seems dry, add milk. Spoon mixture into lightly greased 3-quart baking dish. Bake, covered, at 300°F for 25–35 minutes, until thoroughly heated. *Serves 10.*

*Gaye S. LeBoutillier, St. Dunstan's Episcopal Church, Ellsworth, Maine*

# Marit's Fish Casserole

Fish and macaroni in a nutmeg cream sauce.

1 **pound uncooked white fish fillets**
4 **teaspoons butter**
3 **tablespoons flour**
1½ **cups milk**
½ **teaspoon salt**
1½ **teaspoons nutmeg**

2 **eggs, separated**
1 **cup elbow macaroni**
4 **American or provolone cheese slices**
3 **tablespoons plain dry bread crumbs**

Cut fish into small pieces. Melt butter in saucepan over medium heat. Add flour and stir 1 minute. Whisk in ¾ cup milk until lumps disappear. Whisk in salt, nutmeg, and remaining ¾ cup milk. Cook until thick. Remove from heat and stir in beaten egg yolks.

Cook and drain macaroni. Mix fish, macaroni, and white sauce together. Fold in stiffly beaten egg whites. Pour into buttered 1½ quart casserole and top with cheese slices and bread crumbs. Bake at 350°F for 30 minutes.

## Sauce

¼ **cup melted butter**
2 **tablespoons minced parsley**

1 **tablespoon lemon juice**

Combine butter, parsley, and lemon juice, and keep warm until fish is done. Pour over casserole and serve. *Serves 6.*

*Rebecca Ulrich, Concord Unitarian Church, Concord, New Hampshire*

# Salmon Pudding

1 can (8 ounces) salmon, boned
   and flaked
⅛ teaspoon paprika
⅛ teaspoon dillweed
2 tablespoons lemon juice
¼ teaspoon salt

⅛ teaspoon pepper
2 dashes of Tabasco Sauce
   Dash of Worcestershire sauce
½ cup bread crumbs
½ cup milk, warmed
3 eggs, separated

Mix salmon with paprika, dillweed, lemon juice, salt, pepper, Tabasco Sauce, and Worcestershire sauce. Soak bread crumbs in milk and add to salmon. Add well-beaten egg yolks. Fold in stiffly beaten whites. Bake in greased 2-quart casserole at 350°F for 40 minutes, or until golden brown. *Serves 6.*

*Elizabeth Hughes, Old Brick Church, Clarendon, Vermont*

# Flounder Crowns with Florentine Stuffing

This one could make you famous.

3 pounds flounder fillets, fresh
   or frozen
¾ teaspoon salt
½ cup chopped celery
½ cup butter, melted
1 box (6½ ounces) onion- and
   garlic-salted croutons (4 cups)

1 egg, beaten
1 package (10 ounces) frozen
   chopped spinach, thawed
½ teaspoon salt
¼ teaspoon thyme
⅛ teaspoon pepper

Divide fillets in half lengthwise. Sprinkle with salt. Cook celery in ¼ cup butter until tender. Combine with croutons, egg, spinach, salt, thyme, and pepper, and mix thoroughly. (Makes 4½ cups stuffing.) Place approximately ¾ cup filling on each fillet half. Roll fish around stuffing and secure with toothpicks. Place stuffed fish rolls—"crowns"—in shallow, well-greased 9" × 13" baking dish. You'll have about 16 crowns. Drizzle with remaining ¼ cup butter. Bake at 350°F for about 25 minutes, or until fish flakes easily when tested with fork.

## Sauce

2 tablespoons butter
2 tablespoons flour
1 cup milk
1 egg yolk

2 tablespoons heavy cream
½–1 cup small cooked shrimp
Salt and pepper

Melt butter and blend with flour. Add milk gradually, stirring constantly and cooking until thickened. Remove from heat. Beat egg yolk and mix with a little sauce. Add egg to remainder of sauce, stirring to blend well. Add cream, shrimp, and salt and pepper to taste. Heat through over double boiler and pour over flounder crowns. *Serves 8.*

*Woodmont Congregational Church, Milford, Connecticut*

# Fish Casserole

Served at the Maundy Thursday Supper of Northfield's United Church,
this casserole can be changed by varying the herbs used to flavor it.

1½ pounds haddock fillets, cut into 2" strips
3 cups soft fresh bread, diced and pushed down in cup (about 7 slices)
1 medium onion, minced
Pinch of salt
Pinch(es) of one herb or combination of herbs: sweet

basil, thyme, savory, marjoram, rosemary
2 cans (10¾ ounces each) cream of mushroom soup
½ cup milk
¾ cup cracker crumbs
2 tablespoons butter, cut into small pieces

Lay half the fish on bottom of greased 9" × 13" casserole. Mix bread crumbs with onion, salt, and a pinch or so of herbs. Top fish layer with half this stuffing. Mix 1 can soup with ¼ cup milk and pour over stuffing. Repeat layers, ending with second can of soup mixed with remaining ¼ cup milk. Cover with cracker crumbs and dot with butter. Bake uncovered at 350°F for 1 hour. *Serves 8.*

*Doris Seal, The United Church, Northfield, Vermont*

# Fabulous Flounder Fillets

### Absolutely fantastic!

6 large flounder fillets (about 2 pounds)
½ teaspoon salt

6 slices tomato
12 slices (approximately 4" × 4") Gruyère or Swiss cheese

Sprinkle fillets on both sides with salt, then roll each up. In 9" × 13" greased baking dish, place flounder roll, beside it a tomato slice, and next to that a pair of cheese slices. Begin next row with tomato slice, then cheese, then flounder roll, and start third row with cheese, then flounder, and then tomato. Continue to make total of 6 rows. After all ingredients are used up, there should be a diagonal pattern in the way the flounder, tomato, and cheese line up. Preheat oven to 400°F.

## Sauce

1 can (4 ounces) sliced mushrooms
2 medium onions, sliced
2 tablespoons butter
1½ tablespoons flour
1½ teaspoons salt

¼ cup minced parsley + ¾ cup snipped parsley
1 cup light cream
6 tablespoons sherry
1½ cups uncooked long-grain rice

Drain mushrooms, reserving liquid. In 2-quart saucepan, sauté mushrooms and onion in butter until golden. Stir in flour, salt, and minced parsley, then add cream, reserved mushroom liquid combined with enough water to make ½ cup, and sherry. Stir until all is well-mixed. Bring to boil. Pour over fish, tomato, and cheese. Bake 15–20 minutes, or until fillets are golden and easily flaked with fork but still moist.

Meanwhile, cook rice. Stir snipped parsley into cooked rice. When fish is done, spoon rice along sides of dish. *Serves 6.*

*Don Wyant, Woodmont Congregational Church, Milford, Connecticut*

# Shrimp and Rice Casserole

The dill makes the difference.

1 cup rice, cooked and drained
½ pound sharp Cheddar cheese, grated
2 cups cooked shrimp
4 eggs, separated

¾ cup milk
¼ teaspoon pepper
¼ teaspoon onion salt
¼ teaspoon dillweed

Mix rice, cheese, and shrimp (reserve about 1 cup cheese for top). Mix egg yolks and milk and combine with shrimp mixture. Season with pepper, onion salt, and dillweed. Beat egg whites until stiff and fold in. Turn into greased 2-quart casserole. Sprinkle reserved cheese on top. Bake at 375°F for 30 minutes. *Serves 8.*

*Catherine B. Anderson, United Methodist Church of the Hamptons, Hampton, New Hampshire*

# Gourmet Shrimp

A good dish if you feel like splurging on shrimp without going to a lot of trouble.

2 pounds shelled, deveined medium shrimp (fresh or frozen)
3 quarts boiling water
1¼ teaspoons salt
1 tablespoon + 1 teaspoon lemon juice
3 tablespoons butter
1 cup chopped onion

1 cup chopped green pepper
1 can (10¾ ounces) cream of mushroom soup
1 cup sour cream
⅓ cup ketchup
1 can (6 ounces) sliced mushrooms, drained
⅛ teaspoon pepper
¼ cup dry white wine

Add shrimp to boiling water seasoned with 1 teaspoon salt and 1 tablespoon lemon juice. Boil 3 minutes. Drain and set aside. Melt butter in large skillet over medium heat. Add onion and green pepper. Sauté until onion is transparent. Add soup, sour cream, ketchup, mushrooms, remaining 1 teaspoon lemon juice, remaining ¼ teaspoon salt, pepper, wine, and cooked shrimp. Reduce heat, stir, and simmer gently for 5 minutes. Serve over hot rice. *Serves 8.*

*Lillian Gerlander, Woodmont United Church of Christ, Milford, Connecticut*

# Spicy Shrimp with Mango-Fennel Salsa

This vibrant appetizer looks as good as it tastes. The recipe can easily be doubled.
If you can't find mango, use sweet ripe peaches instead.

8 ounces shelled, deveined raw
shrimp
Salt and pepper
2 tablespoons olive oil
4 garlic cloves, minced
1 fennel bulb, trimmed and diced
6 plum tomatoes, seeded and diced

1 mango, diced
1 cup fresh cilantro, chopped
½ cup fresh basil leaves, coarsely
chopped
2 tablespoons fresh lime juice
1 tablespoon capers, rinsed and drained
½ teaspoon crushed red pepper

Season shrimp with salt and pepper; set aside for 10 minutes. In wok or large skillet, warm 1 tablespoon oil and garlic over medium heat for 1 minute or until sizzling. Turn heat to high. Add fennel; stir-fry for 1 minute. Add tomatoes and mango, stir-fry for 1 minute or until mixture is hot. Season to taste with salt and pepper. Remove and set aside. Add remaining 1 tablespoon oil to wok or skillet and turn heat to high. Add shrimp and stir-fry for 1½ minutes or just until opaque. Return fennel mixture to wok. Add cilantro, basil, lime juice, capers, and crushed red pepper. ***Serves 6–8 as appetizer.***

*Amy Chao, Lord's Grace Christian Church, Mountain View, California*

# Deviled Eggs, Shrimp, and Mushrooms in Cheese Sauce

Serve spooned over toast, English muffins, biscuits, noodles, or rice,
depending on what meal you are serving—breakfast, brunch, lunch, or supper.

6 hard-boiled eggs
3 tablespoons mayonnaise
Pinch of dry mustard
Dash of Tabasco Sauce

Dash of Worcestershire sauce
Salt and pepper
1 cup cooked, drained shrimp
1 cup sliced, cooked, drained mushrooms

Cut shelled eggs in halves and remove yolks. Mix yolks with mayonnaise, mustard, Tabasco Sauce, Worcestershire sauce, and salt and pepper to taste. Refill whites with mixture and place in buttered 1-quart casserole dish, along with shrimp and mushrooms.

# Cheese Sauce

| | |
|---|---|
| 2 tablespoons butter | ½ cup cheese, diced |
| 2 tablespoons flour | Salt and pepper |
| 1 cup milk | |

Melt butter over low heat and gradually blend in flour. Cook gently for a minute or so, then add milk a little at a time, stirring constantly throughout. When sauce has thickened, add cheese and salt and pepper to taste, continuing to stir until cheese is melted.

Pour Cheese Sauce over eggs, shrimp, and mushrooms and bake at 350°F until thoroughly heated and bubbling, about 10–15 minutes. *Serves 6.*

# Shrimp and Blue Cheese Casserole

Mrs. Miller contributed a number of recipes that rated "superb." This one is an incredible combination of ingredients that really works. Very subtle and delicious taste. Try it!

| | |
|---|---|
| 1 pound cooked shrimp, or 1 can (12 ounces) rinsed and drained | ½ cup thinly sliced celery |
| 1 can (16 ounces) cream-style corn | 1 green onion, sliced |
| | 1½ tablespoons melted butter |

Combine shrimp and corn in greased 2-quart casserole. Sauté celery and onion in butter until tender. Add to shrimp.

## Sauce

| | |
|---|---|
| 2 tablespoons butter | ½ teaspoon salt |
| 2½ tablespoons flour | ⅛ teaspoon pepper |
| 1 cup milk | 3 ounces American blue cheese |

Melt butter and blend in flour. Gradually add milk, stirring constantly, until thickened. Stir in salt, pepper, and blue cheese. Cook until cheese is melted. Pour over corn and shrimp and bake at 375°F for 30–40 minutes. Serve with rice or noodles. *Serves 6.*

*Jeannette M. Miller, Morris Congregational Church, Morris, Connecticut*

# Sesame Scallops and Salmon with Cucumber

Use an English or "hothouse" cucumber for this recipe. This long, slender cucumber tends to have fewer seeds and be less bitter than regular cucumbers.

1 pound jumbo scallops
1 tablespoon soy sauce
2 teaspoons toasted sesame oil
½ teaspoon salt
1 tablespoon rice wine or white wine

1 teaspoon pepper
1 pound salmon fillet
3 tablespoons vegetable oil
1 English cucumber, thinly sliced
  Rice wine vinegar (optional)

Cut scallops in half horizontally through middle. In shallow dish, combine soy sauce, sesame oil, and ¼ teaspoon salt. Add scallops; toss to coat. Marinate 30 minutes. In another shallow dish, combine wine, pepper, and remaining ¼ teaspoon salt. Add salmon; toss to coat. Marinate 30 minutes.

Place salmon on baking sheet. Broil 6" from heat source for about 6 minutes or until cooked. Meanwhile, heat vegetable oil in large skillet over high heat. Place scallops in single layer in pan. Fry about 1½ minutes each side or until golden. Arrange salmon in center of platter. Surround with scallops. Arrange cucumber slices in ring around outside; sprinkle lightly with vinegar, if using. *Serves 12–16 as appetizer.*

*Lisa Chen, Allentown Chinese Christian Church, Wescosville, Pennsylvania*

# Salmon Mousse with Cucumber Sauce

A cool summer entrée that can also be made with water-pack tuna,
½ cup chopped celery, and ¼ cup chopped green pepper for variety.

| | |
|---|---|
| 1 tablespoon plain gelatin | 2 teaspoons dillweed |
| 2 tablespoons lemon juice | 1 teaspoon grated horseradish |
| 1 small onion | (optional) |
| ½ cup boiling water | Dash of Tabasco Sauce |
| ½ cup mayonnaise | 1 can (16 ounces) salmon |
| ¼ teaspoon paprika | 1 cup sour cream |

Empty gelatin into blender and soak for 3–5 minutes in a little cold water. Add lemon juice, onion, and water, and cover blender. Blend 40 seconds. Then add mayonnaise, paprika, dillweed, horseradish, if using, Tabasco Sauce, and salmon, and blend again. Add sour cream and blend once more. Pour into oiled mold and refrigerate until firm. Unmold on lettuce and serve with separate bowl of Cucumber Sauce. *Serves 8.*

## Cucumber Sauce

| | |
|---|---|
| ½ cup heavy cream | Dash of pepper |
| 2 tablespoons vinegar | 1 cucumber, peeled, chopped, |
| ¼ teaspoon salt | and drained |

Beat cream until thick but not stiff. Add vinegar gradually while beating. Season with salt and pepper and fold in cucumber.

*Baptist Women's Fellowship, New London, New Hampshire*

# Crispy Tuna Balls
# with Spicy Cheddar Dip

Easy to prepare, these seafood starters are deliciously
different from the usual chips and dip.

1 can (6 ounces) tuna packed in
water, drained and flaked
½ cup plain dry bread crumbs
3 tablespoons mayonnaise
2 tablespoons minced onion
2 tablespoons minced parsley or
cilantro

1 egg, beaten
2 teaspoons dry mustard
¼ teaspoon Tabasco sauce
3 tablespoons butter, melted
¾ cup corn flakes, crushed

In mixing bowl, combine tuna, bread crumbs, mayonnaise, onion, parsley or cilantro, egg, mustard, and Tabasco sauce. Stir to combine. Shape into balls, about 2 teaspoons each. One at a time, use one hand to dip balls in butter and other hand to roll balls in corn flakes to coat. Place 1" apart on ungreased baking sheet. Bake at 450°F for 8–10 minutes or until hot and crispy. Serve with Spicy Cheddar Dip (see below).

## Spicy Cheddar Dip

1 can (10¾ ounces) Cheddar or
Pepper-Jack cheese soup

¼ cup salsa, mild or hot

In bowl, combine soup and salsa. For warm dip, use a microwaveable bowl and heat in microwave until warm, about 30 seconds. ***Serves 6 (3 tuna balls per serving).***

*Melinda Ingalls, Gay Street United Methodist Church, Mount Vernon, Ohio*

**Meatballs with Sweet and Sour Sauce, page 14**

**Snowtime Beef Casserole, page 17**

**Arcadian Shepherd's Pie, page 22**

**Cannelloni, page 26**

**Ham and Chicken Luncheon Dish, page 35**

California Oven-Fried Chicken, page 61

**Chicken Pie with Crust, page 63**

**Chicken Marengo, page 73**

**Paella Valenciana, page 75**

**Three-Cheese Deviled Eggs, page 83**

**Kedgeree, page 90**

**Flounder Crowns with Florentine Stuffing, page 92**

**Baked Beans, page 118**

**Pennsylvania Dutch Green Beans, page 121**

**Carrot Casserole, page 124**

**Autumn Leaves, page 133**

# Vegetable Sides and Casseroles

Most cooks spend the majority of time in the kitchen fixing an entrée of meat, poultry, or fish, and allow only a few minutes for the vegetables. But some of the vegetable casseroles in this chapter are interesting enough in their own right to consider building a meal around.

Baked Apple and Carrot Casserole  118

Baked Beans  118

Grace Manney's Baked Beans  119

Black Beans and Rice  119

Stewed Green Beans  120

Harvard Beets  120

Pennsylvania Dutch Green Beans  121

Orangey Beets  121

John Russell's Mushroom-Rice Casserole 122

Broccoli Casserole  122

Broccoli and Cheese Casserole  123

Stuffed Broccoli  123

Carrot Casserole  124

Carrots Excelsior  124

Far East Celery  125

Eggplant Casserole  125

Corn-Zucchini Bake  126

Eggplant Italiano  127

Scalloped Sweet Spanish Onions  128

Onion Pie  128

Savory Onion Kuchen  129

Baked Potatoes Élégant  130

Spinach Rockefeller  130

Soft Clouds  131

Spinach Squares  132

Summer Delight  132

Autumn Leaves  133

Squash and Hominy Dish  134

Tomato-Corn Rarebit  134

Tomato-Cheese Crunch  135

Mixed Vegetable Casserole  135

Vegetable Cobbler  136

Mixed Vegetables Italienne  136

Roasted Herbed Vegetables  137

T. L. C. Vegetable Casserole  138

7-Minute Zucchini  138

Italian Zucchini Casserole  139

Lemon-Spinach Rice  139

Spanish Rice  140

Spanish Rice II  140

# Baked Apple and Carrot Casserole

A perfect companion for baked beans, ham, or pork.

6 apples, cored, peeled, and
  thinly sliced
2 cups cooked carrot slices
⅓ cup brown sugar

2 tablespoons flour
Salt
¾ cup orange juice

Place half the apples in greased 2-quart baking dish and cover with half the carrots. Mix brown sugar, flour, and salt to taste, and sprinkle half the mixture over carrots. Repeat layers and pour orange juice over top. Bake at 350°F for 45 minutes. *Serves 6.*

*Alma L. Hedrick, Harwinton Congregational Church, Harwinton, Connecticut*

# Baked Beans

Some require an onion in their baked beans; to others, this is heresy.
Include it or not, as you will, in this fine recipe.

1 pound dry navy or pea beans
6 cups water
½ pound salt pork, cut into
  ½" dice
1 small onion, peeled

⅓ cup molasses
¼ cup sugar
1 teaspoon dry mustard
¼ teaspoon pepper

Soak beans overnight in water. Place beans with soaking water in large kettle (add water to cover if necessary). Bring to boil; lower heat and simmer until beans are tender. Drain, reserving liquid. Place salt pork, onion, and beans in 2-quart bean pot or casserole. Combine molasses, sugar, mustard, pepper, and 1 cup of reserved bean liquid. Pour over beans. Stir thoroughly. Add just enough bean liquid to cover beans. Cover pot or casserole and bake at 300°F for 2 hours. Add liquid if necessary and stir. Continue baking 1½–2 hours longer, or until beans are tender. Bake uncovered for last half-hour. *Serves 8.*

*Mary Nichol, First Presbyterian Church, Monroe, New York*

# Grace Manney's Baked Beans

Both Grace and her recipe are well-known at the Mendon Community Church.

1 pound yellow-eye beans
1 cup sugar
1 teaspoon salt

1 teaspoon dry mustard
⅓ pound salt pork, thinly sliced

Soak beans overnight. Leave in soaking water and add sugar, salt, and mustard. Add water as necessary to cover beans. Cook until beans are tender. Turn into bean pot or Dutch oven, arranging salt pork slices on top. Cover and bake at 275°F for 6–8 hours, adding water from time to time when dry. *Serves 6–8.*

*Ruth French, Mendon Community Church, Mendon, Vermont*

# Black Beans and Rice

Use any of this interesting dish left over to make a super soup.

1 pound black beans, washed and dried
6 cups water
1 cup chopped onion
1 green pepper
1 clove garlic
½ cup olive oil
2 bay leaves

2 teaspoons salt
¼ teaspoon pepper
1 smoked ham bone (optional)
1 slice bacon, minced
¼ cup wine vinegar
Cooked rice
1 hard-boiled egg, sliced
Raw onion rings

Cover beans with water. Bring to boil, and boil 2 minutes. Cover. Let stand 1 hour. Sauté onion, green pepper, and garlic in olive oil for 5 minutes. Add to beans with bay leaves, salt, pepper, ham bone, if using, and bacon. Bring to boil and simmer, covered, for 2 hours. Add water if necessary. Add wine vinegar. Before serving, remove and discard bay leaves. Serve with hot cooked rice. Garnish with hard-boiled egg slices and onion rings. *Serves 8.*

*Beth Bartlett, Concord Unitarian Church, Concord, New Hampshire*

# Stewed Green Beans

Beans in a minty tomato sauce.

2 pounds fresh green beans
½ cup olive oil
2 cans (6 ounces each) tomato
  paste
1 large onion, chopped

2 teaspoons minced fresh mint
  leaves, or ½ teaspoon (heaping)
  dried mint
1 teaspoon garlic powder
  Salt and pepper

Sauté beans in oil until bright green and tender. Stir in tomato paste, onion, mint, garlic powder, and salt and pepper to taste. Add enough water to cover beans. Simmer until cooked to preference. *Serves 8.*

*Kathleen Adams, Park Street Baptist Church, Pittsfield, New Hampshire*

# Harvard Beets

Make with either canned or freshly cooked beets. If you use canned, reserve the liquid to use instead of the water below; if you use fresh, add the beets to the sauce immediately after slicing. Tangy and colorful.

2 tablespoons cornstarch
2 tablespoons sugar
1½ teaspoons salt
  Pinch of pepper

⅔ cup water
½ cup vinegar
2 cups sliced beets

In saucepan, mix together cornstarch, sugar, salt, pepper, water, and vinegar. Heat and cook, stirring, until mixture thickens and boils gently. Continue to cook, still stirring, for 1 minute more. Stir in beets, heat thoroughly, and serve. (Good cold, too.) *Serves 6.*

*Edna W. Warner, Foxon Congregational Church, East Haven, Connecticut*

# Pennsylvania Dutch Green Beans

A fine way to renew interest in overabundant green beans from the garden.

1 pound fresh green beans, cut into short lengths and cooked, or 2 packages (10 ounces each) frozen cut green beans, cooked, or 2 cans (16 ounces each) cut string beans
6 slices bacon
2 medium onions, chopped
4 teaspoons cornstarch
1 teaspoon salt
½ teaspoon dry mustard
2 tablespoons brown sugar
2 tablespoons vinegar

Drain beans and reserve 1 cup water fresh or frozen beans were cooked in, or ½ cup liquid from can. Set aside. Fry bacon until crisp and drain on paper towel. Sauté onions in bacon fat until golden. In small bowl, mix cornstarch, salt, mustard, brown sugar, and vinegar. Add reserved liquid from beans and beat until smooth. Then add this mixture to bacon fat in pan and boil until thickened slightly. Add string beans and stir well. Crush bacon and sprinkle bacon bits on top of casserole. *Serves 8.*

*Jeannette M. Miller, Morris Congregational Church, Morris, Connecticut*

# Orangey Beets

Similar to Harvard Beets, but uses orange juice instead of vinegar.

1½ tablespoons butter
⅓ cup brown sugar
1½ teaspoons cornstarch
⅔ cup orange juice
2 tablespoons grated orange rind
3 cups diced, cooked beets, or canned, drained
4 shakes each salt and pepper

Melt butter. Mix brown sugar and cornstarch. Stir into butter. Add orange juice gradually and cook, stirring constantly, until thickened. Blend in 1 tablespoon orange rind and beets. Shake salt and pepper and remaining 1 tablespoon orange rind over all. *Serves 8.*

*Mary Wakefield, First Congregational Church, Rindge, New Hampshire*

# John Russell's Mushroom-Rice Casserole

This homey, baked side dish pairs well with chicken, ham,
roast beef, and other church supper mainstays.

½ cup butter or margarine
1½ cups chopped green onions, white and light green parts
8 ounces fresh mushrooms, sliced
2 cups uncooked medium or long grain rice

2 cans (14½ ounces each) beef broth
2 cups water
1 teaspoon salt
1 teaspoon pepper
Paprika or minced parsley

In large skillet, melt butter or margarine over medium-high heat. Add green onions and sauté for 5 minutes or until softened. Add mushrooms and sauté for 5 minutes or until mushrooms are browned and no liquid remains. Stir in rice and cook until rice is lightly browned. Stir in broth, water, salt, and pepper; pour into greased 9" × 13" baking dish. Cover tightly with aluminum foil. Bake at 350°F for 50 minutes. Check rice doneness by carefully lifting foil away from you to avoid steam. If needed, re-cover and bake 10 more minutes or until rice is very tender. Sprinkle with paprika or parsley. *Makes 10–12 servings.*

*Nancy Eichler, Roswell Presbyterian Church, Roswell, Georgia*

# Broccoli Casserole

Serve as a main dish, or halve to serve 8 as a side dish.

2 packages (10 ounces each) frozen broccoli
1 can (10¾ ounces) cream of mushroom soup
1 cup mayonnaise
2 eggs, beaten

1 cup grated sharp cheese
Pepper
4 tablespoons chopped onion
Crushed Ritz crackers for topping
4 tablespoons butter

Cook broccoli for 5 minutes in boiling salted water. Drain well. Combine soup, mayonnaise, eggs, cheese, pepper to taste, and onion. Mix well. Add broccoli and turn into greased 2-quart baking dish. Sprinkle with crushed Ritz crackers and dot with butter. Bake at 350°F for 30 minutes, or until it bubbles and browns. *Serves 8.*

*Kate Barnes, St. Paul's Episcopal Church, Fort Fairfield, Maine*

# Broccoli and Cheese Casserole

An unusual casserole that's a little like a soufflé, but not as fluffy.

3 eggs
1 cup cottage cheese
½ cup Cheddar cheese
3 tablespoons flour

2 teaspoons salt
Dash of pepper
2 packages (10 ounces each)
   frozen broccoli

Beat eggs, then add cottage cheese, Cheddar, flour, salt, and pepper. Beat well together. Cook broccoli as directed and drain well. Add to egg mixture. Pour into greased baking dish and bake at 350°F for 30–35 minutes. *Serves 6–8.*

*Betty Fainelli, Harwinton Congregational Church, Harwinton, Connecticut*

# Stuffed Broccoli

Creamed broccoli with crunch and crumbs.

2 packages (10 ounces each)
   frozen chopped broccoli
4 tablespoons butter

¼ cup flour
2 chicken bouillon cubes
2 cups milk

Cook broccoli according to package directions. Drain and set aside. Melt butter. Add flour and mix. Add bouillon cubes and milk. Cook until sauce thickens. Grease 2-quart baking dish and place broccoli in it. Pour sauce over.

## Topping

2 cups seasoned stuffing mix
6 tablespoons butter

⅔ cup water
⅔ cup chopped walnuts

Combine stuffing mix with butter, water, and walnuts. Place on top of sauce, and bake at 350°F for 20–30 minutes. *Serves 6–8.*

*Lina Storrs, Center Congregational Church, Torrington, Connecticut*

# Carrot Casserole

Carrots enlivened with onion and horseradish. Fix ahead and heat when ready.

2 bunches (2 pounds) carrots
4 tablespoons grated onion
1½ teaspoons horseradish
½ cup mayonnaise

1 teaspoon salt
¼ teaspoon pepper
1 cup dry bread crumbs
½ cup melted butter

Scrape, dice, and boil carrots in salted water until crisply done. Drain, reserving ½ cup liquid. Place carrots in greased 2-quart casserole. In small bowl, mix reserved carrot liquid, onion, horseradish, mayonnaise, salt, and pepper. Pour over carrots. Top with bread crumbs and pour melted butter over all. Bake at 375°F about 20 minutes, or until slightly brown and bubbly. *Serves 6.*

*Shirley T. Oladell, Harwinton Congregational Church, Harwinton, Connecticut*

# Carrots Excelsior

Colorful and custardy.

2½ cups carrots, cooked, mashed, and seasoned with salt and pepper
2 egg yolks, beaten
1½ cups milk

1 cup bread crumbs
1 tablespoon finely chopped onion
2 egg whites

Combine carrots, egg yolks, milk, bread crumbs, and onion. Beat egg whites until stiff, and fold lightly into carrot mixture. Turn into buttered 1½-quart casserole. Bake at 350°F for 45–60 minutes, or until knife inserted comes out clean. Serve hot. *Serves 6–8.*

*Mrs. Albert G. Clark, United Church of Christ, Keene, New Hampshire*

# Far East Celery

Delicious served with steak or chicken.

4 cups celery, cut into 1" pieces
1 can (5 ounces) water chestnuts, drained and sliced
1 can (10¾ ounces) cream of chicken soup

1 small jar pimiento, drained and chopped
2 tablespoons butter
½ cup slivered almonds
½ cup bread crumbs

Cook celery in small amount of boiling salted water for about 8 minutes. Drain. In buttered 1-quart casserole, mix celery, water chestnuts, soup, and pimiento.

Melt butter in skillet and lightly brown almonds. Add bread crumbs and sprinkle mixture over casserole. Bake at 350°F for 35 minutes. *Serves 6.*

# Eggplant Casserole

For a different note at a potluck supper.

½ of 10¾-ounce can golden mushroom soup
½ cup mayonnaise
1 egg, beaten
1 tablespoon grated onion
1 cup shredded cheese

1 medium eggplant, peeled, diced, and cooked in boiling salted water for 10–15 minutes
¾ cup crushed Ritz crackers (about 15 crackers)
1 tablespoon butter

Mix soup, mayonnaise, egg, onion, and cheese with eggplant. Place in greased 1½-quart casserole and cover with cracker crumbs. Dot with butter. Bake at 350°F for 25 minutes. *Serves 6.*

*Betty C. Rollins, The Congregational Church, Atkinson, New Hampshire*

# Corn-Zucchini Bake

A nice combination. Also try topped with tomato sauce.

3–4 medium zucchini (1 pound)
¼ cup chopped onion
2 tablespoons melted butter
2 eggs, beaten
2 tablespoons flour
1 package (10 ounces) frozen whole-kernel corn, or 2 cups fresh corn cut from cob, cooked and drained
1 cup (4 ounces) shredded Swiss cheese

¼ teaspoon salt
¼ cup fine dry bread crumbs
1 teaspoon oregano or Italian seasoning (optional)
2 tablespoons grated Parmesan cheese
Tomato halves
Parsley

Wash zucchini; do not pare. Slice about 1" thick. Cook, covered, in small amount of boiling salted water until tender (15–20 minutes). Drain and mash with fork. Sauté onion in 1 tablespoon butter until tender. Combine eggs, flour, mashed zucchini, onion, corn, Swiss cheese, and salt. Turn into greased 1-quart casserole or 7" × 7" baking dish. Combine bread crumbs, oregano or Italian seasoning, if using, and Parmesan cheese with remaining 1 tablespoon melted butter. Sprinkle over corn mixture. Place on baking sheet. Bake at 350°F for 40 minutes if using 1-quart casserole, or for 25–30 minutes if using square baking dish—or until knife inserted comes out clean. Let stand 5–10 minutes before serving. Garnish with tomato halves and parsley. *Serves 6.*

*Mrs. L. Bouchard, St. Paul's Church, Lancaster, New Hampshire*

# Eggplant Italiano

Cheese-filled battered eggplant rolls with a tomato-saucy flair.

## Filling

1 cup grated mozzarella cheese
½ cup grated Parmesan cheese
⅓ cup cottage or ricotta cheese
½ teaspoon salt

¼ teaspoon pepper
½ teaspoon basil or oregano
1 tablespoon chopped parsley

## Batter

1 egg
2 tablespoons flour

⅓ cup milk
1 tablespoon cooking oil

## Other

2 small eggplants
¼ cup cooking oil
2 tablespoons butter

Flour
2 cans (6 ounces each) tomato sauce

Combine mozzarella, Parmesan, cottage cheese or ricotta, egg, salt, pepper, basil or oregano, and parsley. Make smooth paste and chill. For batter, combine egg, flour, milk, and oil, and beat until smooth. Peel eggplants and cut lengthwise into thin slices. Heat oil and butter to 360°F. Dip eggplant slices in flour, then in batter, and sauté in hot oil until browned on both sides. Drain on paper towels. Place 2 tablespoons chilled filling mixture on each slice and roll loosely, placing seam-side down in buttered 9" × 13" baking dish. Cover with tomato sauce. Bake at 375°F for 15 minutes. *Serves 8.*

*Margaret Michaelsen, The Congregational Church, North Bennington, Vermont*

# Scalloped Sweet Spanish Onions

Onions and cheese in a lovely crumb-topped custard.
Prepare a day ahead and bake when convenient.

¼ cup butter + 2 tablespoons
butter, melted
3 medium Spanish onions, sliced
¼ cup chopped green pepper
2 tablespoons chopped pimiento
1 cup grated Swiss cheese

1 cup cracker crumbs
2 eggs, beaten
¾ cup light cream
1 teaspoon salt
⅛ teaspoon white pepper

Melt ¼ cup butter in skillet. Add onions and green pepper and cook until tender. Stir in pimiento. Place half of mixture in shallow greased baking dish. Sprinkle with ½ cup Swiss cheese and ½ cup cracker crumbs. Repeat layers of onions and cheese. Beat eggs with cream, salt, and pepper. Pour over onions in baking dish. Combine remaining ½ cup cracker crumbs with remaining 2 tablespoons melted butter. Sprinkle over top. Bake at 325°F for 25 minutes, or until set. Serve hot. *Serves 6–8.*

*Mrs. Albert G. Clark, United Church of Christ, Keene, New Hampshire*

# Onion Pie

A marvelously hearty treat for onion fans. Serve with a fresh green salad.

## Crust

6 tablespoons butter
1¼ cups flour

½ teaspoon salt
2–4 tablespoons ice water

Crumble butter into flour and mix with salt. Add ice water as necessary to form into ball. Spread pastry directly into 9" greased pie tin, pressing lightly into place with your fingers.

## Filling

8 cups sliced onions
4 tablespoons butter
1 tablespoon cooking oil

Salt, pepper, and nutmeg
3 egg yolks, beaten until thick
½ cup heavy cream

Sauté onions in butter and oil in heavy frying pan. Cook, covered, over medium-low heat until onions are quite soft and pale gold (about 30 minutes). Stir occasionally to prevent sticking. Season to taste with salt, pepper, and nutmeg. Stir in egg yolks and cream. Pour into pastry shell and bake at 400°F for 30 minutes. *Serves 6–8.*

*Moira Burnham, Church of the Epiphany, New York, New York*

# Savory Onion Kuchen

¾ cup warm water
1 package dry yeast
2 teaspoons sugar
1 teaspoon salt
4 tablespoons butter, softened
2¼ cups flour

3 cups sliced onions
1 egg
¼ cup sour cream
Sesame, caraway, celery, or dill seed

Measure warm water into large warmed bowl. Sprinkle in yeast and stir until dissolved. Stir in sugar, ½ teaspoon salt, and 1 tablespoon soft butter. Add 1 cup flour and beat until smooth. Then beat in enough additional flour to make a soft dough. Turn dough onto lightly floured board and knead until smooth (about 5 minutes). Place dough in greased bowl, turning to grease surface evenly. Cover and let rise in warm place for about 30 minutes.

Sauté onions in remaining 3 tablespoons butter. Cool. Beat egg with sour cream and remaining ½ teaspoon salt until smooth. Add cooled onions.

Punch down dough. Place in greased 9" × 13" pan. Pat out dough to cover bottom and 1" up sides of pan. Spread onion mixture on dough and sprinkle with your chosen seasoning seeds. Let rise in warm place for 20 minutes. Bake at 375°F for 45 minutes, or until crust is golden brown. Cool slightly on rack before cutting and serving. *Serves 6.*

# Baked Potatoes Élégant

So much easier to eat in company than plain baked potatoes.

6 medium baking potatoes*
½ cup sour cream
1 package (3 ounces) cream
  cheese, softened
2 tablespoons milk

3 tablespoons butter, softened
1 teaspoon onion salt
  Salt and pepper
2 tablespoons chopped pimiento
  (optional)

Bake potatoes at 375°F until done. Cut slice from top of each and scoop out insides. Mash and mix with sour cream, cream cheese, milk, butter, onion salt, and salt and pepper to taste. Beat until smooth and fluffy. Stir in pimiento, if using. Fill potato shells. Return to oven and bake 15 minutes, or until potatoes are heated through. For variety, try topping stuffed potatoes with crumbled crisp bacon, chives, shredded cheese, or sour cream. **Serves 6.**

*Barbara Lockhart, United Church of Christ, Keene, New Hampshire*

*Do not use russets, or the filling will be gluey.

# Spinach Rockefeller

A light and zesty dish to please all spinach lovers. Serve with sliced chicken or ham.

2 packages (10 ounces each)
  frozen chopped spinach
2 eggs, separated
½ cup melted butter
¾ cup cracker or bread crumbs
¼ cup grated onion

⅛ teaspoon thyme
½ teaspoon garlic powder
2 dashes of Tabasco Sauce
½ teaspoon salt
¼ teaspoon pepper
¼ cup Parmesan cheese

Cook spinach and drain well. Beat egg yolks and mix into spinach. Combine butter, crumbs, onion, thyme, garlic powder, Tabasco Sauce, salt, pepper, and Parmesan. Mix into spinach. Beat egg whites until stiff, and fold into spinach mixture. Pour into greased 2-quart casserole. Bake at 350°F for 30 minutes. **Serves 6.**

*Betsy High, United Methodist Church of the Hamptons, Hampton, New Hampshire*

# Soft Clouds

A potato dish that lives up to its name.

| | |
|---|---|
| 6 medium potatoes, peeled, boiled, and drained | ¼ cup grated Romano cheese |
| 2 eggs, beaten | 1 tablespoon parsley |
| 4 tablespoons butter | ½ teaspoon garlic salt |
| ½ cup grated Velveeta cheese | Salt and pepper |

In mixing bowl, combine potatoes, eggs, butter, Velveeta, Romano, parsley, garlic salt, and salt and pepper to taste. Whip with electric mixer until smooth. Transfer to greased 1½-quart baking dish. Bake at 350°F for 30 minutes. **Serves 6–8.**

*Grace P. Van Etten, St. Mary's Church, Marlboro, New York*

# Spinach Squares

This easy semi-quiche is good served either as a vegetable dish
or with cheese sauce as a main course.

4 tablespoons butter
3 eggs
1 cup flour
1 cup milk
1 teaspoon salt
1 teaspoon baking powder

1 pound mild Cheddar cheese,
  grated
2 packages (10 ounces each)
  frozen spinach, thawed,
  drained, and chopped

Melt butter in 9" × 13" baking dish in 350°F oven and remove. In large bowl, beat eggs well.
Add flour, milk, salt, and baking powder. Mix well. Add cheese and spinach. Mix well. Spoon
into baking dish and level. Bake at 350°F for 35 minutes, or until top is slightly browned. Take
out, cool for 45 minutes, and cut into squares. (This freezes well. After thawing, reheat at 325°F
for approximately 12 minutes.) *Serves 8.*

*Kathleen Adams, Park Street Baptist Church, Pittsfield, New Hampshire*

# Summer Delight

A happy choice for supper during that late-summer glut of garden squash.

6 cups (2 pounds) diced young
  summer squash
¼ cup chopped onion
1 can (10¾ ounces) cream of
  chicken soup
1 cup sour cream

1 cup shredded carrots
2 cups prepared stuffing mix
  (cornmeal is best)
¼ pound butter, melted
  Chopped parsley

Cook squash and onion in boiling water for 5 minutes. Drain. Combine soup, sour cream, and carrots. Gently fold in squash and onion. Combine stuffing mix with melted butter. Put ⅔ of stuffing mixture into greased 2-quart casserole, spoon in squash mixture, and top with rest of stuffing. Bake at 350°F for 25 minutes. Sprinkle with parsley. *Serves 6–8.*

*Evelyn I. Johnson, Our Savior Lutheran Church, Hanover, New Hampshire*

# Autumn Leaves

This colorful casserole brings to mind the bright reds and yellows of fall.

| | |
|---|---|
| 2 cups diced summer squash | ½ cup cream |
| 1 cup finely chopped onion | 1 teaspoon basil |
| 6 medium tomatoes, skinned and cut up | 1 tablespoon parsley |
| | Black pepper |
| 6 tablespoons butter | 4 cups cooked rice |
| ¼ cup flour | ¼ cup Parmesan cheese |
| 2 cups chicken broth | |

Sauté squash, onion, and tomatoes in 2 tablespoons butter until tender. Melt remaining 4 tablespoons butter in saucepan. Blend in flour. Gradually add chicken broth, stirring until thickened. Stir in cream, basil, and parsley. Season to taste with pepper. Mix vegetables with rice and sauce. Turn into buttered 2-quart casserole. Sprinkle with Parmesan cheese. Bake at 350°F until bubbling and heated through. *Serves 6–8.*

*E. M. Charlton, St. Matthew's Church, Bedford, New York*

# Squash and Hominy Dish

Filling enough for the entrée; fine as a vegetable, too.

2 pounds zucchini or summer squash
1 large onion, chopped
4 tablespoons butter
½ cup water
2 cans (16 ounces each) hominy, drained

2 jalapeño peppers, seeded and chopped (wear plastic gloves when handling)
1½ cups sour cream
1 teaspoon salt
2 cups grated sharp cheese
Crushed corn chips for topping

Combine zucchini or squash, onion, butter, and water in skillet, and cook slowly until tender. Add hominy, peppers, sour cream, salt, and 1 cup cheese. Pour into greased 3-quart casserole, top with remaining 1 cup cheese, and sprinkle with crushed corn chips. Bake at 325°F for 1 hour. *Serves 8.*

*Phyllis Shattuck, All Saints Episcopal Church, Pasadena, California*

# Tomato-Corn Rarebit

Tasty and easily transportable.

2 teaspoons chopped onion
1½ tablespoons butter
3 tablespoons flour
1 cup canned tomatoes
1 cup drained canned corn

½ teaspoon salt
1 package (8 ounces) processed cheese, shredded
6–8 slices toast or double-size saltines

Sauté onion in butter until onion is soft. Blend in flour; add tomatoes (with juice), corn, and salt. Cook slowly for 10 minutes. Add cheese and cook over low heat, stirring often, until cheese melts completely. (Too high heat will curdle it.) Serve on saltine crackers or toast points. *Serves 6.*

*Mrs. Albert G. Clark, United Church of Christ, Keene, New Hampshire*

# Tomato-Cheese Crunch

Great with garden-ripe tomatoes.

6 medium tomatoes, peeled
½ cup thinly sliced onion

1 cup grated Cheddar cheese
2 cups crushed potato chips

Slice tomatoes ½" thick. Arrange half of slices in bottom of greased 2-quart casserole. Spread half the onion and half the cheese over tomatoes, ending with half the chips. Repeat layers, ending with remaining chips. Bake at 350°F for 30 minutes. *Serves 6.*

*Jean Cole, Concord Unitarian Church, Concord, New Hampshire*

# Mixed Vegetable Casserole

Vegetables in a mildly mustardy cream sauce.
Make with your own combinations of leftover vegetables, too.

1 package (10 ounces) frozen peas
1 package (10 ounces) frozen lima beans
1 cup chopped celery
1 cup pared and sliced carrots
⅓ cup + 2 tablespoons butter

⅓ cup flour
3 cups milk
1½ teaspoons salt
½ teaspoon paprika
½ teaspoon dry mustard
1½ cups cracker crumbs

Cook frozen vegetables in one pot and celery and carrots in another, until almost tender. Drain and reserve. Melt ⅓ cup butter in saucepan. Add flour and blend; then, stirring constantly, gradually add milk and stir until thickened. Add salt, paprika, and dry mustard. Melt remaining 2 tablespoons butter and mix with crumbs in bowl. Turn vegetables into 2-quart buttered baking dish. Pour white sauce over and top with buttered crumbs. Bake at 375°F for 20 minutes, or until bubbling around edges. *Serves 6.*

*Mrs. Henry Delay, Harwinton Congregational Church, Harwinton, Connecticut*

# Vegetable Cobbler

Tasty and filling as a meatless but balanced meal.

4 cups cooked mixed vegetables
(limas, peas, string beans, corn,
and/or carrots)
1½ cups stock
1 teaspoon oregano, dillweed, or
thyme
½ teaspoon pepper

1½ cups whole wheat flour
2 teaspoons baking powder
1 teaspoon salt
½ cup cornmeal
2 eggs, beaten
1 cup milk or broth
¼–½ cup grated sharp cheese

Grease 9" × 13" dish. Heat vegetables in stock, and pour all into greased dish. Stir together oregano, dillweed, or thyme; pepper; flour; baking powder; salt; and cornmeal. Add eggs and milk or broth, and mix until well-distributed. Spread batter over vegetables. Bake at 425°F for 20–25 minutes. Immediately after removing from oven, sprinkle with grated cheese. *Serves 8–10.*

*Stephanie Gross, Episcopal Church of St. John Baptist, Thomaston, Maine*

# Mixed Vegetables Italienne

Companionable contrasts. No need to peel young zucchini.

¼ cup salad oil
1 can (16 ounces) tomatoes
1 beef bouillon cube
4 cups zucchini, cut into
1" cubes (about 1¼ pounds)
1½ cups green pepper cut into
1" pieces (about ½ pound)
1 cup sliced carrots

1 cup peeled, diced potatoes
1 cup coarsely chopped onion
1 teaspoon oregano
1½ teaspoons salt
⅛ teaspoon pepper
1 cup frozen peas
½ teaspoon cornstarch, mixed
into 1 teaspoon water

In saucepan, combine oil, tomatoes (with juice), bouillon cube, zucchini, green pepper, carrots, potatoes, onion, oregano, salt, and pepper. Cover and bring to boil. Reduce heat and simmer. After 15 minutes, add frozen peas. Continue to simmer, covered, until vegetables are tender. Thicken with cornstarch. *Serves 6.*

*Mary Nichol, First Presbyterian Church, Monroe, New York*

# Roasted Herbed Vegetables

Oven cooking caramelizes the natural sugars of root vegetables
and deepens their flavors. If the seasoning mix herbes de Provence is not available,
substitute one teaspoon each of thyme, sage, and rosemary.

| | |
|---|---|
| 3 **cups 1" cubed carrots** | 2 **tablespoons coarsely chopped** |
| 3 **cups 1" cubed turnips** | **garlic (optional)** |
| 3 **cups 1" cubed red potatoes** | 1 **tablespoon herbes de Provence** |
| 2 **large sweet onions, each cut** | 1 **teaspoon salt** |
| **into 8 wedges** | 1 **teaspoon pepper** |
| ⅓ **cup olive oil** | ¼ **cup minced parsley** |

Place carrots, turnips, potatoes, onion, oil, garlic (if using), herbes de Provence, salt, and pepper in 11" × 15" (5-quart) lasagna dish. Toss to coat vegetables with oil and seasonings. Roast at 375°F for about 1 hour, turning vegetables occasionally. If vegetables are browning too quickly, occasionally add 2 tablespoons hot water to pan.

Remove when vegetables are well browned and tender. Add parsley and toss. *Serves 8–10.*

# T. L. C. Vegetable Casserole

Tomatoes, Limas, and Celery make a fine cold-weather supper.

1 cup dry lima beans
2 cups diced celery
½ cup minced green pepper
4 medium onions, sliced

2 cups canned tomatoes
Salt and pepper
1 tablespoon butter
2 slices bacon

Wash and soak beans overnight in cold water. In morning, add water as needed to cover, and simmer until tender or until bean skins shrivel when blown upon. Drain off water. Add celery, green pepper, onions, tomatoes (with juice), and salt and pepper to taste. Dot with butter. Place in greased 2-quart casserole. Top with bacon slices. Bake at 350°F for about 1 hour, or until bacon is crisp and vegetables are cooked. *Serves 6.*

*Mrs. Albert Marcks, St. Mary's Church, Marlboro, New York*

# 7-Minute Zucchini

A rapidly made and out-of-the-ordinary zucchini dish.

6 cups zucchini, peeled and
  coarsely grated (about 2
  pounds)
1 teaspoon salt
½ pound sliced mushrooms, or
  1 can (4 ounces), drained

¼ cup butter
¼ cup chopped onions
1 minced clove garlic
½ cup sour cream
1 tablespoon minced fresh basil,
  or 1 teaspoon dried basil

Combine zucchini and salt in strainer and let stand. Heat mushrooms in skillet, shaking over high heat until liquid evaporates. Add butter, onions, and garlic to mushrooms and sauté. Squeeze excess liquid from zucchini. Add to mushroom mixture and stir. Heat 5 minutes. Stir in sour cream and basil. Heat through, but do not boil. *Serves 6.*

*Virginia Ritter Mesics, The United Church of Jaffrey, Jaffrey, New Hampshire*

# Italian Zucchini Casserole

Another reason to rejoice over a bountiful zucchini crop.

2½ pounds zucchini, thinly sliced
½ cup chopped onion
½ cup chopped green pepper
4 tablespoons butter
1 can (3 ounces) sliced mushrooms
1 package dry spaghetti sauce mix

1 cup water
1 can (6 ounces) tomato paste
4 ounces shredded mozzarella cheese
2 tablespoons grated Parmesan cheese

Cook zucchini in boiling salted water for 4–5 minutes. Drain. Sauté onion and green pepper in butter until tender. Remove from heat and add mushrooms, sauce mix, water, tomato paste, and mozzarella. Gently stir in zucchini. Transfer to greased 7" × 11" baking dish, and sprinkle with Parmesan cheese. Bake at 350°F for 30–35 minutes. *Serves 8.*

*Evelyn Shaw, Pilgrim Congregational Church, New Haven, Connecticut*

# Lemon-Spinach Rice

Makes a wonderful partner to Rosemary Lamb Stew (page 49).

1½ cups uncooked long-grain rice
3 cups water
1 teaspoon salt
3 eggs, lightly beaten
1 package (10 ounces) frozen chopped spinach, cooked and drained

¾ cup grated Parmesan or Cheddar cheese
¼ teaspoon pepper
2 tablespoons parsley
2½ tablespoons lemon juice

Cook rice by simmering, covered, in boiling salted water until all water is absorbed. Stir spinach and salt into cooked rice. In a 2-quart casserole, mix egg with cheese, pepper, parsley, and lemon juice. Add rice mixture and mix well. Bake at 350°F for 30 minutes. *Serves 6.*

# Spanish Rice

Smooth, creamy rice heated up with peppers. Olé!

1 cup chopped onions
¼ cup butter
4 cups freshly cooked rice
2 cups sour cream
1 cup creamed cottage cheese
1 large bay leaf, crumbled
½ teaspoon salt

½ teaspoon pepper
1 can (12 ounces) Tuscan peppers, or 2 cans (4 ounces each) chilies, chopped
2 cups grated sharp cheese
Parsley

Sauté onions in butter. Stir in rice, sour cream, cottage cheese, bay leaf, salt, and pepper. In 2-quart crockery casserole or 9" × 13" baking pan, layer half the rice, the Tuscan peppers or chilies, and 1 cup grated cheese. Again layer remainder of rice and top with remaining 1 cup cheese and parsley. Bake in preheated 375°F oven for 25 minutes, or until hot and bubbly. *Serves 8.*

*Catherine P. Newell, Concord Unitarian Church, Concord, New Hampshire*

# Spanish Rice II

A more traditional version.

3 slices bacon
1 cup uncooked long-grain rice
2 cups water
1 teaspoon salt
½ cup chopped onion
½ cup chopped celery

⅓ cup chopped green pepper
1 can (16 ounces) tomatoes
1 teaspoon sugar
1 teaspoon chili powder
½ teaspoon Worcestershire sauce
½ cup grated Cheddar cheese

Cook bacon until crisp and crumble. Reserve bacon fat. Set aside. Combine rice, water, and salt. Bring to boil. Stir briefly and reduce heat. Cover tightly and simmer until all liquid is absorbed—about 14 minutes. Sauté onion, celery, and green pepper in reserved bacon fat until tender. Add cooked rice, tomatoes (with juice), sugar, chili powder, Worcestershire sauce, and bacon bits. Transfer to greased casserole. Top with grated cheese. Bake at 350°F for about 20 minutes, or until bubbly. *Serves 6.*

*Dorothy Freitag, Our Savior Lutheran Church, Hanover, New Hampshire*

# Soups and Salads

Nothing comforts the soul like a steaming bowl of soup. Three supremely satisfying ones are included here. If it's a heartier stew you're after, see the recipes in Beef (page 1); Ham, Pork, and Lamb (page 34); and Chicken and Turkey (page 51).

When it comes to salads, there are two schools of thought. One considers fruit with or without gelatin, marshmallows, or other sweet additions to be salads. The other believes that salads are vegetable rather than fruit. Period. To please both sides, this chapter includes both vegetable salads and fruit salads. No matter what side you take, you'll certainly find good things to eat.

French Onion Soup  142

Thick Spiced Lentil Soup  142

Sausage Chowder  143

Bean Salad  143

Molded Beet Salad  144

Copper Pennies  144

Greek Cabbage Salad  145

Turkish Eggplant Salad  146

24-Hour Layered Salad  146

Marinated Vegetable Salad  147

Asian Wilted Greens Salad  147

Mixed Salad  148

Sauerkraut Salad  148

Green Pea Salad  149

Super Salad Sandwich  149

Salad Excelsior  150

Spinach Salad  150

Golden Potato Salad  151

Main Dish Potato Salad  152

Hot Potato Salad  152

Spaghetti Salad  153

Hot German Potato Salad  153

Danish Potato Salad  154

Everlasting Cole Slaw  154

Cabbage Slaw  155

Dill Dip  155

3 Weeks Cole Slaw  156

Chili Dip  156

Astoria Salad  157

Cranberry Salad  157

Christmas Fruit Salad  158

Blueberry Salad  158

Foam Over the Sea  159

5-Cup Salad  160

Spicy Peach Salad  160

Strawberry Nut Salad  161

Jellied Vegetable Salad  161

# French Onion Soup

An old favorite.

8 onions, thinly sliced
4 tablespoons butter
9 cups water
8 beef bouillon cubes

2 cups flavored croutons,
or 8 slices toasted bread (any
kind), crust trimmed
Sliced or grated Muenster or
Swiss cheese

Sauté onions in butter until golden. Boil water and add bouillon cubes. Add onions and simmer for 1½ hours on top of stove. Just before serving time, pour soup into individual crocks or bowls, sprinkle in croutons or lay toasted bread on top of soup, and cover with cheese (any desired amount). Place crocks or bowls on cookie sheet. Heat at 350°F for 3–5 minutes, or put under broiler for 1–2 minutes—until cheese is melted. *Serves 8.*

*Mark and Janet Dodge, Sacred Heart Church, Monroe, New York*

# Thick Spiced Lentil Soup

Hearty and lively.

½ pound dry lentils
5–6 cups water
2 onions, chopped
1 bay leaf
2 cloves garlic
1 can (8 ounces) tomato sauce

1 teaspoon pickling spice (tied up
in cheesecloth bag)
¼ cup vinegar
¼ cup olive oil
Salt and pepper

Pick over and wash lentils. Add water to cover, onions, bay leaf, garlic, tomato sauce, pickling spice, vinegar, oil, and salt and pepper to taste. Simmer until lentils are cooked. Before serving, remove and discard bay leaf and pickling spice. *Serves 6–8.*

*Virginia Colivos, Greek Orthodox Church of the Annunciation, Dover, New Hampshire*

# Sausage Chowder

A three-in-one dish: soup, stew, and chowder.

| | |
|---|---|
| ½ **pound bulk sausage** | ¾ **teaspoon salt** |
| 1½ **cups cooked kidney beans** | ¼ **teaspoon garlic salt** |
| 1½ **cups canned tomatoes** | ¼ **teaspoon thyme** |
| 2 **cups water** | ¼ **teaspoon pepper** |
| 1 **small onion, chopped** | ½ **cup diced potatoes** |
| 1 **bay leaf** | ¼ **cup chopped green pepper** |

Cook sausage in skillet until brown. Pour off fat. In large kettle, combine beans, tomatoes (with juice), water, onion, bay leaf, salt, garlic salt, thyme, and pepper. Simmer 1 hour covered. Add potatoes and green pepper. Cook until tender. Before serving, remove and discard bay leaf. *Serves 6.*

*Bev McKeone, Center Congregational Church, Torrington, Connecticut*

# Bean Salad

A three-bean salad that can become four with chickpeas.

| | |
|---|---|
| 1 **can (16 ounces) kidney beans, drained** | 1 **can (16 ounces) chickpeas, drained (optional)** |
| 1 **can (16 ounces) yellow string beans, drained** | ¾ **cup sugar** |
| 1 **can (16 ounces) green string beans, drained** | ½ **cup vinegar** |
| | ½ **cup salad oil** |

Combine kidney beans, string beans, and chickpeas, if using, in bowl. In saucepan, boil together sugar and vinegar for 10 minutes. Add salad oil and pour over vegetables. Let sit overnight in refrigerator. (Other vegetables may be added as desired, such as onions, peppers, and olives.) *Serves 12–16.*

*Anne Gove, Concord Unitarian Church, Concord, New Hampshire*

# Molded Beet Salad

Colorful and handsome, with just enough "bite."

3 cups shredded canned or
   cooked beets
½ cup sugar
½ cup vinegar
2 tablespoons plain gelatin

½ cup cold water
1½ teaspoons salt
1½ cups finely chopped celery
2 tablespoons grated horseradish
1 tablespoon grated onion

Drain beets, reserving 1½ cups juice. Combine beets, sugar, and vinegar. Chill for 1 hour. Dissolve gelatin in water. Heat reserved beet juice and salt to boiling. Remove from heat and add gelatin. Stir until incorporated. Cool until syrupy. Add beets, celery, horseradish, and onion to gelatin mixture. Mix well. Pour into oiled 1½-quart mold. Chill until firm. Unmold on bed of lettuce or watercress. *Serves 8.*

*Women's Association of The Congregational Church, Amherst, New Hampshire*

# Copper Pennies

A fitting name for a tasty carrot salad.

2 pounds carrots, pared and cut
   into round slices
1 green pepper, seeded and
   chopped

1 onion, chopped
½ cup chopped celery

## Dressing

1 can (10¾ ounces) tomato soup
½ cup salad oil
¾ cup sugar
¾ cup vinegar

1 teaspoon Worcestershire sauce
1 teaspoon prepared mustard
   Salt and pepper

Boil carrot slices in salted water until almost tender. Drain and combine with green pepper, onion, and celery. Mix well together soup, oil, sugar, vinegar, Worcestershire sauce, mustard, and salt and pepper to taste. Pour over vegetables and refrigerate until well-chilled. Will keep in refrigerator a week or more. *Serves 8–10.*

*Regina Stanhope, Our Savior Lutheran Church, Hanover, New Hampshire*

# Greek Cabbage Salad

Not a cole slaw, but just as refreshing.

| | |
|---|---|
| 1 **medium head cabbage, shredded** | ½ **pound feta cheese, crumbled** |
| 1–2 **cloves garlic, crushed** | **Salt and pepper** |
| 2–3 **teaspoons dillweed** | ¼–⅓ **cup olive oil** |

Toss cabbage, garlic, dillweed, and feta. Season to taste with salt and pepper. Add enough oil just to coat ingredients (to make it look dressed but not soupy). Chill several hours. *Serves 6–8.*

*Susan Cronewett, Our Savior Lutheran Church, Hanover, New Hampshire*

# Turkish Eggplant Salad

A real conversation piece and change of pace.

| | |
|---|---|
| 1 good-size eggplant | Salt and pepper |
| ¼ cup olive oil | Parsley |
| ⅔ cup feta cheese, crumbled | Ripe black olives |
| Lemon juice | |

Bake eggplant at 400°F until soft and skin crumbles. Peel, remove seeds, cool, and dice. Whip eggplant in blender with oil to make smooth paste. Add feta and lemon juice to taste and mix well. Season to taste with salt and pepper and spread mixture on flat serving dish (lined with lettuce or watercress, if desired). Garnish with parsley and olives. *Serves 6–8.*

*Belkis H. Vassaf, Concord Unitarian Church, Concord, New Hampshire*

# 24-Hour Layered Salad

A delightful mix of vegetables, cheese, and bacon.

| | |
|---|---|
| 1 head lettuce, torn into bite-size pieces | 1 small sweet red pepper, chopped |
| 1 head cauliflower, broken into florets | 2 cups mayonnaise |
| ¼ cup sliced green onions and tips | 2 tablespoons sugar |
| 1 package (10 ounces) frozen peas, thawed | 1 cup shredded Cheddar cheese |
| | 8 slices bacon, cooked and crumbled |

In large bowl, layer ingredients in order given; *do not mix.* Tightly cover bowl with plastic wrap or lid. Refrigerate overnight. Toss before serving. *Serves 8–10.*

*Lina Storrs, Center Congregational Church, Torrington, Connecticut*

# Marinated Vegetable Salad

Use these vegetables or experiment with your own combinations.

½ cup salad oil
½ cup vinegar
½ cup sugar
2 cups whole cooked green beans
1 cup sliced cooked carrots

1 cup sliced celery
1 cup green pepper, sliced or cut into strips
1 medium Spanish onion, sliced

Prepare dressing of oil, vinegar, and sugar mixed together. Mix green beans, carrots, celery, green pepper, and onion into dressing and keep pressed down with plate on top. Refrigerate overnight. Drain well before serving. ***Serves 8–10.***

*Susan Cronewett, Our Savior Lutheran Church, Hanover, New Hampshire*

# Asian Wilted Greens Salad

A useful salad to serve with an Asian entrée.

3 cups torn lettuce
3 cups torn fresh spinach
1 cup bias-sliced celery
2 medium tomatoes, cut into wedges
¾ cup chopped green pepper
½ cup sliced radishes
⅓ cup sliced green onion

1 envelope (6 ounces) Italian salad dressing mix
⅓ cup salad oil
¼ cup vinegar
4 teaspoons sugar
½ teaspoon salt
1 can (16 ounces) Chinese chop suey vegetables, drained

In large salad bowl, combine lettuce, spinach, celery, tomatoes, green pepper, radishes, and onion. In saucepan, combine salad dressing mix, oil, vinegar, sugar, salt, and Chinese vegetables. Heat to boiling and pour over salad mixture. Toss gently to coat. Serve at once. ***Serves 8.***

*Betsy High, United Methodist Church of the Hamptons, Hampton, New Hampshire*

# Mixed Salad

A luncheon salad with plenty of protein.

1 small head lettuce
2 medium tomatoes, skinned
1 small cucumber, pared
2 hard-boiled eggs
¼ pound crisp cooked bacon

1½ cups cooked chicken or tuna
½ cup Cheddar cheese
2 tablespoons chopped onion
1 cup garlic dressing

Rip lettuce leaves into small pieces and place in large salad bowl. Finely chop tomatoes, cucumber, eggs, bacon, chicken or tuna, and cheese. Arrange each in row across lettuce, ending with onion. Pour dressing over salad and toss lightly. *Serves 6.*

*Carol Jensen, United Church of Hardwick, Hardwick, Vermont*

# Sauerkraut Salad

Most people feel strongly about sauerkraut . . . either you *love* it or you *hate* it.
Here's a recipe for those who love it.

1¼ cups sugar
½ cup salad oil
½ cup vinegar
1 can (16 ounces) sauerkraut,
   drained, rinsed, and snipped

1 cup diced celery
1 onion, chopped
1 cup diced green
   pepper

Mix sugar, oil, and vinegar. Pour over sauerkraut, celery, onion, and green pepper in bowl. Mix and let stand several hours or overnight in refrigerator. Drain before serving. *Serves 8–10.*

*Joanna Miller, Dublin Community Church, Dublin, New Hampshire*

# Green Pea Salad

Serve as is or on lettuce.

2 packages (10 ounces each) frozen peas, defrosted
1 cup celery, finely cut
½ cup scallions, finely cut

1 pound bacon, cooked and crumbled
1 cup sour cream
Salt

Combine peas, celery, scallions, bacon, sour cream, and salt to taste. Chill thoroughly. *Serves 8.*

*Catherine B. Anderson, United Methodist Church of the Hamptons, Hampton, New Hampshire*

# Super Salad Sandwich

Also good served on lettuce without bread and garnished with slices of lemon or avocado.

1 can (6½ ounces) tuna, drained and flaked
1 cup cottage cheese
2 chopped hard-cooked eggs
1 large tomato, chopped and drained
½ cup shredded natural Cheddar cheese
1 teaspoon lemon-pepper

marinade, or 1 teaspoon garlic salt + dash of lemon juice
¼ cup chopped celery
2 green onions, sliced
⅓ cup mayonnaise
¼ teaspoon salt
16 slices whole grain bread, toasted and buttered
½ cup fresh alfalfa sprouts

Mix together tuna, cottage cheese, eggs, tomato, Cheddar, marinade or garlic mixture, celery, onions, mayonnaise, and salt. Chill. Spread mixture on 8 slices of toast, then top with sprouts and remaining toasted slices. *Serves 8.*

*Evelyn H. Chase, Concord Unitarian Church, Concord, New Hampshire*

# Salad Excelsior

Served for lunch with a creamy Italian, Caesar, or other cheesy dressing and hot garlic bread, this is a complete meal. Augment, if you wish, with soup and dessert.

1 pound fresh spinach
1 head garden lettuce
4 hard-boiled eggs, quartered
4 tomatoes, skinned and sliced
1 can (8½ ounces) artichoke hearts, drained
1 cup cooked (or canned, rinsed, and drained) medium shrimp

1 cup creamy Italian or Caesar dressing
½ pound bacon, cooked crisp and crumbled
1 cup toasted and buttered croutons

Wash spinach and garden lettuce leaves. Drain. Remove thick stems from spinach and tear into pieces. Tear garden lettuce into pieces. Put in clean towel or towels and refrigerate to crisp. Line large bowl with mixture of crisped lettuce and spinach. Add eggs, tomatoes, artichoke hearts, and shrimp. Toss with dressing, mixing well to coat all ingredients. Sprinkle bacon and croutons over top. *Serves 8.*

# Spinach Salad

To ensure crisp spinach, wrap washed and stemmed leaves in a clean towel and refrigerate for at least an hour before using in salad.

1 pound fresh spinach
2 hard-boiled eggs, chopped
½ of 5-ounce can water chestnuts, sliced thin

5 strips bacon, cooked and crumbled

## Dressing

½ cup sugar
1 cup salad oil
⅓ cup ketchup
½ cup vinegar

2 tablespoons Worcestershire sauce
1 medium onion, grated

Wash, drain, and remove hard stems on spinach. Combine spinach with eggs, water chestnuts, and bacon. Mix together sugar, oil, ketchup, vinegar, Worcestershire sauce, and onion and pour over spinach. Toss and serve. **Serves 6.**

*Jean Cole, Concord Unitarian Church, Concord, New Hampshire*

# Golden Potato Salad

A cold potato salad with a creamy mayonnaise dressing.

6 cups peeled, diced, and boiled potatoes
½ cup diced cucumber
½ cup chopped onion
2 tablespoons chopped chives
⅔ cup mayonnaise

⅓ cup yogurt
2 tablespoons cider vinegar
1 tablespoon prepared mustard
1½ teaspoons salt
¼ teaspoon pepper
Paprika

Combine potatoes, cucumber, onion, and chives in large bowl. Blend mayonnaise, yogurt, vinegar, mustard, salt, and pepper in small bowl. Pour over potato mixture and blend thoroughly. Refrigerate several hours. Sprinkle with paprika before serving. **Serves 6–8.**

*Carol Jensen, United Church of Hardwick, Hardwick, Vermont*

# Main Dish Potato Salad

This salad recipe, over 50 years old and handed down from the Bedford Men's Club (now disbanded), is now served at the Unity Club Harvest Supper every October to 450–600 people. Here, it is cut down to serve 8.

| | |
|---|---|
| 2 pounds potatoes, peeled | 1 pimiento, diced |
| 3 stalks celery, chopped | Salt and pepper |
| 1 pound rump veal (or lean pork) | 1 cup whipped salad dressing |
| 1 large onion, grated | 1 head lettuce |

Cook potatoes, cool, and dice. Mix in celery. Cook veal, cool, and dice. Add onion and pimiento with veal to potatoes. Season to taste with salt and pepper, then mix with salad dressing and serve on bed of lettuce. ***Serves 8.***

*Bedford Presbyterian Church, Bedford, New Hampshire*

# Hot Potato Salad

Made with onion and hard-boiled eggs.

| | |
|---|---|
| 6 medium potatoes, chopped | 1 egg, beaten |
| 2 hard-boiled eggs, chopped | ¼ cup cider vinegar |
| 4 slices bacon, diced | 1¾ teaspoons salt |
| ¼ cup minced onion | |

Cook potatoes. Add chopped eggs. Fry bacon and onion until delicate brown. Strain, reserving bacon fat. Add fat slowly to beaten egg and beat well. Add vinegar and salt and pour mixture over potatoes. Mix lightly to blend well; heat in double boiler. Serve hot. ***Serves 6.***

*Mary Kay Royer, Center Congregational Church, Torrington, Connecticut*

# Spaghetti Salad

Essentially a "potato" salad—but with pasta!

1 package (8 ounces) thin
  spaghetti
4 hard-boiled eggs
1 green pepper, finely cut
1 stalk celery, finely cut
1 teaspoon finely grated or
  minced onion

Salt and pepper
½ of 5-ounce jar green olives,
  finely cut, and a few slices for
  top of salad
½ cup whipped salad dressing
  (*not* mayonnaise)

Cook spaghetti, drain, and rinse with cold water. Drain again. Add eggs, green pepper, celery, onion, salt and pepper to taste, olives, and salad dressing. Mix thoroughly. Chill in refrigerator for a few hours before serving to allow flavors to blend. Top with remaining olive slices. *Serves 6–8.*

*Mrs. Albert G. Clark, United Church of Christ, Keene, New Hampshire*

# Hot German Potato Salad

"A New Year's tradition from my mother-in-law's family," featuring chicory.

14 medium potatoes, peeled and
   cut into large chunks
⅓ pound bacon, cut with kitchen
   shears into ¼" squares
¼ cup bacon fat

¼ cup cider vinegar
¼ cup water
2 cups snipped chicory
2 tablespoons sugar
  Salt and pepper

Boil potatoes until slightly firmer than required for mashing. Fry bacon pieces over medium-low heat until crisp (reserve ¼ cup fat). Mix vinegar and water. As soon as potatoes are done, drain, dump into large bowl, and immediately add chicory, bacon pieces, vinegar and water, hot bacon fat, and sugar. Toss well and season to taste with salt and pepper. *Serves 8.*

*Mary Wakefield, First Congregational Church, Rindge, New Hampshire*

# Danish Potato Salad

A cooked dressing without mayonnaise over a cold salad
with hard-boiled eggs and radishes.

¼ cup vinegar
¼ cup water
¼ cup sugar
¼ teaspoon salt
   Dash of pepper
1 teaspoon prepared mustard
2 eggs, well-beaten

1 cup whipped salad dressing
4 cups peeled, cooked, diced potatoes
2 hard-boiled eggs, chopped
½ cup chopped cucumbers
1 tablespoon minced onion
1 tablespoon chopped green pepper
3–4 diced or sliced radishes

Combine vinegar, water, sugar, salt, pepper, and mustard in saucepan. Bring to boil. Reduce heat and gradually beat in eggs. Cook, stirring constantly, until slightly thickened. Remove from stove and beat in salad dressing. Toss together potatoes, hard-boiled eggs, cucumbers, onion, green pepper, and radishes. Pour dressing on potato mixture and toss gently. Adjust seasonings if necessary. Refrigerate for several hours. *Serves 6–8.*

*Beatrice Benjamin, The United Church, East Calais, Vermont*

# Everlasting Cole Slaw

1 head cabbage
1 small onion, finely chopped
2 carrots, grated
2 stalks celery, diced
1 cup chopped black olives
   (optional)
1 sweet pepper, diced

½ cup sugar
⅔ cup vinegar
1 cup salad oil
1 teaspoon mustard
1 teaspoon celery seed
1 tablespoon salt

Finely shred cabbage. Add onion, carrots, celery, olives, if using, and pepper. Add sugar and turn into 11" × 15" pan. Mix vinegar, oil, mustard, celery seed, and salt in saucepan. Bring to boil. Pour hot liquid over vegetables. Mix well, cover, and refrigerate. *Serves 8–10.*

*Naomi Crook, Chocorua Community Church, Chocorua, New Hampshire*

# Cabbage Slaw

1 cup mayonnaise
½ cup milk
½ cup seedless raisins
½ cup drained crushed pineapple

1 medium dark green cabbage, shredded
1 red apple, or 3 red and 3 green cherries

In large mixing bowl, combine mayonnaise and milk to make thick dressing. Stir in raisins and pineapple. Add cabbage and mix well. Cut apple into wedges, leaving skin on. In decorative design, place apple wedges or cherries on cabbage. *Serves 8–10.*

*Flora C. Hammond, Unitarian Universalist Church, Keene, New Hampshire*

# Dill Dip

1 cup mayonnaise
2 teaspoons dill seed
1 cup plain yogurt

1 tablespoon minced green onion
2 teaspoons salt

Beat together mayonnaise, dill seed, yogurt, onion, and salt until well-blended. *About 2 cups.*

*Carolyn Ramsbotham, St. Thomas More Church, Durham, New Hampshire*

# 3 Weeks Cole Slaw

3 pounds white cabbage, chopped
1 green pepper, chopped (optional)
2 white onions, chopped
1½–2 cups sugar

1 cup salad oil
1 cup cider vinegar
1 teaspoon celery seed
2 teaspoons salt

Combine cabbage, green pepper, if using, onions, and sugar. Mix well. Mix oil, vinegar, celery seed, and salt and bring to hard boil. Pour over cabbage mixture and stir very well. Store in refrigerator in airtight container. Let stand at least 3 days as flavor improves as it ages. Will keep refrigerated for a month. ***Serves 10.***

*Pauline Hammond, Free Will Baptist Church, Northwood, New Hampshire*

# Chili Dip

Use this dip with a crudité, or raw vegetable, platter. Arrange broccoli or cauliflower florets, slivered peeled carrots, celery ribs, quartered tomatoes, sliced cucumber, cut fresh green beans, cut-up green pepper, turnip strips, radishes, or mushroom slices on a large plate or platter with a bowl of dip in the center or on the side. Do the same with the recipe for Dill Dip (page 133).

1 cup mayonnaise or sour cream
2 tablespoons grated onion
2 teaspoons vinegar
2 teaspoons chives (dried or fresh)
2 teaspoons chili sauce

½ teaspoon curry powder
½ teaspoon salt
¼ teaspoon red-pepper flakes, crushed
½ teaspoon thyme

Combine mayonnaise or sour cream, onion, vinegar, chives, chili sauce, curry powder, salt, red-pepper flakes, and thyme. ***About 1¼ cups.***

*Janet Dodge, Sacred Heart Church, Monroe, New York*

# Astoria Salad

A fruit salad, but not sweet, except for the apples.

4 large red apples, cored and cut up into small pieces but left unpeeled
2 stalks celery, finely chopped

½ cup chopped walnuts
½ cup cubed cheese
½ cup raisins

## Dressing

¼ cup yogurt
¼ cup mayonnaise

¼ cup sour cream

Combine apples, celery, walnuts, cheese, and raisins in bowl. Mix well together yogurt, mayonnaise, and sour cream and add to salad. Toss and serve on lettuce. *Serves 6.*

*Carolyn Myrick, Temple Congregational Church, Temple, New Hampshire*

# Cranberry Salad

A can of whole-berry cranberry sauce can be used in this recipe, but then omit the sugar.

2 packages (3 ounces each) lemon gelatin
2 cups boiling water
1 cup sugar
2 cups ground fresh cranberries

1 cup drained crushed pineapple
1 cup finely diced celery
½ cup chopped nuts (any kind)
1 cup orange juice

Soak gelatin in a little bit of cold water for 3–5 minutes, then dissolve gelatin in boiling water. Add sugar and stir until sugar is dissolved. Add cranberries, pineapple, celery, nuts, and orange juice. Refrigerate until partially congealed. Stir and return to refrigerator until set. Serve on lettuce. *Serves 10–12.*

*Jeannette M. Miller, Morris Congregational Church, Morris, Connecticut*

# Christmas Fruit Salad

Adds a colorful note to a holiday table setting.

1½ pounds red grapes, seeded and halved
1 can (8½ ounces) pineapple chunks

4 oranges, peeled, seeded, and cut up small
½ cup sugar

## Dressing

1 tablespoon butter
1 tablespoon flour
½ cup sugar
¼ teaspoon dry mustard
1 egg, beaten

¼ teaspoon pepper
¼ cup vinegar
2 tablespoons water
1 cup cream, whipped

Combine grapes, pineapple (with juice), oranges, and sugar and let stand overnight in refrigerator. Meanwhile, melt butter in top of double boiler and add flour. Add sugar, mustard, egg, pepper, vinegar, and water. Cook, stirring, until smooth and thickened. Cool and refrigerate overnight. Drain juice from fruit in morning. Add whipped cream to dressing. Mix dressing and fruit, and serve on lettuce or as fruit cup. *Serves 6–8.*

*Rosamond Wehrwein, Swanzey Congregational Church, Swanzey, New Hampshire*

# Blueberry Salad

A nifty idea for a fruit salad.

2 packages (3 ounces each) black raspberry gelatin
2 cups boiling water
1 can (20 ounces) crushed pineapple

1 can (16 ounces) blueberries, or 1½ cups fresh blueberries + ½ cup water

# Topping

8 ounces soft cream cheese

8 ounces sour cream

½ cup sugar

1 teaspoon vanilla

½ cup chopped walnuts

Soak gelatin in a little bit of cold water for 3–5 minutes, then mix gelatin and boiling water and stir until gelatin is dissolved. Add pineapple (with juice) and canned blueberries (with juice) or fresh berries and water. Pour into 9" × 13" pan and chill until congealed. Cream together cream cheese, sour cream, sugar, and vanilla, and spread over gelatin. Sprinkle with chopped walnuts. Refrigerate. **Serves 8–10.**

*Marcia Fletcher, St. Anne's Episcopal Church, Calais, Maine*

# Foam Over the Sea

An apt name for a pretty gelatin salad. The dressing is important to the dish.

1 package (3 ounces) lime gelatin

1 cup boiling water

1 cup pear juice (drained from canned pears)

½ teaspoon vinegar

½ teaspoon ground ginger, or 1 teaspoon chopped crystalline ginger

1 package (3 ounces) cream cheese, softened

2 cups drained and diced canned pears

2 tablespoons honey

1 cup mayonnaise

Soak gelatin in a little bit of cold water for 3–5 minutes, then dissolve gelatin in boiling water and add pear juice and vinegar. Pour half of gelatin into flat 6" × 10" glass dish and refrigerate until set. Cool remaining gelatin until syrupy and whip. Work ginger and cream cheese into gelatin as you whip. Fold in pears. Spread mixture over gelatin that has set in refrigerator. Chill. To make dressing, whip together honey and mayonnaise. Serve salad with lettuce and dressing. **Serves 6.**

*Carolyn Buck, Wapping Community Church, South Windsor, Connecticut*

# 5-Cup Salad

Vary this by using other fruits by the cupful as well—
apple wedges, banana slices, grapes, or whatever is in season.

1 cup drained crushed pineapple
1 cup grated coconut
1 cup drained mandarin oranges

1 cup miniature marshmallows
1 cup sour cream

In a large bowl, mix together pineapple, coconut, oranges, marshamallows, and sour cream. Let stand overnight. Serve on lettuce. *Serves 6–8.*

*Shirley T. Oladell, Harwinton Congregational Church, Harwinton, Connecticut*

# Spicy Peach Salad

Peachy keen. Serve on lettuce with cottage cheese or yogurt.

1 package (3 ounces) peach gelatin
¼ cup sugar
¼ teaspoon cinnamon
⅛ teaspoon cloves
1 cup boiling water

¾ cup peach syrup (drained from canned peaches)
2 tablespoons vinegar
1 can (16 ounces) sliced peaches, drained

Soak gelatin in a little bit of cold water for 3–5 minutes. Mix sugar, cinnamon, cloves, and gelatin and dissolve in water. Add peach syrup and vinegar. Chill, stirring occasionally, as spices are apt to settle. When *slightly* thickened, add peaches. Stir and chill until firm. *Serves 6.*

*Gladys Priest, Foxon Congregational Church, East Haven, Connecticut*

# Strawberry Nut Salad

A great combination of tastes.

2 packages (3 ounces each) strawberry gelatin
1 cup boiling water
2 packages (10 ounces each) frozen strawberries, thawed
1 cup drained crushed pineapple
3 medium bananas, mashed
1 cup chopped pecans
1 pint sour cream

Soak gelatin in a little bit of cold water for 3–5 minutes, then mix gelatin with boiling water in large bowl. Fold in strawberries, pineapple, bananas, and pecans. Pour half of mixture into 9" × 13" baking dish or metal mold. Refrigerate 1 hour. Spread sour cream over top. Layer balance of mixture on top of sour cream and refrigerate overnight or for several hours. Serve on lettuce or plain. *Serves 12.*

*Elnor Hayward, First Baptist Church, Concord, New Hampshire*

# Jellied Vegetable Salad

Traditional at church suppers. Included in this section because the vegetables are embedded in sweet gelatin.

1 package (3 ounces) lemon gelatin
½ teaspoon salt
1 cup boiling water
1 cup cold water
½ cup shredded cabbage
½ cup shredded carrots
2 tablespoons French dressing

Soak gelatin in a little bit of cold water for 3–5 minutes, then dissolve gelatin and salt in boiling water. Add cold water. Refrigerate until partially jelled. Meanwhile, marinate cabbage and carrots in French dressing for 15 minutes. Add vegetables to gelatin and stir to distribute evenly. Chill until firm. Cut into squares and serve plain or on lettuce. *Serves 6.*

*Marcia Fletcher, St. Anne's Episcopal Church, Calais, Maine*

# Breads and Breadstuffs

This chapter has the most magnificently de-*luscious* ideas for pancakes, doughnuts, muffins, quick breads, yeast breads, coffee cakes, rolls, and biscuits. You won't find these recipes anywhere else. Some are quite surprising inventions—like Squash Biscuits, somewhere between a yeast and quick bread, and so light they are hard to believe; and Deli-Cakes, probably the most airborne pancake alive.

Deli-Cakes  163

Bread Crumb Pancakes  163

Five-Grain Pancakes  164

Flora's Doughnuts  164

Milk Chocolate Doughnuts  165

Apple Muffins  165

Potato Doughnuts  166

Corn Muffins  166

Blueberry Muffins  167

Apple Bread  167

Patty's Pumpkin Muffins  168

Beer Bread  168

Blueberry Bread  169

Blueberry-Pineapple Loaf  169

Cornbread  170

Irish Oatmeal Bread  170

Date Nut Bread  171

Sausage Cake  171

Zucchini Bread  172

Quick Graham Bread  172

Pineapple-Raisin Tea Ring  173

Julekage (Scandanavian Christmas Bread)  174

Apple Coffee Cake  175

Cherry Coffee Cake  175

Danish Kringle  176

Crumb Cake  177

Danish Puff  178

Sour Cream Coffee Cake  178

Rhubarb Coffee Cake  179

Swedish Coffee Ring  180

Walnut-Raisin Coffee Cake  181

Dill Bread  182

Maple Oatmeal Bread  182

Molasses-Bran Bread  183

Oatmeal Bread  184

Feather-Light Dinner Rolls  184

Rindge Rye Bread  185

Butter Dips  185

White Bread  186

Cinnamon Rolls  186

Refrigerator Rolls  187

Orange Bow Knots  188

Raised Rolls  189

Squash Biscuits  189

Cinnamon Roll-Ups  190

# Deli-Cakes

Cooked like pancakes, but the stiffly-beaten egg whites folded in make these cakes unique. Incredibly light and tender, they are a perfect foil for creamed toppings or sweet fruit sauces, and the contributor's own invention.

½ cup flour
1 teaspoon baking powder
½ teaspoon salt
2 large or 3 medium eggs, separated

2 tablespoons melted butter
⅔ cup milk
1 tablespoon sugar or honey (optional)

Combine flour, baking powder, and salt. Beat egg yolks, and add along with butter and milk. If you plan to use as dessert cakes, you may add the sugar or honey. Beat egg whites until stiff. Fold into mixture. Drop in 3"–4" rounds on greased and heated griddle. Brown lightly on both sides over medium heat. Serve warm, topped with hot applesauce flavored with cinnamon and nutmeg, or with hot blueberries. Or serve with creamed mushrooms or ground ham, with sausages, and of course, with maple syrup. Or use to make strawberry shortcake. **Makes about 18 cakes.**

*Walter Clement, United Methodist Church, Plymouth, New Hampshire*

# Bread Crumb Pancakes

Delicate and delicious pancakes that taste very much like French toast. You must use *fresh* bread crumbs.

1½ cups fresh bread crumbs
2 cups buttermilk or soured milk
1 cup flour
1½ teaspoons salt

2 eggs, beaten
1 teaspoon baking soda, dissolved in ¼ cup hot water

Combine bread crumbs, buttermilk or sour milk, flour, salt, and eggs. Mix well. Add baking soda just before frying pancakes. **Serves 6.**

*Marcia Fletcher, St. Anne's Episcopal Church, Calais, Maine*

# Five-Grain Pancakes

2 cups buttermilk
1 cup sour cream
2 eggs
½ teaspoon salt
2 tablespoons sugar
¼ cup bran cereal
1 cup white flour

¼ cup rye flour
¼ cup soy meal flour
¼ cup buckwheat flour
¼ cup cornmeal
2 teaspoons baking soda,
   dissolved in ¼ cup warm water

In large bowl, combine buttermilk, sour cream, eggs, salt, and sugar. Add cereal. Sift flours and cornmeal together and beat into liquid mixture. Stir in baking soda. Cook as any pancake on hot skillet. Skillet is ready for pancakes when drops of cold water shaken onto it jump and bounce rather than just boil. Serve with butter and jam and/or maple syrup. *Makes about 36 pancakes 4" in diameter.*

*Lillian Farrar, United Church of Christ, Keene, New Hampshire*

# Flora's Doughnuts

Even if you've never tried doughnuts before, these are "easy as pie" and scrumptious.

3 cups flour
½ teaspoon salt
3 teaspoons baking powder
½ teaspoon cinnamon

⅔ cup sugar
2 eggs, beaten
2 tablespoons shortening, melted
1 cup milk

Sift together flour, salt, baking powder, and cinnamon. Add sugar and mix to soft dough with eggs, shortening, and milk. Roll out to ½" thickness on well-floured surface. Cut out doughnuts. Fry in 2" hot (360°F) fat until brown on both sides. Drain and serve plain or sprinkled with sugar. For a fancier touch, frost when cool with mixture of maple syrup and confectioners' sugar. *Makes about 24 doughnuts.*

*Flora C. Hammond, Unitarian Universalist Church, Keene, New Hampshire*

# Milk Chocolate Doughnuts

An oldie that's a real goodie.

2 squares unsweetened chocolate
1 cup sugar
1 egg
1 teaspoon baking soda

1 teaspoon baking powder
2–3 cups flour
1 teaspoon salt
1 cup soured milk

Melt chocolate over hot water and mix with sugar in large bowl. Add egg and mix well. Combine baking soda, baking powder, 2 cups flour, and salt, and add alternately with milk to sugar mixture. Add as much of remaining 1 cup of flour as needed to make soft dough. Roll to ½" thickness, cut out, and fry in deep fat (370°F) for total of 3–5 minutes, turning each doughnut as it rises. Roll in granulated sugar when hot and confectioners' sugar when cold. ***Makes 2 dozen.***

*Mrs. Almond Hager, United Church of Christ, Keene, New Hampshire*

# Apple Muffins

A change from blueberry muffins and lighter than doughnuts.

1⅛ cups flour
1¾ teaspoons baking powder
¼ teaspoon salt
¼ teaspoon cinnamon
¼ teaspoon nutmeg
2 tablespoons shortening

¼ cup + 1 tablespoon sugar
1 egg, beaten
½ cup milk
1 cup apples, cored, peeled, and finely chopped

Sift flour, baking powder, salt, ⅛ teaspoon cinnamon, and ⅛ teaspoon nutmeg. Cream shortening with ¼ cup sugar. Add egg, then flour mixture, alternating with milk. Fold in apples and fill greased muffin cups two-thirds of the way. Combine remaining 1 tablespoon sugar, ⅛ teaspoon cinnamon, and ⅛ teaspoon nutmeg and sprinkle over tops. Bake at 375°F for 20–25 minutes. ***Makes 10 muffins.***

*Ruth Colby, First Congregational Church of Pembroke, Pembroke, New Hampshire*

# Potato Doughnuts

Such a wonderful texture.

3 eggs
¾ cup sugar
3 tablespoons soft butter
⅓ cup milk
2¾ cups flour
4 teaspoons baking powder
1 teaspoon salt

½ teaspoon nutmeg
1 teaspoon mace
½ teaspoon cinnamon
1 cup plain mashed potatoes
(containing no milk, butter, or
seasonings)

Beat eggs well. Beat in sugar and butter. Stir in milk, flour, baking powder, salt, nutmeg, mace, and cinnamon, and beat in until smooth. Add potatoes and blend well. Chill 2–3 hours. Turn out about a third of the dough at a time onto a lightly floured board. Dust sparingly with flour. Roll out to ⅓" thickness and cut with floured cutter. Fry in deep fat or oil (375°F). As doughnuts rise, turn them. Cook 2–3 minutes total until light golden brown. Lift out and drain on paper toweling. Dust with sugar or cinnamon sugar. ***Makes about 3 dozen.***

*Mary Wakefield, First Congregational Church, Rindge, New Hampshire*

# Corn Muffins

A real honey of a corn muffin.

¼ cup oil
1¼ cups milk
1 egg
¼ cup honey

1 cup yellow cornmeal
3 teaspoons baking powder
½ teaspoon salt
1¼ cups sifted flour

Blend oil, milk, egg, and honey into cornmeal, baking powder, salt, and flour. Do not overmix. Bake in greased muffin pans at 425°F for 20–25 minutes. ***Makes 12 large muffins.***

*Carol Jensen, The United Church of Hardwick, Hardwick, Vermont*

# Blueberry Muffins

Blueberries can be fresh, frozen, or canned (drain canned blueberries before using),
but of course right off the bush is best!

| | |
|---|---|
| 3 tablespoons butter, melted | 1 tablespoon baking powder |
| 3½ tablespoons sugar | ½ teaspoon salt |
| 1 egg, beaten | 1 cup milk |
| 2 cups flour | 1 cup blueberries |

Combine butter, sugar, and egg. Sift together flour, baking powder, and salt. Add alternately to egg mixture with milk. Beat until batter is full of bubbles. Stir in blueberries. Fill greased muffin tins three-quarters of the way and bake at 350°F for about 30 minutes. *Makes 12 muffins.*

*Mildred D. Chamberlain, The Congregational Church, South Hero, Vermont*

# Apple Bread

A nice change from banana bread—good for showers and bake sales—
or after school with milk!

| | |
|---|---|
| 4 cups flour | 1 cup cooking oil |
| 2 teaspoons baking soda | ¼ cup sour cream |
| 2 teaspoons cinnamon | 2 teaspoons vanilla |
| 1 teaspoon salt | 2 cups chopped apples |
| 2 cups sugar | 1 cup chopped nuts (any kind) |
| 4 eggs, beaten | |

Sift flour and baking soda, cinnamon, and salt. Combine sugar with eggs, oil, sour cream, and vanilla. Beat well. Blend in flour mixture. Fold in apples and nuts and pour into 2 greased and floured loaf pans. Bake at 350°F for 1 hour, or until done. *Makes 2 loaves.*

*Caroline Hunt, First Baptist Church, Hudson, New Hampshire*

# Patty's Pumpkin Muffins

Just as good without the raisins.

1 cup raisins
½ cup hot water
2 eggs
1 cup solid-pack canned pumpkin
1¼ cups sugar
¾ teaspoon cloves

¾ teaspoon cinnamon
½ teaspoon salt
⅓ cup cooking oil
1¾ cups flour
1½ teaspoons baking powder
½ teaspoon baking soda

Soak raisins in water for 5 minutes. Do not drain. In large mixing bowl, beat eggs; stir in pumpkin, sugar, cloves, cinnamon, and salt. Add oil, mixing well. Stir together flour, baking powder, and baking soda. Add to pumpkin mixture with half the raisin-water mixture. Mix well. Add remaining raisin mixture. Stir well. Fill greased muffin pans two-thirds of the way. Bake at 400°F for about 25 minutes. *Makes 12 large or 16 medium muffins.*

*Gladys Priest, Foxon Congregational Church, East Haven, Connecticut*

# Beer Bread

Slices better when cool but is delicious hot from the oven. Especially good toasted.

4 cups flour
2 tablespoons baking powder
2 teaspoons salt

¼ cup sugar
1 can (12 ounces) beer
1 egg, slightly beaten

Mix flour, baking powder, and salt with sugar. Add beer and egg both at once and stir. You may have to knead last of flour in with hands. Place in greased 9" × 5" loaf pan and bake at 375°F until done—about 1 hour and 10 minutes. Remove from pan immediately and cool. *Makes 1 loaf.*

*Dianne Johnson, Dublin Community Church, Dublin, New Hampshire*

# Blueberry Bread

We think perhaps it's the molasses that makes this so good—but does not darken it.

2 cups flour
¼ cup sugar
½ teaspoon baking soda
½ teaspoon salt
¼ cup molasses

1 cup soured milk or yogurt
2 tablespoons butter, melted
1 egg, beaten
1 cup blueberries

Sift together flour, sugar, baking soda, and salt. Combine molasses, sour milk or yogurt, butter, and egg and mix well. Stir in dry ingredients and beat to blend. Fold in blueberries. Turn into greased 9" × 9" pan and bake at 350°F for 40 minutes. *Serves 9.*

# Blueberry-Pineapple Loaf

An attractive loaf for breakfast or tea. Good toasted, too, with butter or cream cheese. Tastes more blueberry than pineapple.

¾ cup sugar
1 egg
2 tablespoons melted butter
¾ cup pineapple juice
2 cups flour

½ teaspoon salt
2 teaspoons baking powder
½ cup drained crushed pineapple
½ cup fresh or frozen blueberries
½ cup nuts (any kind)

Combine sugar and egg; cream with butter. Add pineapple juice. Combine flour, salt, and baking powder, and add to sugar mixture. Then stir in pineapple, blueberries, and nuts; pour into greased 8" × 4" loaf pan. Bake at 350°F for 1 hour. *Makes 1 medium loaf.*

*Arlene Gilman, Woodstock Baptist Church, Woodstock, New Hampshire*

# Cornbread

Makes a big batch of sweeter-than-usual cornbread that children love.
Reduce the sugar to ½ cup for a standard cornbread.

¾ cup sugar
2 eggs, beaten
2 cups flour
1 cup yellow cornmeal

1 tablespoon baking powder
¼ teaspoon salt
2½ tablespoons melted butter
1½ cups milk

Mix sugar with eggs. Sift together flour, cornmeal, baking powder, and salt, and add to egg mixture. Stir in butter and milk. Beat up quickly. Bake in greased 9" × 13" pan at 350°F for about 30 minutes. *Serves 8–12.*

*Evelyn Shaw, Pilgrim Congregational Church, New Haven, Connecticut*

# Irish Oatmeal Bread

A hearty oatmeal quick bread, chewy and moist.

3 cups flour
1½ tablespoons baking powder
1 teaspoon salt
1¼ cups rolled oats
½ cup raisins (optional)

1 egg
¼ cup honey
1½ cups milk
1 tablespoon melted butter

Sift together flour, baking powder, and salt. Add oats and raisins, if using. Beat egg lightly, then add honey and milk and beat until well-blended. Add dry ingredients and stir just until all is moistened. Turn into greased 9" × 5" loaf pan. Brush top of loaf with melted butter and bake at 350°F for 1 hour to 1 hour and 15 minutes. *Makes 1 large loaf.*

*Mrs. Charles Wilson, Center Congregational Church, Torrington, Connecticut*

# Date Nut Bread

¾ cup cut-up dates
1 cup boiling water
1 cup brown sugar
1 egg, beaten
2 cups flour

½ teaspoon baking soda
½ teaspoon salt
½ teaspoon baking powder
¾ cup chopped walnuts
2 tablespoons cooking oil

Cover dates with boiling water. Add brown sugar and egg. Mix well. Sift flour, baking soda, salt, and baking powder together and add to date mixture, along with walnuts and oil. Turn into greased 9" × 5" loaf pan and bake at 350°F for 45 minutes. ***Makes 1 large loaf.***

*Priscilla Downing, Killingworth Congregational Church, Killingworth, Connecticut*

# Sausage Cake

Very similar to zucchini or pumpkin bread—and no, you cannot taste the sausage!

1 pound loose pork sausage
1½ cups brown sugar
1½ cups sugar
2 eggs, lightly beaten
3 cups sifted flour
1 teaspoon ginger

1 teaspoon pumpkin pie spice
1 teaspoon baking powder
1 teaspoon baking soda
1 cup strong cold coffee
1 cup raisins
1 cup chopped walnuts

Combine meat with brown sugar and sugar until well-blended. Add eggs and beat well. Sift together flour, ginger, pumpkin pie spice, and baking powder. Stir baking soda into coffee. Add flour mixture and coffee alternately to meat mixture, beating well after each addition. Pour boiling water over raisins to cover and let stand 5 minutes. Drain well and pat dry with paper towel. Fold raisins and walnuts into batter. Turn into well-greased and floured Bundt pan (9-cup size). Bake at 350°F for 1½ hours, or until done. Cool 15 minutes before turning out of pan. To store, wrap tightly in plastic wrap and refrigerate. ***Makes 1 round loaf.***

*Marcia Gehrke, United Methodist Church of the Hamptons, Hampton, New Hampshire*

# Zucchini Bread

One of the best.

3 eggs
¾ cup cooking oil
1½ cups sugar
2 cups chopped zucchini
  (approximately ¼" dice)
2 teaspoons vanilla
3 cups flour
1 teaspoon salt

1 teaspoon baking soda
½ teaspoon baking powder
1 teaspoon cinnamon
¾ cup chopped nuts (any kind),
  optional
¾ cup raisins or cut-up dates
  (optional)

Mix eggs, oil, sugar, zucchini, and vanilla. Sift together flour, salt, baking soda, baking powder, and cinnamon, and add to egg mixture. Stir in nuts and/or raisins or dates, if desired. Turn into 2 greased 8" × 4" loaf pans and bake at 350°F for 50–60 minutes. *Makes 2 medium loaves.*

*Barbara Lockhart, United Church of Christ, Keene, New Hampshire*

# Quick Graham Bread

Easy to make bread with a firm texture and a rich molasses-y taste. Perfect with baked beans.

3 cups graham flour
½ cup cornmeal
1 cup whole wheat flour
½ cup sugar
1 teaspoon salt
½ cup molasses

1 egg, beaten
2 teaspoons baking soda,
  dissolved in 1 cup soured milk
2 cups milk
½ cup raisins (optional)

Combine graham flour, cornmeal, whole wheat flour, sugar, and salt. Combine molasses, egg, baking soda mixture, and milk. Stir in dry ingredients, adding raisins, if using. Turn into greased 9" × 5" loaf pan and bake at 350°F for 50–60 minutes. *Makes 1 large loaf.*

*Florence Smith, Harwinton Congregational Church, Harwinton, Connecticut*

# Pineapple-Raisin Tea Ring

A real conversation piece until everyone takes the first bite—then just munching sounds!

| | |
|---|---|
| 2 yeast cakes | 2 eggs |
| ¼ cup lukewarm water | 5–5½ cups sifted flour |
| 1 cup scalded milk | 6 tablespoons brown sugar |
| 1 teaspoon salt | 2 teaspoons cinnamon |
| ½ cup sugar | 2 tablespoons chopped nuts |
| 4 tablespoons butter + | (any kind) |
| 2 tablespoons melted butter | Maraschino cherry halves |

Soften yeast in water. Combine milk, salt, sugar, and 4 tablespoons butter in large bowl. Cool to lukewarm. Stir in eggs and softened yeast. Gradually add flour. Knead on lightly floured board until smooth and satiny. Place in greased bowl; cover and let rise in warm place until doubled in size (1½ hours).

Divide dough in half. Roll out one portion on floured board to 20" × 12" rectangle. Brush with 1 tablespoon melted butter. Spread with half of Pineapple-Raisin Filling (see below). Combine brown sugar and cinnamon and sprinkle half over filling on dough. Roll dough the long way as for jelly roll. Shape into ring on greased baking sheet. With scissors, make cuts 1" apart through top of ring to within 1" from bottom. Alternate cut slices, bringing one to center and next to outside of ring. Cover. Repeat with remaining dough. Let rise in warm place until light and doubled in size—45–60 minutes. Bake at 375°F for 20–25 minutes. Let cool on racks. Frost with Confectioners' Sugar Glaze (see page 181) while warm; sprinkle with chopped nuts. Garnish with maraschino cherry halves. *Makes 2 rings.*

## Pineapple-Raisin Filling

| | |
|---|---|
| 1 can (20 ounces) crushed | ¾ cup sugar |
| pineapple, well-drained | ½ cup seedless raisins |
| 1 tablespoon cornstarch | |

Mix together pineapple, cornstarch, and sugar. Cook over medium heat until thickened. Add raisins.

*Peg Rodenhiser, The Congregational Church, New Ipswich, New Hampshire*

# Julekage (Scandinavian Christmas Bread)

Brian Anderson shares this special bread each holiday season with his church.

| | |
|---|---|
| 1 package regular or Rapid Rise yeast | ½ teaspoon salt |
| ¼ cup warm water | 1 egg, slightly beaten |
| 1 cup warm milk | ½ cup raisins |
| 2 tablespoons vegetable shortening or softened butter | ¼ cup fruitcake mix or chopped citron |
| ½ cup sugar | ¼ cup quartered red candied cherries |
| ½ teaspoon cardamom | 3½–3¾ cups flour |
| | Vegetable oil |

In small measuring cup, dissolve yeast in water; set aside 5 minutes or until bubbly. In large bowl, combine milk with shortening or butter; stir to melt. Stir in sugar, cardamom, and salt. Stir in yeasty water, egg, raisins, fruitcake mix or citron, and cherries. Mix in 3 cups of flour, 1 cup at a time, mixing well after each addition.

Use remaining ¾ cup flour to generously coat work surface and scrape remainder to side. Turn dough onto surface. With well-floured hands, knead dough. Work in only enough remaining flour to prevent sticking. Continue kneading about 8 minutes or until dough is smooth ball. Place in large oiled bowl, cover and set aside 1 hour or until doubled in bulk. Punch down dough, knead lightly, shape into ball and place in bowl. Coat lightly with oil, cover and set aside 1 hour or until doubled in bulk again. Punch down dough and knead lightly. Shape into ball and place in oiled 9" round cake pan. Oil top lightly. Cover and set aside 1 hour or until doubled in bulk once more. Bake at 350°F for 40–45 minutes or until browned. Loaf will sound hollow when tapped. If top is browning too quickly, cover loosely with aluminum foil. Remove and transfer to cooling rack. Spread with Vanilla Glaze (see below).

## Vanilla Glaze

| | |
|---|---|
| 1 cup sifted confectioners' sugar | 1 teaspoon vanilla |
| 1 tablespoon milk | Red and green candied cherries |

In bowl, whisk confectioners' sugar, milk, and vanilla until smooth. Add a few drops more milk to make glaze that drips easily from a spoon. Pour glaze over loaf, spreading with back of spoon and allowing glaze to drip down sides. If desired, cut strips of red and green candied cherries. Arrange like poinsettias on top of loaf. Allow to set 30 minutes before slicing. ***Makes 1 round loaf.***

*Brian Anderson, Evangelical Lutheran Church, Frederick, Maryland*

# Apple Coffee Cake

Make this for coffee hour on Sunday morning. Be sure cake is cold before turning out. If turned out hot, it will break up.

5 tablespoons sugar
2 teaspoons cinnamon
3 cups flour
1 cup sugar
1 cup cooking oil
4 eggs

¼ cup orange juice
2½ teaspoons vanilla
3 teaspoons baking powder
1 teaspoon salt
5 apples, peeled, cored, and thinly sliced

Combine sugar and cinnamon and set aside. In large bowl, combine flour, sugar, oil, eggs, orange juice, vanilla, baking powder, and salt. Beat well. Grease 10" tube pan. Pour in one-third of the batter, half the apples, and one-third of the cinnamon and sugar alternately until all ingredients are used. Bake at 350°F for 1 hour and 10 minutes.

*Laura Goodenough, The Congregational Church, Winchester Center, Connecticut*

# Cherry Coffee Cake

Pretty and cheery—really more a cake than a bread, but super with coffee.

1¾ cups flour
1 cup sugar
1 teaspoon baking powder
¼ teaspoon baking soda
¼ teaspoon salt
½ cup + 2 tablespoons butter

½ cup milk
1 egg
1 teaspoon vanilla
¼ teaspoon lemon extract
1 can (21 ounces) cherry pie filling

Grease and flour 9" × 9" baking pan. Sift together 1¼ cups flour, ½ cup sugar, baking powder, baking soda, and salt. Add ½ cup butter, milk, egg, and vanilla and beat until well-mixed. Turn into baking pan, spreading batter evenly. In small bowl, combine remaining ½ cup flour, ½ cup sugar, and 2 tablespoons butter until mixture is like coarse crumbs. Sprinkle half on top of batter. Stir lemon extract into pie filling. Spread over crumbs on batter. Sprinkle rest of crumb mixture over top. Bake at 350°F for 1 hour, or until top is light golden. Cut into squares. ***Serves 9.***

*Mrs. L. Bouchard, St. Paul's Church, Lancaster, New Hampshire*

# Danish Kringle

This rich Danish pastry—pronounced "KRING-la"—graces many a church table throughout the upper Midwest.

| | |
|---|---|
| 1 package (¼ ounce) active dry yeast | 1 teaspoon salt |
| 8 tablespoons sugar | 1 cup vegetable shortening |
| ½ cup warm water | 1 cup warm milk |
| 4 cups flour | 3 egg yolks, beaten |
| | 2 tablespoons butter, softened |

Dissolve yeast and 1 tablespoon sugar in water. In mixing bowl, combine flour, salt, and 5 tablespoons of remaining sugar. With pastry blender or fork, cut shortening into flour mixture until reduced to pea-sized pieces. Add milk, egg yolks, and yeast mixture. Beat with spoon until mixture forms a thick batter. Transfer to large greased bowl; cover and refrigerate overnight.

With spatula, scrape dough onto a well-floured work surface. Dust dough with flour. Knead very lightly for about 1 minute or until dough forms a ball. (Dough will be very soft and fragile.) Divide into 4 balls. Place 3 balls back in refrigerator. Roll or pat remaining ball with well-floured rolling pin or hands into a 10" × 14" rectangle. With floured offset spatula, transfer to greased baking sheet. Spread ½ tablespoon butter lengthwise down center of dough. Sprinkle with ½ tablespoon of remaining sugar. Spread one-quarter of Almond Custard Filling (see below) lengthwise down center. Lift and fold one long edge to mid-line of filling. Repeat with other side. Fold short edges gently to form seal (it is not necessary to seal center seam). Repeat with remaining dough, butter, sugar, and filling on 3 greased baking sheets. Cover and set aside to rise for 2 hours or until doubled in bulk. Bake kringles at 325°F for 30–35 minutes or until golden. Remove from oven to cool. Drizzle Kringle Icing (see below) over kringles.

## Almond Custard Filling

| | |
|---|---|
| ½ cup sugar | 1 cup half-and-half |
| 2 tablespoons cornstarch or 4 tablespoons flour | 2 egg yolks, beaten |
| Dash of salt | 2 tablespoons butter |
| | 1½ teaspoons almond extract |

In top of double boiler or metal bowl set over simmering water, combine sugar, cornstarch or flour, and salt. In mixing cup, combine half-and-half and egg yolks; whisk gradually into dry ingredients. Cook over medium heat, whisking constantly, about 4 minutes or until thickened. Remove from heat and whisk in butter and almond extract. Set aside to cool. Cover and refrigerate overnight.

# Kringle Icing

1 cup confectioners' sugar
4–5 teaspoons milk

¼ teaspoon vanilla

In bowl, whisk confectioners' sugar, 4 teaspoons milk and vanilla until smooth. Add 1 teaspoon milk if icing is too thick. ***Makes 4 kringles.***

*Darline Struve, St. Stephen's Lutheran Church, Clinton, Iowa*

# Crumb Cake

Good served either warm or cold, as a breakfast coffee cake, or as a dinner dessert.

¾ cup butter
1½–2 cups brown sugar (depending on sweetness desired)
2½ cups flour
1 teaspoon baking soda
1 cup buttermilk or soured milk

1 egg, beaten
1 teaspoon vanilla
½ teaspoon salt
½ cup chopped nuts (any kind), optional

Combine butter, brown sugar, and flour, and work together until crumbly. Reserve 1 cup of mixture for topping. Beat baking soda into buttermilk or soured milk and add to flour mixture along with egg, vanilla, and salt. Stir (do not beat) all ingredients together until batter is smooth. Pour into greased 9" × 13" cake pan. Sprinkle reserved crumb topping over batter. If desired, nuts can be added to crumbs before sprinkling. Bake at 350°F for 35–40 minutes. ***Serves 24.***

*Helen Michaels, St. Dominic's Catholic Church, Sheboygan, Wisconsin*

# Danish Puff

Danish pastry from "scratch." The only sugar is in the icing.

2 cups sifted flour
1 cup butter
2–3 tablespoons (approximately)
   + 1 cup water

3 eggs
1 teaspoon almond extract
Chopped nuts (any kind) or
coconut

Measure 1 cup flour into bowl. Cut in ½ cup butter. Sprinkle with 2 tablespoons water and mix with fork. (You may need to add 1 tablespoon more water.) Shape into ball and divide in half. Pat dough with hands into 2 long strips, 12" × 13" each. Place strips 3" apart on ungreased baking sheet.

Combine remaining ½ cup butter and 1 cup water in saucepan. Bring to rolling boil, and remove from heat. Stir in remaining 1 cup flour immediately to keep it from lumping. When smooth and thick, add 1 egg at a time, beating until smooth after each addition. Add almond extract and mix again. Divide in half and spread one-half evenly over each piece of pastry on the baking sheet. Bake at 350°F for about 60 minutes, or until topping is crisp and nicely browned.

Frost with Confectioners' Sugar Glaze (see page 181) or with Thin Chocolate Icing. (Melt 1 square unsweetened chocolate with 1 teaspoon butter. Remove from heat and add 1 cup confectioners' sugar and 2 tablespoons boiling water. Blend until smooth.) Sprinkle with chopped nuts or coconut. *Serves 8–10.*

*Sara Houlberg, The Congregational Church, Sherman, Connecticut*

# Sour Cream Coffee Cake

This chef has a way with coffee cake.

½ cup butter
1 cup sugar
2 eggs
1 teaspoon vanilla
2 cups flour, sifted
1 teaspoon baking powder

1 teaspoon baking soda
1 cup sour cream
½ cup brown sugar
1 teaspoon cinnamon
½ cup chopped walnuts

Cream together butter, sugar, eggs, and vanilla. Combine flour, baking powder, and baking soda. Add alternately with sour cream to butter mixture. Mix well. Grease and lightly flour 10" tube pan. Put half of batter in pan. Combine brown sugar, cinnamon, and walnuts. Sprinkle batter with half of brown sugar mixture. Repeat. Bake at 350°F for 45 minutes. Serve hot with butter. **Serves 12.**

*Thomas A. Nerbonne, United Baptist Church, Concord, New Hampshire*

# Rhubarb Coffee Cake

Mrs. Farr says, "This recipe always makes a big hit at our church breakfasts. It makes a large cake that is quite different and very moist."

| | |
|---|---|
| 2 cups sifted flour | ¼ teaspoon cloves |
| 1½ cups sugar | 2 eggs |
| 1 teaspoon baking soda | ½ cup cooking oil |
| 1 teaspoon salt | ⅓ cup milk |
| 1 teaspoon cinnamon | 2 cups fresh rhubarb, cut into |
| ¼ teaspoon allspice | ½" pieces |

Sift flour, sugar, baking soda, salt, cinnamon, allspice, and cloves together in mixing bowl. Place eggs, oil, and milk in another bowl and beat together. Then add to dry ingredients. Fold in rhubarb. Turn into greased 9" × 13" pan. Make Topping (see below) and spoon over batter. Bake at 350°F for 50 minutes. **Serves 18–24.**

## Topping

| | |
|---|---|
| ⅔ cup flour | 4 tablespoons butter |
| ½ cup brown sugar | ¼ cup chopped nuts (any kind) |

Combine flour, brown sugar, and butter with fork. Add nuts and stir.

*Lillian Farr, All Saints Episcopal Church, Wolfeboro, New Hampshire*

# Swedish Coffee Ring

A time-saving means to a handsome end.

**Dough made from 1 package hot roll mix, or 1 roll frozen white bread dough, thawed**
**¼ cup melted butter**

**½ cup firmly packed brown sugar**
**½ cup flaked coconut, or ½ cup chopped nuts (any kind)**
**1 teaspoon cinnamon**

Turn out dough on floured breadboard and roll into rectangle ¼"–½" thick. Spread butter on dough. Combine brown sugar, coconut or nuts, and cinnamon. Sprinkle over dough. Roll up on long side as for jelly roll, wetting edges to seal. Place on greased baking sheet, bringing ends together to form ring.

With scissors, cut 1" slices almost through ring. Turn each cut piece on its side. Cover with clean towel and let rise in warm place until doubled in bulk, about 1 hour. Bake at 375°F for 25 minutes, or until golden brown. While still warm, brush top with Glaze (see below) and sprinkle with flaked coconut, if desired. *Serves 8.*

## Confectioners' Sugar Glaze

Gradually add about 1 tablespoon hot milk or water to 1 cup sifted confectioners' sugar in bowl. Blend well.

*Mrs. Edward B. Riley, First Congregational Church, Concord, New Hampshire*

# Walnut-Raisin Coffee Cake

Quite impressive when done properly. For Christmas, make poinsettias with red and green slivered maraschino cherries put into pan first of all.

| | |
|---|---|
| 2 cups warm water | 2 eggs, beaten |
| 2 packages dry yeast | 1 cup cold water |
| 1 tablespoon salt | ½ cup melted butter |
| 1 tablespoon + 2 cups sugar | 1½–2 teaspoons cinnamon |
| Sprinkle of ginger | Raisins |
| 8 cups (approximately) flour | Chopped walnuts |
| 1 cup shortening | |

Put warm water in large bowl and sprinkle with yeast, salt, 1 tablespoon sugar, and ginger. Let set until yeast rises to top of water. Add about 2 cups flour, enough to make a sponge dough that will drop from spoon in a mound. Let rise until bubbly. Combine shortening, 1 cup sugar, eggs, and cold water. Add to yeast mixture. Mix well. Add rest of flour (more if necessary) to make soft, nonsticky dough. Cover with cloth and let rise. Punch down and let rise again. With floured hands, roll dough into balls a little larger than a walnut. Roll balls in melted butter. Combine remaining 1 cup sugar with cinnamon and roll dough balls in this mixture. Place balls in layers in greased 10" tube pan, topping each layer with a few raisins and chopped walnuts. Fill pan one-half to two-thirds of the way. Let rise until doubled in bulk. Bake at 375°F for 40–45 minutes. (If top browns too fast, reduce heat to 350°F for remainder of baking time. Turn out of pan to cool. *Serves 8–10.*

*Peg Rodenhiser, The Congregational Church, New Ipswich, New Hampshire*

# Dill Bread

Great for lunch or brunch. Best served warm from oven.

1 package dry yeast
¼ cup lukewarm water
1 cup cottage cheese, heated to warm
2 tablespoons sugar
2 tablespoons grated onion, or 1 tablespoon minced dry onion

1 tablespoon butter
2 teaspoons dill seed
1 teaspoon salt
¼ teaspoon baking soda
1 egg
2¼–2½ cups flour

Soften yeast in lukewarm water and combine in mixing bowl with cottage cheese, sugar, onion, butter, dill seed, salt, baking soda, and egg. Stir in flour. Knead well. Let rise in warm place until doubled in bulk (about 1 hour). Punch down and knead again. Form into loaf and place in greased and floured 9" × 5" loaf pan. Let rise in warm place for 30 minutes. Bake at 350°F for 50 minutes. *Makes 1 large loaf.*

*Mrs. Burton Erickson and Eleanor Wells, First Congregational Church, Concord, New Hampshire*

# Maple Oatmeal Bread

A good substantial bread subtly flavored with maple. Terrific with peanut butter.
If you like your bread sweet, include the honey.

2 packages dry yeast
¼ cup lukewarm water
Pinch of sugar
1 cup rolled oats (not quick)
1 cup maple syrup
1 cup hot strong coffee
¾ cup boiling water

¼ cup honey (optional)
⅓ cup shortening
2 teaspoons salt
4½ cups white flour
2 eggs, lightly beaten
2 cups whole wheat flour

Dissolve yeast in lukewarm water with sugar for 10 minutes or until foamy. In large bowl, combine oats, maple syrup, coffee, water, honey, if using, shortening, and salt. Stir until shortening is melted and let cool until lukewarm. Stir in 1 cup white flour, eggs, and yeast mixture, and beat with electric mixer until smooth. Add remaining 3½ cups white flour and whole wheat flour, 2 cups at a time, and beat dough until smooth and elastic. Form dough into ball, transfer to greased bowl, and turn to coat both sides. Let dough rise, covered, for 1 hour and 30 minutes, or until doubled in bulk. Punch down dough. Divide between 2 buttered 9" × 5" loaf pans, and let rise, covered, for 1 hour. Bake at 350°F for 45 minutes. Turn out on racks to cool. *Makes 2 large loaves.*

*Carol Jensen, The United Church of Hardwick, Hardwick, Vermont*

# Molasses-Bran Bread

Easy to make and very good.

| | |
|---|---|
| ¾ **cup bran cereal** | 2 **packages dry yeast** |
| ½ **cup molasses** | ½ **cup warm water** |
| 2 **tablespoons butter** | 4 **cups white flour** |
| 2 **teaspoons salt** | 3 **cups whole wheat flour** |
| 2 **cups boiling water** | |

In large bowl, combine bran, molasses, butter, salt, and boiling water. Cool to lukewarm. Dissolve yeast in warm water and stir into bran mixture. Stir in white and whole wheat flours. Place dough in greased bowl and turn to coat evenly. Cover with damp cloth and let rise until double. Punch down. Divide dough in half. Place each half in well-greased 9" × 5" loaf pan. Cover with damp cloth and let rise until double. Bake at 400°F for 45 minutes. Turn out on wire rack and brush tops with melted butter. *Makes 2 large loaves.*

*Carol Jensen, The United Church of Hardwick, Hardwick, Vermont*

# Oatmeal Bread

Light-textured and golden oatmeal loaves.

| | |
|---|---|
| 1 cup rolled oats | 2 cups boiling water |
| ½ cup molasses | 1 package dry yeast |
| 2 teaspoons butter | ½ cup warm water |
| 1 tablespoon butter | 5–5½ cups flour |

Combine oats, molasses, salt, butter, and boiling water. Stir and let stand until lukewarm. Mix yeast with warm water and stir into oatmeal. Add 4½ cups flour. Beat well and knead in bowl (dough will be sticky). Let rise until doubled in bulk. Punch down and add enough remaining flour to make dough firm enough to knead on floured board. Shape into loaves and put into 2 greased 8" × 4" loaf pans. Let rise until light and nearly doubled. Bake at 350°F for 50 minutes. ***Makes 2 medium loaves.***

*Helen Poole, Harwinton Congregational Church, Harwinton, Connecticut*

# Feather-Light Dinner Rolls

A well-named recipe. Makes 18 medium or 24 small rolls.

| | |
|---|---|
| 1 package dry yeast | ¼ cup sugar |
| ¼ cup lukewarm water | 1 teaspoon salt |
| ¼ cup shortening | 1 egg, beaten |
| ¾ cup scalded milk | 3½–3¾ cups flour |

Dissolve yeast in water. Melt shortening in scalded milk and add sugar, salt, and egg. When mixture has cooled to lukewarm, add dissolved yeast. Stir in flour and knead 5–10 minutes, or until dough is smooth. Let rise until doubled in bulk (45–60 minutes). Form rolls—18 medium or 24 small—and place on greased baking sheet. Let rise until light (about 45 minutes). Bake at 375°F for 10–15 minutes, or until done. ***Makes 18–24 rolls.***

*Liese Shewmaker, Our Savior Lutheran Church, Hanover, New Hampshire*

# Rindge Rye Bread

1 package dry yeast
1¾ cups warm water
1 cup rye flour
2½ cups white flour

2 tablespoons soft shortening
1 teaspoon salt
2 tablespoons honey
Melted butter

Dissolve yeast in water. Combine rye and white flours and set aside. Add shortening, salt, honey, and half of the flour to yeast and beat 2 minutes at medium speed. Add remaining flour and blend with spoon, scraping bowl frequently. Cover with cloth and let rise in warm place until doubled in bulk (about 30 minutes). Stir batter down by beating about 25 strokes. Spread batter into greased 8" × 4" loaf pan. (Batter is sticky—use floured hand to pat into shape.) Cover with cloth again and let rise to ¼" from top of pan (40–45 minutes). Bake at 375°F for 45 minutes, or until loaf sounds hollow when tapped on the bottom. Brush with melted butter and cool on rack. ***Makes 1 medium loaf.***

*Mary Wakefield, First Congregational Church, Rindge, New Hampshire*

# Butter Dips

Tender tidbits of biscuit dough baked in butter.

½ cup butter
2 cups + ¼ cup flour
1 tablespoon sugar

3½ teaspoons baking powder
1½ teaspoons salt
1 cup milk

Preheat oven to 400°F. Place butter in 9" × 13" baking dish and melt in oven. Take dish out of oven when butter has melted. Meanwhile, sift flour, sugar, baking powder, and salt together. Add milk and stir with fork just until all is moistened. Turn onto floured board and roll into rectangle approximately 9" × 13". Score with knife into ¾" strips lengthwise and crosswise every 2", going almost but not quite through dough. Lift scored dough (in 2 halves is easiest) on pancake turners and place on melted butter in baking dish. Bake at 400°F for 15–20 minutes. ***Enough to serve 8.***

*Flora C. Hammond, Unitarian Universalist Church, Keene, New Hampshire*

# White Bread

Nice flavor and texture. Can be used to make either rolls or one large loaf.

3½ cups hot water
½ cup sugar
1 tablespoon rendered chicken
   fat or soft shortening

1 tablespoon salt
2 packages dry yeast
8 cups flour

Combine hot water with sugar, chicken fat or shortening, and salt. Cool to lukewarm and stir in yeast. Let stand until foamy, then add 4 cups flour. Keep adding flour until mixture can be kneaded by hand and is not sticky but nice and smooth. Knead well and put in greased bowl covered with damp towel and set in warm place to rise until doubled in bulk. Punch down and shape into loaf (or rolls). Place in greased 9" × 5" loaf pan and let rise again until light. Bake at 400°F for about 20–25 minutes, or until done (loaf should sound hollow when tapped on bottom). ***Makes 1 large loaf.***

*Jan Shoup, Center Congregational Church, Torrington, Connecticut*

# Cinnamon Rolls

A nice surprise to serve for lunch.

1 yeast cake
4 tablespoons lukewarm water
1 cup scalded milk
½ cup shortening

½ cup sugar
2 eggs, beaten
1 teaspoon salt
4½ cups flour

Crumble yeast and add water. Let stand 5 minutes. Mix milk with shortening, cool to lukewarm, and add to yeast. Stir in sugar, eggs, salt, and 2 cups flour. Beat 3 minutes, then add remaining 2½ cups flour. Mix well, cover with cloth, and let stand until dough has doubled in bulk.

# Filling

**4 tablespoons butter, melted**
**½ cup sugar**

**1 teaspoon cinnamon**

Roll dough ¼" thick and spread with melted butter. Mix sugar and cinnamon and sprinkle over buttered dough. Roll up dough tightly and cut roll into ⅓" slices. Flatten down and place flat side up in greased pan. Let rise until doubled in size. Bake at 400°F for 20 minutes.

*Eva Day, The Unitarian Church, Peterborough, New Hampshire*

# Refrigerator Rolls

We think the melt-in-the-mouth quality of these superb rolls
has something to do with the built-in butter.

**¼ cup sugar**
**½ teaspoon salt**
**13½ tablespoons butter**
**1 cup boiling water**

**1 package dry yeast**
**¼ cup warm water**
**1 egg, beaten**
**3½ cups flour**

Mix sugar, salt, 1½ tablespoons butter, and boiling water. Cool to lukewarm. Dissolve yeast in water and add to sugar mixture. Add egg and stir in flour. Refrigerate overnight. Punch down and knead lightly on floured board. Shape into rolls. Cut remaining butter into teaspoon-size pieces and put 1 piece into center of each roll. Place on greased baking sheet. Let rise until doubled in bulk. Bake at 400°F for 10–12 minutes. ***Makes 3 dozen rolls.***

*Edna Foss, Suncook United Methodist Church, Suncook, New Hampshire*

# Orange Bow Knots

Excellent coffee roll, and sure seller at bake sales, too.

1 yeast cake
¼ cup warm water
1 cup milk, scalded
½ cup shortening
⅓ cup sugar
1 teaspoon salt

5–5½ cups sifted flour
2 eggs, well-beaten
¼ cup orange juice
2 tablespoons grated orange
   rind

Soften yeast in warm water. Combine milk, shortening, sugar, and salt. Cool to lukewarm. Stir in about 2 cups flour and beat well. Add eggs. Stir in yeast, orange juice and rind, and remaining flour. Mix well. Cover and let rest for 10 minutes. Knead on lightly floured board. Place in greased bowl and let rise in warm place until doubled. Punch down, cover, and let rest 10 minutes. Roll dough out ½" thick. Cut into 10" strips, ½" wide. Tie each strip in a knot. Arrange on greased baking sheet. Cover and let rise until doubled. Bake at 400°F for 12–15 minutes. Spread with Orange Topping (see below). ***Makes about 24.***

# Orange Topping

2 tablespoons orange juice
1 teaspoon grated orange rind

1 cup confectioners' sugar

Combine orange juice, orange rind, and confectioners' sugar. Blend well.

# Raised Rolls

Serve plain or iced with a butter frosting.

½ cup scalded milk
¼ cup shortening
2 tablespoons sugar
1½ teaspoons salt

½ cup cold water
1 package dry yeast
1 egg
3 cups flour

Combine scalded milk, shortening, sugar, and salt. Cool to lukewarm by adding water. Add yeast and egg and mix well. Then add flour. Mix well and turn onto floured board. Roll dough out to ¼" thickness. Cut rolls with biscuit cutter and place in greased pan. Let rise until doubled in size. Bake at 400°F for 15–20 minutes. ***Makes 1 dozen rolls.***

*Jeannette M. Miller, Morris Congregational Church, Morris, Connecticut*

# Squash Biscuits

An airy and flavorsome cross between a biscuit and a roll. "A must for Thanksgiving dinner."

½ cup milk
½ cup sugar
1 teaspoon salt
1 cup cooked, mashed winter squash
½ yeast cake

½ cup warm water
5 cups flour
½ teaspoon baking soda
⅓ cup melted shortening
½ cup melted butter

Scald milk. Add sugar, salt, and squash, and cool to lukewarm. Dissolve yeast in warm water and add to squash mixture. Sift 2 cups flour with baking soda. Combine with squash mixture, blending thoroughly. Add shortening and beat well. Stir in remaining 3 cups flour to make soft dough. Cover and let rise until doubled in bulk. Punch down and let rise again. Shape on floured board into biscuits, dip in melted butter, and arrange on baking pan. Let rise once more until light. Bake at 375°F for about 20 minutes, or until lightly browned. ***Makes 3 dozen.***

*Priscilla Downing, Killingworth Congregational Church, Killingworth, Connecticut*

# Cinnamon Roll-Ups

A delightful snack to serve at coffee hour following a church service—
or at any other "coffee."

1 loaf thin-sliced white sandwich
  bread (about 20 slices)
  Milk
1 package (8 ounces) cream
  cheese, softened

½ cup melted butter
¾ cup sugar mixed with 1
  teaspoon cinnamon
  Sour cream

Remove crusts from bread slices. Roll each slice flat with rolling pin. Blend just enough milk with softened cream cheese to make it easily spreadable. Spread 1 side of each bread slice with cream cheese. Roll up each slice, cheese side in. Roll in melted butter, then roll in sugar mixed with cinnamon. Cut each roll into 2 pieces. Bake on cookie sheet at 400°F for 12–15 minutes. Serve warm with sour cream for dipping. Roll-ups can be made ahead of time, refrigerated, and baked just before serving. Can also be frozen. If freezing, freeze before cutting. *Yields 40 tidbits; serves 8 or more.*

*Nancy A. Burton, St. Andrew's Church, Newcastle, Maine*

# Cakes

For a special occasion, or to make an ordinary occasion a little more special, what is more elegant than a cake? The recipes in this chapter will become traditions in your family—like Jeannette Miller's Birthday Cake, a light, white-frosted yellow cake; or the smoothly delectable, classic Red Velvet Cake.

From Apricot Pound Cake (so moist you can serve it for a week), to the one-pan Wacky Cake that takes only minutes to prepare, to the aristocratic high-rise Walnut Cake, each cake here is a family-pleaser that will command high praise—and high prices at bake sales, too!

Apple Upside-Down Cake  192

Special Applesauce Cake  192

Tempting Bishop's Cake  193

Apricot Pound Cake  193

Birthday Cake  194

Broiler Cake  195

Red Velvet Cake  196

Extra-Rich Chocolate Cake  197

Fruit Cocktail Cake  197

Satin's Velvet Robe Cake  198

Chocolate Roll  199

Bohemian Coffee Cake  200

Cottage Pudding  201

Fruit Torte  202

Key Lime Cake  202

Mayonnaise Cake  203

Molasses Cake  204

Mother's Hot Weather Cake  204

Fresh Pear Cake  205

Sauerkraut Surprise Cake  206

Pineapple Nut Cake  207

Pineapple Upside-Down Cake  208

Poppy Seed Cake  208

Pound Cake  209

Pumpkin Cake  210

Oatmeal Cake  211

Scripture Cake  212

Sponge Cake with Orange Sauce  229

White Cake  230

Yogurt Cake Dessert  230

Upside-Down Gingerbread  232

Wacky Cake  232

Walnut Cake  233

# Apple Upside-Down Cake

Serve with coffee and heavy cream, whipped or not, for dessert.

¾ **cup butter**
¾ **cup brown sugar**
½ **teaspoon cinnamon**
3 **cups sliced apples**
1¼ **cups flour**
1 **cup sugar**

1½ **teaspoons baking powder**
¾ **cup milk**
⅓ **cup shortening**
1 **egg**
1 **teaspoon vanilla**

In greased 8" × 8" cake pan, melt butter and mix in brown sugar and cinnamon. Put sliced apples in mixture and stir until apples are coated. Mix flour, sugar, baking powder, milk, shortening, egg, and vanilla, and spread over apple mixture. Bake at 350°F for about 35 minutes, or until cake mixture is light brown and firm to the touch. Let cool 20 minutes, then turn out on plate.

*Joanne Earle, Old Brick Church, Clarendon, Vermont*

# Special Applesauce Cake

A fruitcake-textured spice cake that keeps well.

3½ **cups flour**
1 **teaspoon baking soda**
½ **teaspoon salt**
2 **teaspoons cinnamon**
1 **teaspoon cloves**
2 **teaspoons nutmeg**

1 **cup butter**
1 **cup sugar**
2 **eggs, beaten**
2 **cups warm applesauce**
1 **cup coarsely chopped walnuts**
1 **cup raisins**

Sift together flour, baking soda, salt, cinnamon, cloves, and nutmeg. Cream butter and sugar. Add eggs. Alternately stir in sifted dry ingredients and applesauce. Stir in walnuts and raisins. Mix well. Pour into well-greased 10" tube pan. Bake at 350°F for 60–70 minutes. Cool 20 minutes, then turn out of pan.

*Karen Russo, The Congregational Church, East Hampton, Connecticut*

# Tempting Bishop's Cake

An enticing concoction somewhere between a fruitcake and a chocolate-chip cookie.

1½ cups flour
1½ teaspoons baking powder
½ teaspoon salt
1 package (6 ounces) chocolate bits
2 cups chopped nuts (any kind)

1 cup cut-up dates
1 cup halved maraschino or glacé cherries
3 eggs
1 cup sugar

Sift together flour, baking powder, and salt. Add chocolate bits, nuts, dates, and cherries. In another bowl, beat eggs and sugar. Add to dry ingredients and fold in. Fill two 8" × 4" greased loaf pans three-quarters of the way and bake at 325°F for 45 minutes, or until done.

*Nancy A. Burton, St. Andrew's Church, Newcastle, Maine*

# Apricot Pound Cake

Dense, moist, and a bit different—keeps well, too.

1 cup butter
3 cups sugar
6 eggs
½ teaspoon rum extract
1 teaspoon orange extract
½ teaspoon lemon extract
¼ teaspoon almond extract

1 teaspoon vanilla extract
1 teaspoon butter extract
3 cups sifted flour
¼ teaspoon baking soda
½ teaspoon salt
1 cup sour cream
½ cup apricot nectar

Cream butter and sugar until light and fluffy. Add eggs, 1 at a time, beating well after each addition. Add rum, orange, lemon, almond, vanilla, and butter extracts. Then combine flour, baking soda, and salt, and mix together sour cream and apricot nectar. Add alternately to butter mixture and beat well. Pour into greased and floured 10" tube pan. Bake at 325°F for 60–70 minutes. Cool before serving.

*Marcia Fletcher, St. Anne's Episcopal Church, Calais, Maine*

# Birthday Cake

Mrs. Miller has made generations of birthday cakes;
this is a fine yellow cake with a white boiled frosting that is good for birthdays—
and almost any other occasion.

| | |
|---|---|
| 1 cup butter | 2¾ cups flour |
| 2 cups sugar | 3 teaspoons baking powder |
| 4 eggs | ½ teaspoon salt |
| 1 teaspoon vanilla | 1 cup milk |

Cream butter and sugar and beat in eggs and vanilla. Sift together flour, baking powder, and salt. Add alternately with milk to creamed mixture. Beat well until light. Pour batter into 2 greased and floured 9" layer-cake pans. Bake at 350°F for 35 minutes. Cool, then spread with White Frosting (see below).

# White Frosting

| | |
|---|---|
| 1 cup sugar | 2 teaspoons vanilla |
| ½ cup white corn syrup | 4 egg whites, beaten stiff |
| ¼ cup water | Grated coconut (optional) |

In saucepan, combine sugar, corn syrup, and water and boil until a teaspoonful stays together in cold water. Remove from stove and add vanilla. Start beating egg whites again, and while beating, very slowly in a thin stream pour cooked syrup into egg whites. Keep beating until frosting is thick enough to spread. Spread frosting between layers, on top, and on sides of cake. If desired, sprinkle coconut between layers and on top and sides of cake.

*Jeannette M. Miller, Morris Congregational Church, Morris, Connecticut*

# Broiler Cake

A great cake with an out-of-this-world topping. Serve warm.

## Cake

| | |
|---|---|
| 3 eggs | Pinch of salt |
| 1½ cups white sugar | 6 tablespoons butter |
| 1½ cups flour | ⅔ cup milk |
| 1½ teaspoons baking powder | 1 teaspoon vanilla |

Beat eggs and add sugar. Sift flour, baking powder, and salt together, and stir into egg mixture. Melt butter, add milk, and bring to boil. Add to flour and egg mixture along with vanilla. Bake in greased 9" × 13" pan at 325°F for 30 minutes. Make Topping (see below).

## Topping

| | |
|---|---|
| ½ cup + 2 tablespoons butter, melted | 1 cup chopped pecans |
| 1½ cups brown sugar | 1 cup shredded coconut or crushed, drained pineapple |
| ½ cup cream | |

Beat together butter, brown sugar, and cream. Add pecans and coconut or pineapple. Spoon over hot cake and place under broiler until brown.

*Marjorie M. Stultz, Concord Unitarian Church, Concord, New Hampshire*

# Red Velvet Cake

A subtly delicious cake that looks like its name; the frosting sets it off like white ruching.

½ cup shortening
1½ cups sugar
2 eggs, beaten
2 cups flour
1 tablespoon cocoa

½ teaspoon salt
1 cup buttermilk
1 ounce red food coloring
1 teaspoon baking soda
1 tablespoon vinegar

Cream shortening and sugar and add eggs. Sift flour, cocoa, and salt together, and mix buttermilk with coloring. Add dry ingredients alternately with liquid ingredients to creamed mixture. Beat well. Dissolve baking soda in vinegar and fold into batter. Grease and flour two 9" layer-cake pans. Bake at 350°F for 30–35 minutes. Remove from pans, cool, and spread with Vanilla Filling and Frosting (see below).

## Vanilla Filling and Frosting

¼ cup flour
1 cup milk
⅛ teaspoon salt
½ cup shortening

½ cup softened butter
1 cup sugar
1 tablespoon vanilla
Grated coconut (optional)

In small saucepan, blend flour with milk and salt and cook over low heat, stirring, until of pudding consistency. Cool. In large mixer bowl, cream together shortening, butter, sugar, and vanilla. Add cooled flour mixture and beat until smooth. Spread between layers and over top and sides of cake. Sprinkle coconut on top, if desired. Refrigerate cake.

*Winona Gilman, Old Brick Church, Claredon, Vermont*

# Extra-Rich Chocolate Cake

Baked in a tube pan or in 4 layers, this makes a nice high cake, easily sliced.
To make a 4-layer cake, divide the batter between 2 cake pans.
Cut each finished cake horizontally to make 4 layers.

2½ cups flour
2 teaspoons baking soda
¾ cup cocoa
½ teaspoon salt
1 cup butter

2 cups + 2 tablespoons sugar
4 eggs, well-beaten
1 cup soured milk
1 teaspoon vanilla
1 cup boiling water

Sift flour once; add baking soda, cocoa, and salt. Sift together 3 times. Cream butter; add sugar. Cream until light. Add eggs and beat. Add flour and sour milk alternately. Add vanilla and boiling water and beat. Bake in greased 10" tube pan at 375°F for about 45 minutes. Frost as desired.

*Peg Rodenhiser, The Congregational Church, New Ipswich, New Hampshire*

# Fruit Cocktail Cake

Serve warm or cold for festive occasions.

1 cup flour
1 cup sugar
1 teaspoon baking soda
¼ teaspoon salt
1 egg, beaten

1 teaspoon vanilla
2 cups fruit cocktail, drained,
  with ½ cup syrup reserved
¾ cup brown sugar
½ cup chopped nuts (any kind)

Combine flour, sugar, baking soda, and salt. Add egg, vanilla, fruit cocktail, and syrup. Beat well. Put in greased 9" × 13" pan and spread brown sugar and nuts on top of batter. Bake for 1 hour at 350°F (325°F if using glass pan). Top with ice cream or whipped cream.

*Mildred G. Quayle, Good Shepherd Episcopal Church, Houlton, Maine*

# Satin's Velvet Robe Cake

High-rising and delicious; belongs in everyone's chocolate cake collection.

1½ teaspoons baking soda
1⅔ cups cold water
½ cup butter
1¾ cups sugar
1 teaspoon salt

1 teaspoon vanilla
½ cup cocoa
2½ cups sifted flour
3 egg whites

Combine baking soda and ⅓ cup cold water; stir to dissolve and set aside. Cream butter. Gradually add 1 cup sugar and cream until fluffy. Blend in salt and vanilla. Mix cocoa with another ⅓ cup cold water. Beat into creamed mixture. Add flour alternately with remaining 1 cup cold water. Beat egg whites until soft peaks form, then beat in remaining ¾ cup sugar. Fold into batter. Add baking soda and water mixture; mix well. Pour into two 9" layer pans or one 9" × 13" pan, greased. Bake at 350°F for 30 minutes. Cool on racks and frost with Cocoa Frosting (see below).

## Cocoa Frosting

¼ cup butter
3½ cups confectioners' sugar
1½ teaspoons vanilla

½ cup cocoa
¼ teaspoon salt
⅓ cup milk

Combine butter, sugar, vanilla, cocoa, salt, and milk. Beat together until well-blended.

*Peg Rodenhiser, The Congregational Church, New Ipswich, New Hampshire*

# Chocolate Roll

Airy and light as a feather, it literally melts in your mouth.

5 egg whites
1 cup sifted confectioners' sugar
3 tablespoons cocoa

5 egg yolks, beaten
½ pint heavy cream, whipped and
flavored with sugar and vanilla

Beat egg whites till frothier; add sugar and beat until stiff. Add cocoa, mix well. Fold in egg yolks. Grease jelly-roll (10" × 15") pan. Cut wax paper to fit. Grease and flour wax paper–lined pan. Spread mixture in pan and bake at 375°F for 20 minutes. Turn out on dish towel sprinkled with confectioners' sugar. Cover with damp towel until cool. Spread with whipped cream. Roll up (using dish towel to help) on long side. Cut in half and frost with Chocolate-Roll Icing (see below).

## Chocolate-Roll Icing

2–3 tablespoons milk
1 cup sifted confectioners' sugar

1 tablespoon cocoa

Combine milk, sugar, and cocoa, and mix until smooth.

*Arlene Foulds, Center Congregational Church, Torrington, Connecticut*

# Bohemian Coffee Cake

Despite its name, in America, this is definitely a dessert cake—
but also a sweet treat served with coffee. A handsome item for any occasion.

| | |
|---|---|
| 2½ cups flour | 2 eggs |
| 1 cup brown sugar | 1 cup cooking oil |
| 1 cup sugar | 1 teaspoon vanilla |
| 1 teaspoon salt | 1 cup buttermilk |
| 1 teaspoon cinnamon | 1 cup chopped nuts (any kind) |
| 1 teaspoon nutmeg | 1 cup grated coconut |
| 1 teaspoon baking soda | |

Combine flour with brown sugar, sugar, salt, cinnamon, nutmeg, and baking soda. Mix well. In separate bowl, beat eggs well, then beat in oil, vanilla, and buttermilk. Stir into dry ingredients until well-blended. Add ¾ cup nuts and coconut. Grease and flour a 10" tube pan. Turn batter into tube pan and bake at 350°F for 1 hour. Remove from pan and cool on rack. Spread with Cream Cheese Frosting (see below) and sprinkle with remaining ¼ cup nuts.

## Cream Cheese Frosting

| | |
|---|---|
| 1 package (3 ounces) cream cheese, softened | ½ box confectioners' sugar |
| ½ teaspoon vanilla | 2 tablespoons butter |

Blend cream cheese, vanilla, sugar, and butter together, and beat until of spreadable consistency.

*Marcia Fletcher, St. Anne's Episcopal Church, Calais, Maine*

# Cottage Pudding

Children usually love this old favorite, which is not a pudding at all but a mild cake
served with different sauces. Use vanilla instead of lemon extract to flavor cake
if you elect to serve it with a vanilla or chocolate sauce.

## Cake

¼ cup shortening
1 cup sugar
1 egg
¼ teaspoon lemon extract,
or ½ teaspoon vanilla

1¾ cups flour
2½ teaspoons baking powder
½ teaspoon salt
⅔ cup milk

Cream shortening and sugar. Add egg and lemon extract or vanilla and beat well. Sift flour
together with baking powder and salt. Add to creamed mixture alternately with milk, beating
after each addition. Bake in greased 8" × 8" or 9" × 9" pan at 350°F for 35 minutes, or until
done. Cut into squares and serve with Lemon Nutmeg Sauce (see below).

## Lemon Nutmeg Sauce

½ cup sugar
1 tablespoon cornstarch,
dissolved in ¼ cup cold water
⅛ teaspoon salt
1¼ cups boiling water

3 tablespoons butter
1 teaspoon grated lemon rind
2 tablespoons lemon juice
½ teaspoon nutmeg

Mix sugar, cornstarch, and salt in saucepan. Gradually add boiling water, stirring constantly.
Bring mixture to boil while continuing to stir. Turn down heat and simmer 5 minutes. Blend
in butter, lemon rind and juice, and nutmeg. Pour hot sauce over each cake square.

*Gladys Priest, Foxon Congregational Church, East Haven, Connecticut*

# Fruit Torte

Taking advantage of American packaged foods,
this is super quick and easy to prepare but tasty, too.

1 can (16 ounces) apple pie
   filling
1 can (16 ounces) crushed
   pineapple

1 package (15 ounces) lemon
   cake mix
½ cup butter
   Whipped cream

In a greased 10" × 15" pan, layer apple pie filling and pineapple (with juice). Sprinkle cake mix over fruit. Cut butter into bits and dot over top. Bake at 375°F for 45 minutes, or until golden brown. Top with whipped cream and cut into squares.

*Elvira Howe, The Congregational Church, Laconia, New Hampshire*

# Key Lime Cake

A lovely cake for spring or summer—to make in a flat or tube pan.

1 package (3 ounces) lime gelatin
1½ cups sugar
2 cups flour, sifted
⅔ teaspoon salt
1 teaspoon baking powder
½ teaspoon baking soda
5 eggs
1⅓ cups cooking oil
¾ cup orange juice

½ teaspoon vanilla
1 teaspoon lemon extract
⅓ cup lime juice and ⅓ cup sifted
   confectioners' sugar (optional)
1 cup whipping cream,
   ⅛–¼ teaspoon green food
   coloring, and fresh lime slices
   (optional)

Soak gelatin in a little bit of cold water for 3–5 minutes. Combine sugar, flour, salt, baking powder, baking soda, and gelatin in mixing bowl. Add eggs, oil, orange juice, vanilla, and lemon extract. Beat until well-blended. Now, depending on the type of cake you wish:

1. Pour batter into greased 9" × 13" pan and bake at 350°F for 25–30 minutes. Let cool in pan for 15 minutes. Prick cake all over with fork. Drizzle well with lime juice mixed with confectioners' sugar.

2. Pour batter into greased 10" tube cake pan and bake at 350°F for 45–50 minutes. Cool. Whip cream and tint green. Use whipped cream to completely frost cake. Garnish with fresh lime slices (and a violet or two, if they are out!).

*Ruth A. Palmer, St. John's Episcopal Church, Bethesda, Maryland*

# Mayonnaise Cake

Moist and light cocoa-colored, with an unexpected zing.

| | |
|---|---|
| 2 cups sifted flour | ¼ cup cocoa |
| 1 cup sugar | 1 cup cold water |
| 1½ teaspoons baking soda | 1 cup mayonnaise |

Mix together flour, sugar, baking soda, and cocoa. Beat cold water and mayonnaise together. Add to dry ingredients and mix well. Pour into greased pans (two 8" layer-cake pans or one 8" × 12" sheet-cake pan). Bake at 350°F for 45 minutes, or until cake springs back in center.

*Dianne Johnson, Dublin Community Church, Dublin, New Hampshire*

# Molasses Cake

Similar to gingerbread but lighter in texture.
Cake can be frosted or served with lemon sauce or whipped cream.

1 cup butter
1½ cups sugar
3 eggs
¾ cup molasses
3¾ cups sifted flour
¾ teaspoon baking soda

¾ teaspoon salt
2 teaspoons cinnamon
1 teaspoon cloves
1 teaspoon ginger
¾ cup milk

Cream butter and sugar. Add eggs and beat until fluffy. Add molasses and blend well. Sift flour, baking soda, salt, cinnamon, cloves, and ginger together. Add to mixture alternately with milk. Turn into buttered 9" × 13" pan. Bake at 350°F for about 35 minutes, or until toothpick inserted in center comes out clean.

*Naomi Crook, Chocorua Community Church, Chocorua, New Hampshire*

# Mother's Hot Weather Cake

A quick, easy, and quite impressive spice cake.

½ cup shortening
1 cup brown sugar
1 egg
1 egg yolk
1⅓ cups cake flour
½ teaspoon salt

½ teaspoon baking soda
½ teaspoon baking powder
½ teaspoon cloves
½ teaspoon cinnamon
½ cup soured milk

## Topping

1 egg white
½ cup brown sugar

¼ cup chopped nuts (any kind)

Cream shortening with brown sugar. Beat egg with egg yolk, and add to creamed mixture. Sift together cake flour, salt, baking soda, baking powder, cloves, and cinnamon. Add to creamed mixture alternately with milk. Grease and flour an 8" × 8" or 9" × 9" pan and line with waxed paper well up on sides of pan. Turn batter into pan. Make topping by beating egg white until stiff, then beating in brown sugar, adding a little at a time while beating. Spread over cake batter. Sprinkle nuts over top. Bake at 350°F for 40 minutes, or until done.

*Marianne Jewell, United Methodist Church of the Hamptons, Hampton, New Hampshire*

# Fresh Pear Cake

Both light and moist, spicy yet pear-y, and altogether remarkable. Keeps well, too—though there is usually little left to keep.

| | |
|---|---|
| 2 cups sugar | 1 teaspoon salt |
| 3 eggs, well-beaten | 1 teaspoon vanilla |
| 1½ cups cooking oil | 2 teaspoons cinnamon |
| 3 cups flour | 3 cups thinly sliced pears, cored |
| 1 teaspoon baking soda | and peeled |

Combine sugar, eggs, and oil. Beat well. Combine flour, baking soda, and salt. Add to sugar mixture, 1 cup at a time, mixing well after each addition. Stir in vanilla, cinnamon, and pears. Turn into well-greased 10" Bundt or tube pan. Bake at 350°F for 1 hour. Remove from pan and allow to cool. Pour Confectioners' Sugar Glaze on top (see below).

## Confectioners' Sugar Glaze

1¼ cups sifted confectioners' sugar     2–4 tablespoons milk

Combine sugar and milk, blending until smooth.

*Joan Young, The Unitarian Church, Franklin, New Hampshire*

# Sauerkraut Surprise Cake

A novelty cake well worth serving to both delight and mystify your friends.
Most will guess the secret ingredient to be coconut!
The frosting is tart-sweet and very important to the cake.

| | |
|---|---|
| ½ cup butter | ¼ teaspoon salt |
| 1½ cups sugar | ½ cup cocoa |
| 3 eggs | 1 cup water |
| 1 teaspoon vanilla | 1 can (8 ounces) sauerkraut, |
| 2 cups sifted flour | drained, rinsed, and finely |
| 1 teaspoon baking powder | snipped |
| 1 teaspoon baking soda | |

In large mixing bowl, cream butter and sugar until light. Beat in eggs one at a time; add vanilla. Sift together flour, baking powder, baking soda, salt, and cocoa. Add to creamed mixture alternately with water, beating after each addition. Stir in sauerkraut. Turn into greased and floured 9" × 13" baking pan. Bake at 350°F for 35–40 minutes. Cool in pan. Frost with Sour Cream Chocolate Frosting (see below).

# Sour Cream Chocolate Frosting

| | |
|---|---|
| 1 package (6 ounces) semisweet chocolate pieces | 1 teaspoon vanilla |
| 4 tablespoons butter | ¼ teaspoon salt |
| ½ cup sour cream | 2½–2¾ cups confectioners' sugar, sifted |

Melt chocolate and butter. Blend in sour cream, vanilla, and salt. Gradually add confectioners' sugar until frosting is of spreading consistency. Beat well.

*Marcia Gehrke, United Methodist Church of the Hamptons, Hampton, New Hampshire*

# Pineapple Nut Cake

A very moist cake with a delicious frosting.

2 cups flour
2 cups crushed pineapple, drained
2 cups sugar

2 teaspoons baking soda
2 eggs
1 cup walnuts

Grease and flour 9" × 13" pan. Combine flour, pineapple, sugar, baking soda, eggs, and walnuts, and pour into pan. Bake at 350°F for about 40 minutes. Cool and frost cake with Vanilla Frosting (see below).

## Vanilla Frosting

1 package (8 ounces) cream cheese
½ cup butter

1 tablespoon vanilla
1½–2 cups confectioners' sugar

Whip cream cheese and butter together. Then add vanilla and enough sugar to make icing spreadable.

*Avis M. Ayotte, St. Mark's Church, Augusta, Maine*

# Pineapple Upside-Down Cake

A fluffy white cake with a caramelized pineapple topping.

3 tablespoons butter
½ cup brown sugar
6 or 9 slices pineapple (depending on size of pan)
6 or 9 cherries
1 egg
½ cup sugar

¼ cup milk
1 cup flour
1 teaspoon baking powder
⅛ teaspoon salt
1 tablespoon melted shortening
1 teaspoon vanilla

Melt butter in large ovenproof skillet. Add brown sugar. Stir until melted. Cover with pineapple slices. Place cherries in holes of pineapple slices. Set aside.

Beat egg lightly and add sugar. Beat well. Sift flour together with baking powder and salt. Add milk alternately with flour mixture. Beat well; add shortening and vanilla. Pour over pineapple. Cover and bake at 350°F for 30 minutes. Turn out upside down on plate and serve with whipped cream.

*Dianne Johnson, Dublin Community Church, Dublin, New Hampshire*

# Poppy Seed Cake

A superb cake far easier to make than most of its ilk.

1 box (18½ ounces) yellow cake mix
1 package (3½ ounces) instant vanilla pudding
½ cup cooking oil
½ cup sherry

1 cup sour cream
¼ cup poppy seeds
4 eggs, separated
1 teaspoon cream of tartar
½ cup chopped walnuts

Stir together cake mix, pudding, oil, sherry, sour cream, and poppy seeds. Add egg yolks and beat 2 minutes. Beat egg whites with cream of tartar until stiff and fold into first mixture. Fold in walnuts. Bake in 10" Bundt or tube pan at 350°F for 40–50 minutes.

*Gladys Priest, Foxon Congregational Church, East Haven, Connecticut*

# Pound Cake

Makes a nice sound pound cake. Freezes well, too.

| | |
|---|---|
| 1¼ cups sugar | 2 cups flour |
| ⅔ cup shortening | ½ teaspoon baking powder |
| 3 eggs | 1 teaspoon salt |
| ⅔ cup milk | |
| 1 teaspoon lemon or vanilla extract | |

Cream sugar and shortening. Beat in eggs. Add milk and extract. Combine flour with baking powder and salt and stir into batter. Mix well. Pour into greased and floured large loaf pan (or use 2 small ones). Bake at 300°F for 1 hour and 25 minutes.

*Jeannette M. Miller, Morris Congregational Church, Morris, Connecticut*

# Pumpkin Cake

Good frosted or simply served with whipped cream.

½ cup butter
1¼ cups sugar
2 eggs
1 cup solid-pack canned
　pumpkin
2 cups flour
½ teaspoon cinnamon

½ teaspoon ginger
½ teaspoon nutmeg
½ teaspoon salt
3 teaspoons baking powder
¾ cup milk
½ cup chopped nuts (any kind)
½ teaspoon baking soda

Cream butter and sugar, add eggs, and beat. Stir in pumpkin. Sift together flour, cinnamon, ginger, nutmeg, salt, and baking powder. Add dry ingredients alternately with milk to pumpkin mixture. Then add nuts and baking soda; mix until well-blended and pour into greased and floured 10" × 10" pan. Bake at 350°F for 35 minutes. Cool and frost with Orange Frosting (see below).

# Orange Frosting

1 pound confectioners' sugar
1 package (8 ounces) cream
　cheese

2 teaspoons vanilla
　Orange juice

Combine sugar, cream cheese, and vanilla with enough orange juice to make spreadable.

*Donna Riley, United Church of Christ, Littleton, New Hampshire*

# Oatmeal Cake

A moist and spicy dessert cake with a coconut-nut topping

1¼ cups boiling water
1 cup quick rolled oats
½ cup butter
1 cup sugar
1 cup brown sugar
2 eggs

1⅓ cups flour
¼ teaspoon salt
1 teaspoon baking soda
Scant teaspoon cinnamon
1 teaspoon vanilla

Pour boiling water over oats. Set aside to cool. Cream butter with sugar and brown sugar and beat in eggs. Mix in cooled oats. Add flour, salt, baking soda, cinnamon, and vanilla. Mix well. Pour into greased 7" × 11" pan, and bake at 350°F for 40 minutes, or until done. Cool and cover with Coco-Nut Topping (see below).

# Coco-Nut Topping

4 tablespoons butter
1 cup brown sugar
½ teaspoon vanilla

2 tablespoons cream
½ cup grated coconut
½ cup chopped nuts (any kind)

Place butter, brown sugar, vanilla, cream, coconut, and nuts in saucepan and stir together until butter melts. Spread over cool Oatmeal Cake.

*Pauline Hammond, Free Will Baptist Church, Northwood, New Hampshire*

# Scripture Cake

Certainly a must for a potluck cookbook!
(But in this case, the Bible does not tell you everything.)

1 cup Judges 5:25 last clause (butter)

1 cup Jeremiah 6:20 (sugar)

1 tablespoon I Samuel 14:25 (honey)

3 Jeremiah 17:11 (eggs)

1 cup I Samuel 30:12 second food (raisins)

1 cup Nahum 3:12 (figs), chopped

¼ cup Numbers 17:8 (almonds), blanched and chopped

2 cups I Kings 4:22 (flour)
II Chronicles 9:9 (spices, such as cinnamon and nutmeg)
Pinch of Leviticus 2:13 (salt)

1 teaspoon Amos 4:5 (leavener, such as baking soda)

3 tablespoons Judges 4:19 last sentence (milk)

Cream Judges (butter), Jeremiah (sugar), and I Samuel (honey). Beat in the 3 Jeremiahs (eggs), one at a time. Add I Samuel (raisins), Nahum (figs), and Numbers (almonds), and beat again. Sift together I Kings (flour), II Chronicles (spices), Leviticus (salt), and Amos (leavener, or baking soda). Add to first mixture. Lastly, add Judges (milk). Bake at 325°F for 1½ hours, or until done.

French Onion Soup, page 142

**Molded Beet Salad, page 144**

24-Hour Layered Salad, page 146

**Salad Excelsior, page 150**

**Danish Potato Salad, page 154**

**Astoria Salad, page 157**

**Dill Bread, page 182**

**Deli-Cakes, page 163**

**Orange Bow Knots, page 188**

**Tempting Bishop's Cake, page 193**

Clockwise from bottom right: Apricot Coconut Squares, page 236; Chocolate Layer Bars, page 239; Easiest Peanut Butter Cookies Ever, page 244; and Double-Chocolate Chip Pecan Cookies, page 309

223

**Brownies, page 238**

**Key Lime Pie, page 263**

**Kentucky Bourbon Pumpkin Pie, page 266**

**Mile-High Strawberry Pie, page 271**

**Old-Fashioned Biscuits, page 291**

# Sponge Cake with Orange Sauce

A nice high sponge cake happily set off by the sauce and whipped cream.

| | |
|---|---|
| 4 large or 5 medium eggs, separated | 1 teaspoon lemon extract |
| 2 cups sugar | 2½ cups sifted cake flour |
| 1 cup boiling water | 1½ teaspoons baking powder |
| 1 teaspoon vanilla | ½ teaspoon salt |
| | 1 cup heavy cream |

Beat egg whites until foamy. Still beating, gradually add ¼ cup sugar and continue beating until stiff. Beat egg yolks until thick and lemon-colored. Gradually add boiling water in thin stream to yolks, beating constantly until mixture is foamy and nearly fills large mixing bowl. Add remaining 1¾ cups sugar gradually, beating all the while until thick. Beat in vanilla and lemon extract. Sift together flour, baking powder, and salt, and carefully add to yolk mixture, beating slowly until well-blended. Fold in egg whites. Turn into ungreased 10" tube pan and bake at 325°F for 45–60 minutes. Whip cream and set aside.

## Orange Sauce

| | |
|---|---|
| 1 cup sugar | 2 tablespoons grated orange rind |
| ½ teaspoon salt | 1½ tablespoons lemon juice |
| 2 tablespoons cornstarch | 2 tablespoons butter |
| 1 cup orange juice | |

Mix sugar in saucepan with salt, cornstarch, and orange juice. Cook over medium-high heat, stirring constantly until thickened. Let boil 1 minute, stirring. Remove from heat and add orange rind, lemon juice, and butter. Keep warm.

When cake is done, impale pan upside down on spout of inverted funnel and let cool. Remove from pan when cool and cut into wedges. Serve with warm Orange Sauce and whipped cream.

*Cheryl Tutt, Ascutney Union Church, Ascutney, Vermont*

# White Cake

Frost this 2-egg cake as you wish, or top when cool with hot lemon pie filling.
Makes good cupcakes, too.

| | |
|---|---|
| 2 cups + 2 tablespoons flour | ½ cup shortening |
| 1½ cups sugar | 1 teaspoon vanilla |
| 1 tablespoon baking powder | 1 cup milk |
| ½ teaspoon salt | 2 large eggs |

Sift flour, sugar, baking powder, and salt together. Add shortening, vanilla, milk, and eggs. Then beat by hand or with electric mixer for 3 minutes. Grease and flour two 8" layer-cake pans or one 8" × 12" pan. Turn batter into pans or pan and bake at 350°F for 35–40 minutes. For cupcakes, put paper liners in muffin pans, fill halfway, and bake at 400°F for 18–20 minutes.

*Gladys Congdon, Old Brick Church, Claredon, Vermont*

# Yogurt Cake Dessert

An interesting variation on the Cottage Pudding (page 177) theme.

## Syrup

| | |
|---|---|
| 1¼ cups sugar | 1 tablespoon lemon juice |
| 2 cups water | 1 tablespoon grated orange rind |

Mix sugar and water in saucepan and heat, stirring, until sugar is dissolved. Boil briskly without stirring for 10–15 minutes. Add lemon juice and orange rind. Boil 2 more minutes and set aside to cool.

# Cake

¾ cup sugar
3 eggs
1 cup flour
1 cup yogurt

1 teaspoon baking powder
Whipped cream (optional)
Sliced almonds or coconut for
garnish

Beat sugar into eggs until dissolved. Combine flour with yogurt and baking powder and fold into egg mixture. Pour into greased 8" × 8" or 9" × 9" pan and bake at 350°F for 45 minutes, or until slightly browned and toothpick inserted in center comes out clean.

While cake is still hot, cut into diamonds or squares. Pour cooled syrup over cake pieces. When syrup is absorbed, serve cake with whipped cream, if desired, garnished with almonds or coconut.

*Belkis H. Vassaf, Concord Unitarian Church, Concord, New Hampshire*

# Upside-Down Gingerbread

A novel idea that makes a handsome church supper dessert.

| | |
|---|---|
| 2 tablespoons butter | 2¼ cups flour |
| 1½ cups molasses | ¼ teaspoon salt |
| 6 slices canned pineapple | 1 teaspoon baking soda |
| ¼ cup raisins | 1 teaspoon ginger |
| ¼ cup chopped nuts (any kind) | 1 teaspoon cinnamon |
| 2 tablespoons sugar | ½ teaspoon cloves |
| ½ cup shortening | ¾ cup hot water |
| 1 egg | |

Melt butter in 10"–11" ovenproof frying pan or deep round cake pan. Pour in ½ cup molasses. Arrange pineapple slices in pan, filling in spaces with raisins and nuts. Set in warm place. Cream sugar, shortening, remaining 1 cup molasses, and egg. Sift flour with salt, baking soda, ginger, cinnamon, and cloves, and stir into sugar mixture. Add hot water and pour mixture over fruit. Bake at 350°F for 45–60 minutes. Serve hot with whipped cream.

# Wacky Cake

This eggless brownie-like cake takes only about 10 minutes to make.
You don't even have to grease the pan!

| | |
|---|---|
| 1½ cups flour | 5 tablespoons cooking oil |
| 1 cup sugar | 1 teaspoon vanilla |
| 3 tablespoons cocoa | 1 teaspoon vinegar |
| 1 teaspoon baking soda | 1 cup cold water |
| 1 teaspoon salt | |

Combine flour, sugar, cocoa, baking soda, and salt in bowl, and turn into ungreased 9" × 13" baking pan. Make 3 holes, or wells, in dry ingredients. Pour oil into one, vanilla into another, and vinegar into the third. Pour cold water over all and stir to mix well. Bake at 350°F for about 40 minutes, or until center is firm.

*Thomas A. Nerbonne, United Baptist Church, Concord, New Hampshire*

# Walnut Cake

A beige cake with a gingerbready texture that tastes wonderfully of walnuts.

| | |
|---|---|
| 1 cup walnuts, broken | ½ teaspoon salt |
| Boiling water | 1 tablespoon baking powder |
| ½ cup butter | ½ teaspoon cinnamon |
| 2 cups brown sugar | ½ teaspoon nutmeg |
| 3 eggs, separated | ½ teaspoon cloves |
| 3 cups sifted flour | ¾ cup milk |

Cover broken walnuts with boiling water for a few minutes and drain. Set aside. Cream butter and brown sugar together and add well-beaten egg yolks. Beat egg whites until stiff and set aside. Sift together flour, salt, baking powder, cinnamon, nutmeg, and cloves. Add to creamed mixture alternately with milk. Add walnuts. Fold in egg whites. Bake in 3 greased 8" layer pans at 350°F for 20 minutes, or until lightly brown. Cool and frost with Butter Cream Frosting (see below).

## Butter Cream Frosting

| | |
|---|---|
| 1 cup butter | 6 tablespoons cream |
| 3 cups confectioners' sugar | 1 tablespoon vanilla |

Cream together butter and sugar, then beat in cream and vanilla.

*Dianne Johnson, Dublin Community Church, Dublin, New Hampshire*

# Cookies and Bars

Do you suppose there exists a person who doesn't like cookies? Surely one of the handiest and dandiest of all goodies, cookies and bars tuck neatly into pockets or lunch boxes, preside with delicate grace over the tea table, are the perfect after-school snack, and, of course, make wonderful Christmas or anytime gifts.

Almond Butter Balls  235

Almond Spice Cookies  235

Real Almond Macaroons  236

Apricot-Coconut Squares  236

Chocolate Brownies  237

Brownies  238

Ever-So-Good Golden Brownies  238

Chocolate Layer Bars  239

No-Bake Oatmeal Fudgies  240

No-Bake Carob Oatmeal Bars  240

Oatmeal-Cranberry Bar Cookies  241

Macadamia Rum Balls  242

Easy Filled Drops  242

Forgotten Cookies  243

Easiest Peanut Butter Cookies Ever  244

Great-Great-Grandma's Old-Fashioned Gingersnaps  244

Vermont Ginger Cookies  245

Foxon Ginger Cookies  245

Molasses Cookies  246

Pineapple Cookies  246

Potato Chip Cookies  247

Rich Cookies  247

Sour Cream Cookies  248

Saucy Bars  249

Thumb Cookies  250

Date Balls  250

Frosted Orange Cookies  251

# Almond Butter Balls

A wonderful old-fashioned butter cookie.

¾ cup butter
1 cup brown sugar
1 egg, lightly beaten
1 teaspoon vanilla
2 cups flour

1½ teaspoons baking powder
½ teaspoon salt
½ cup sugar
1½ cups whole almonds

Cream butter and brown sugar. Add egg and vanilla. Sift flour, baking powder, and salt, and add to mixture. Beat well. Form into balls, 1 teaspoon at a time. Roll in sugar. Place on greased cookie sheet. Press whole almond in center of each. Bake at 400°F for 12 minutes. **Makes about 5 dozen.**

*Marion Sarsfield, Woodmont United Church of Christ, Milford, Connecticut*

# Almond Spice Cookies

Can be made way ahead and kept frozen until wanted. No need to thaw dough before baking.

1 cup butter
⅓ cup molasses
1 cup sugar
2 egg yolks
3 tablespoons crystalline ginger, cut up fine

1 tablespoon cinnamon
2 teaspoons cloves
1 teaspoon baking soda
2 cups flour
1 cup slivered almonds

Beat together butter, molasses, sugar, and egg yolks. Stir in ginger. Sift together cinnamon, cloves, baking soda, and flour. Add almonds. Stir into first mixture. Mix well. Pat dough into 2 long rolls about 1½" in diameter. Cover with plastic wrap and freeze. When ready to bake, slice frozen dough into ¼" rounds; place 1" apart on ungreased cookie sheet and bake at 350°F for 8–10 minutes, or until brown and crisp. Cool on racks. **Makes about 6 dozen.**

# Real Almond Macaroons

No flour, no baking powder, no coconut—*real* macaroons.
A treat for any occasion. They will keep well packed in an airtight container.

1 package (7 to 8 ounces) almond
   paste
2 egg whites

1 cup + 2 tablespoons sugar
1 teaspoon vanilla

Put almond paste in bowl and break up into small pieces. Pour egg whites on top of paste. Let stand, covered, in refrigerator 12–24 hours, turning and stirring from time to time. (Egg whites will liquefy almond paste.) Blend whites and almond paste together into smooth paste, and add sugar and vanilla, mixing all well together to form smooth but sticky dough. Line cookie sheet or sheets with aluminum foil. Lightly oil foil. Shape dough into balls the size of large marbles and place on foil 2" apart. Bake at 325°F for 15–20 minutes, or until lightly browned around edges and center is firm. Remove cookie sheet from oven. Transfer foil in one piece with cookies still on it to cooling rack. Re-line cookie sheet with new oiled foil and put in another batch to bake. When first batch of cookies is completely cool, peel macaroons carefully off foil; discard used sheets of foil. (If you try to take macaroons off foil before completely cool, their chewy centers will stick to foil and fragment the cookies.) ***Makes about 3 dozen.***

*O. P. Valhalla, St. Matthew's Church, Bedford, New York*

# Apricot-Coconut Squares

Serve warm to have these at their melt-in-the-mouth best.

1 cup sugar
2 cups flour
¾ cup butter
1 cup grated coconut
½ cup chopped nuts (optional)
1 egg

¼ teaspoon salt
1 teaspoon vanilla
1 jar (10 ounces) apricot jam
   (or substitute your favorite
   fruit jam)

With a fork, mix together sugar, flour, butter, coconut, nuts, if using, egg, salt, and vanilla. Press three-fourths of batter in bottom of greased 9" × 13" pan. Spread jam over top. Spread rest of batter over jam with fork, letting some of jam show through. Bake at 350°F for 25–30 minutes, or until light golden brown. Cool. ***Makes 12–20 bars, depending on size.***

*Mrs. James W. Snow, Jr., Wapping Community Church, South Windsor, Connecticut*

# Chocolate Brownies

Very rich, very sweet, very fudgy, and unsurpassed for those
who like their brownies like that.

| | |
|---|---|
| 1 **cup butter** | 5 **eggs** |
| 1 **package (6 ounces) chocolate bits** | 1 **tablespoon vanilla** |
| | 1½ **cups flour** |
| 3 **cups sugar** | ½ **cup chopped walnuts (optional)** |

Melt together butter and chocolate bits. Remove from heat and add sugar. Beat in eggs, one at a time, and vanilla. Add flour and walnuts, if using, and stir well. Spread on ungreased jelly-roll pan (10" × 15") and bake at 350°F for 25–30 minutes. Do not overbake—they should be fudgy when done. Cool and cut—small, because they *are* rich. ***Makes 32.***

*Diana G. Mac Veagh, Church of the Heavenly Rest, New York City, New York*

# Brownies

Chocolate treats not quite as rich and sweet as those in preceding recipe, but perfect for those who like *their* brownies like *that*.

½ cup butter
4 ounces unsweetened chocolate
4 eggs
2 cups sugar
¼ teaspoon salt

1 teaspoon vanilla
1 cup flour
½ cup semi-sweet chocolate chips
¾ cup chopped nuts (any kind), optional

Melt together butter and chocolate. Beat eggs and add sugar, salt, and vanilla. Beat in chocolate mixture. Stir in flour, chocolate chips, and nuts, if using. Pour into greased 9" × 9" pan and bake at 325°F for 25–30 minutes, or until center is done. Cool and cut into squares. *Makes 18.*

*Inge Schermerhorn, United Church of Christ, North Hampton, New Hampshire*

# Ever-So-Good Golden Brownies

A nice change from chocolate brownies. Rich, fudgy, and butterscotchy-sweet.

½ cup butter
2 cups brown sugar
2 teaspoons vanilla
2 eggs, well-beaten

1½ cups flour
2 teaspoons baking powder
½ teaspoon salt
½ cup chopped nuts (any kind)

Melt butter. Remove from stove and add brown sugar and vanilla. Beat in eggs. Sift together flour, baking powder, and salt, and add to egg mixture. Stir in nuts. Pour into lightly greased 9" × 9" pan. Bake at 350°F for 25–30 minutes. *Makes 18.*

*Mildred Cutter, United Church of Jaffrey, Jaffrey, New Hampshire*

# Chocolate Layer Bars

These rich chocolate treats are doubly delectable.
The moist fudgy center is encased in a crisp cookie shell.

2 cups flour
1 teaspoon baking soda
½ teaspoon baking powder
1 cup butter or margarine, softened
1 cup granulated sugar
1 cup packed light brown sugar
2 eggs, beaten

1 teaspoon vanilla
1 cup walnuts, chopped
1 bag (12 ounces) semi-sweet or
   bittersweet chocolate chips
½ cup butter or margarine
1 can (14 ounces) sweetened
   condensed milk

Line 13" × 9" baking pan with sheet of aluminum foil long enough for lifting flaps after baking; grease foil. In bowl, whisk flour, baking soda, and baking powder; set aside. In mixing bowl, beat butter or margarine until smooth. Add granulated and brown sugars. Beat until smooth. Add eggs and vanilla; mix well. Stir in flour mixture until blended. Stir in walnuts. Spread half of dough into prepared pan; set aside.

In saucepan, melt chocolate and butter or margarine over low heat. Stir in milk until smooth. Pour into pan. Dollop remaining dough over filling, spreading to cover as well as possible (chocolate filling may be visible in some spots). Bake at 375°F for 30 minutes or until topping is browned (filling will still be jiggly). Remove to cool about 1 hour. Using foil flaps, lift entire sheet of cookies out of pan. Cut into 24 bars. Refrigerate in airtight container. *Makes 24.*

*Nancy Eichler, Roswell Presbyterian Church, Roswell, Georgia*

# No-Bake Oatmeal Fudgies

Very easy and very good.

½ cup milk
½ cup cocoa
1½ cups sugar
½ cup butter

½ cup peanut butter
1 teaspoon vanilla
2½ cups quick-cooking oats

In 2-quart saucepan over medium-high heat, mix milk, cocoa, sugar, and butter. Bring to boil and boil for 2 minutes. Remove from heat and stir in peanut butter and vanilla. Then beat in oats. When dough is well-blended, put into greased 8" × 8" pan and cut into bars, or drop by teaspoonsful on waxed paper. Let cool. ***Makes about 32 bars or 40 cookies.***

*Carol Jensen, The United Church of Hardwick, Hardwick, Vermont*

# No-Bake Carob Oatmeal Bars

Similar to preceding recipe, but with the taste of carob rather than chocolate.

⅓ cup milk
¾ cup honey
½ cup carob powder
½ cup butter

1 teaspoon vanilla
½ cup peanut butter
3 cups quick-cooking oats

In 2-quart saucepan over medium-high heat, mix milk, honey, carob powder, and butter. Bring to full boil for 3 minutes, stirring constantly. Remove from heat and add vanilla and peanut butter. Mix well, then stir in oats and blend well. Put into greased 8" × 8" pan and refrigerate. ***Makes 32.***

*Carol Jensen, The United Church of Hardwick, Hardwick, Vermont*

# Oatmeal-Cranberry Bar Cookies

These chewy bars can be adapted with different fruit fillings.
Try dried apricots or raisins in place of cranberries.

| | |
|---|---|
| 2 navel oranges | 1 cup chopped walnuts |
| Water | 1½ teaspoons baking powder |
| 3½ cups (1 pound) dried sweetened cranberries | 1 teaspoon cinnamon |
| ¼ cup granulated sugar | 1 cup butter, softened |
| Salt | 2 cups packed light brown sugar |
| 2 cups flour | 2 eggs, beaten |
| 2 cups rolled oats | 1 teaspoon vanilla |

Grate rind from oranges. Squeeze juice into measuring cup; add enough water to make 1 cup. Place rind, juice-water, cranberries, granulated sugar, and a pinch of salt in medium saucepan. Cook over medium-high heat until boiling. Reduce heat and simmer, stirring occasionally, for 4 minutes or until syrupy. Remove to cool slightly.

In bowl, combine flour, oats, walnuts, baking powder, cinnamon, and pinch of salt. In another bowl, beat butter. Gradually add brown sugar, beating until smooth. Beat in eggs and vanilla until smooth. In three additions, stir in dry ingredients until no flour is visible. Dollop half of batter in greased 13" × 9" pan. With clean, wet hand, spread dough evenly. Cover evenly with cranberry mixture. Dollop remaining dough in tablespoonfuls over cranberries. With clean, wet hand, spread dough evenly. Bake at 350°F for 30 minutes or until puffed and browned. Remove to cool completely before cutting. ***Makes 48 bars.***

# Macadamia Rum Balls

These tropical no-bake cookies develop even more flavor after a few days in the refrigerator. They're ideal for advance preparation.

2 cups sifted graham cracker crumbs, sifted
1 cup sifted confectioners' sugar
2 tablespoons sifted cocoa
1 cup finely chopped macadamia nuts
⅛ teaspoon salt
3 tablespoons honey
2 teaspoons rum extract
4–5 tablespoons cold water
1 cup sweetened, flaked coconut

In bowl, combine crumbs, sugar, cocoa, macadamias, and salt. In small measuring cup, whisk honey, rum extract, and 4 tablespoons water until thoroughly mixed. Add to dry ingredients. Stir until moist enough to clump together. Gradually add up to 1 additional tablespoon water, if needed, to make mixture moist enough to stick together but not so moist that it falls apart. With hands, roll into 1" balls. Roll balls in coconut to coat. Chill in airtight container for 12 hours to firm up. *Makes about 2½ dozen.*

*Li-hwa Ong, Kilohana United Methodist Church, Honolulu, Hawaii*

# Easy Filled Drops

Drop cookies with a date-nut filling

## Filling

2 cups chopped dates
¾ cup sugar
¾ cup water
½ cup chopped nuts (any kind)

Combine dates, sugar, and water in saucepan and cook, stirring constantly, until thick. Remove from stove, stir in nuts, and allow to cool.

# Cookies

3½ cups flour
⅛ teaspoon cinnamon
1 teaspoon salt
1 teaspoon baking soda
1 cup shortening

2 cups brown sugar
2 eggs, beaten
½ cup soured milk or buttermilk
1 teaspoon vanilla

Sift together flour, cinnamon, salt, and baking soda. Cream shortening and brown sugar. Add eggs, milk, and vanilla; stir in dry ingredients and mix well. Drop most of dough by teaspoonfuls on ungreased cookie sheet.

Flatten cookies a little and place ½ teaspoon date filling on top of each. Cover filling with ½ teaspoon more cookie dough. Bake at 350°F for 15 minutes. *Makes 3½ dozen.*

*Bob Gates, Advent Christian Church, Pittsfield, New Hampshire*

# Forgotten Cookies

Don't forget and turn on the oven to cook something else
while these meringuey treats are in residence.

2 egg whites
½ cup sugar
Dash of salt

½ teaspoon vanilla
½ cup semisweet chocolate bits
½ cup chopped walnuts

Preheat oven to 350°F. Beat egg whites until foamy and gradually add sugar, salt, and vanilla, still beating. Beat until stiff. Fold in chocolate bits and walnuts. Place by tablespoonsful on greased cookie sheet. Turn off oven and put cookies in. Leave in oven overnight. *Makes 24.*

*Laura Goodenough, The Congregational Church, Winchester Center, Connecticut*

# Easiest Peanut Butter Cookies Ever

People are always surprised to hear there's no flour in this peanut butter cookie.
It's a sure-fire hit with children and adults alike.

1 jar (8 ounces) creamy peanut
butter
2 cups sugar

2 eggs, beaten
2 teaspoons vanilla

In mixing bowl, combine peanut butter and sugar with fork. Add eggs and vanilla. Beat until smooth. Roll into 1½" balls and place 2" apart on greased cookie sheet. Press cookies with fork in crisscross pattern. Bake at 375°F for 8 minutes or until edges start to color. Remove and allow cookies to cool 5 minutes on sheet before transferring to rack. Continue in batches until all dough is baked. *Makes 3½ dozen.*

*Gayla Magnus, Evangelical Lutheran Church, Frederick, Maryland*

# Great-Great-Grandma's
# Old-Fashioned Gingersnaps

The thin, crispy kind of ginger cookie, today more usually called ginger wafers.

1 cup molasses
½ cup butter
1 tablespoon ginger

1 rounded teaspoon baking soda
3 cups flour

Boil together molasses and butter. Cool. Add ginger, baking soda, and flour. Roll dough thin on floured board and cut with cookie cutters. Bake on ungreased cookie sheet at 350°F for 8–10 minutes. *Makes 4–6 dozen.*

*Helen E. Goodwin, Our Savior Lutheran Church, Hanover, New Hampshire*

# Vermont Ginger Cookies

A cakier cookie covered with sugar grains
and pressed down with a fork like peanut butter cookies.

| | |
|---|---|
| ⅔ cup cooking oil | 2 teaspoons baking soda |
| 1½ cups sugar | ½ teaspoon salt |
| 1 egg | 1 teaspoon cinnamon |
| ¼ cup molasses | 1 teaspoon ginger |
| 2 cups flour | |

In large bowl, mix oil, 1 cup sugar, egg, molasses, flour, baking soda, salt, cinnamon, and ginger. Drop dough by teaspoonsful into dish of remaining ½ cup sugar to coat each cookie. Place on greased cookie sheet and press flat with fork. Bake at 350°F for 8–10 minutes. **Makes 4 dozen.**

*Mildred D. Chamberlain, The Congregational Church, South Hero, Vermont*

# Foxon Ginger Cookies

These crisp cookies are more like what we think of today as gingersnaps.
You can make a fine Icebox Cake by stacking layers of whipped cream
between the cookies and chilling for several hours.

| | |
|---|---|
| 1 cup shortening | 4 cups flour |
| 1 cup sugar | 1 teaspoon baking soda |
| 1 egg | ½ teaspoon salt |
| 1 cup molasses | 1 teaspoon ginger |

Cream shortening and sugar. Add egg and mix well. Beat in molasses. Then combine flour, baking soda, salt, and ginger, and stir into molasses mixture. Roll thin, cut out, and bake on ungreased cookie sheet at 350°F for 10 minutes. **Makes 6–7 dozen.**

*Elizabeth K. Watrous, Foxon Congregational Church, East Haven, Connecticut*

# Molasses Cookies

A *very* good soft molasses cookie with just the right amount of spice.
Is the heated cookie sheet the secret?

| | |
|---|---|
| 3½ cups flour | 1 teaspoon ginger |
| 1 teaspoon baking soda | ½ cup butter |
| ½ teaspoon salt | 1 cup sugar |
| 1½ teaspoons cinnamon | 2 eggs, beaten |
| 1 teaspoon cloves | 1 cup molasses |

Sift flour, baking soda, salt, cinnamon, cloves, and ginger together. Cream butter and sugar. Beat in eggs and molasses. Add flour mixture and stir well. Have all ingredients at room temperature and cookie sheets *hot*. Drop by teaspoonsful on ungreased sheets and bake at 350°F for 10 minutes or less. **Makes 4 dozen.**

*Eva Day, The Unitarian Church, Peterborough, New Hampshire*

# Pineapple Cookies

Light, pretty, and absolutely scrumptious.

| | |
|---|---|
| 1⅔ cups sugar | 2⅔ cups flour |
| ⅔ cup butter | ½ teaspoon baking soda |
| 2 eggs | ½ teaspoon salt |
| ½ cup crushed pineapple (canned in syrup or fresh in natural juice) | 2 teaspoons lemon extract |

Mix sugar, butter, eggs, pineapple (with juice), flour, baking soda, salt, and lemon extract. Drop by teaspoonsful on greased baking sheet. Bake at 350°F for 12–15 minutes, or until lightly brown. Let stand a few seconds before removing to cooling racks. **Makes approximately 6 dozen.**

*Regina Stanhope, Our Savior Lutheran Church, Hanover, New Hampshire*

# Potato Chip Cookies

Hard to tell from the title, but this recipe makes a superb sugar cookie.

1 cup sugar
1 cup light brown sugar
1 cup butter
2 eggs, well-beaten
2 cups flour

1 teaspoon baking soda
2 teaspoon vanilla
1 cup potato chips, finely crushed
¾ cup chopped nuts (any kind), optional

Combine sugar and brown sugar and cream with butter. Beat in eggs. Sift flour and baking soda together and add to creamed mixture. Stir in vanilla, potato chips, and nuts, if using. Drop by teaspoonsful 3" apart on ungreased baking sheet. Bake at 350°F for 10–12 minutes. **Makes 5 dozen.**

*Marion R. Andrew, United Church of Christ, Keene, New Hampshire*

# Rich Cookies

Wonderful thin tea cookies. Before baking, decorate with nuts, candied fruit, raisins, or coconut; after baking, decorate when cool with a chocolate cream frosting.

1 cup butter
⅔ cup sugar
2 eggs, well-beaten

1½ cups flour
1 teaspoon vanilla

Cream butter and add sugar gradually, then eggs, flour, and vanilla. Drop from tip of spoon in small portions on greased baking sheets, 2" apart. Spread thin with knife dipped in cold water and bake at 375°F for about 5 minutes. **Makes 3–3½ dozen.**

*Margaret Michaelsen, North Bennington Congregational Church, North Bennington, Vermont*

# Sour Cream Cookies

The old-fashioned kind, with raisins.

2 cups sugar
1 cup butter
2 eggs
3 cups flour
1 teaspoon baking soda

½ teaspoon salt
1 teaspoon nutmeg
1 cup sour cream
1½ cups raisins

Cream sugar and butter. Add eggs and beat well. Sift together flour, baking soda, salt, and nutmeg, and add alternately with sour cream to creamed mixture. Add raisins. Drop by teaspoonful on ungreased cookie sheet and bake at 375°F for 7 minutes. **Makes 5 dozen.**

*Lillian Farrar, United Church of Christ, Keene, New Hampshire*

# Saucy Bars

Similar in taste and consistency to a carrot cake.
Would also be good with Cream Cheese Frosting (page 176).

½ cup butter
1 cup sugar
1 cup applesauce
1 teaspoon vanilla
2 cups flour
1 teaspoon baking soda

½ teaspoon salt
½ teaspoon cloves
1 teaspoon cinnamon
1 teaspoon nutmeg
¾ cup raisins
½ cup chopped nuts (any kind)

Cream butter and sugar. Add applesauce and vanilla. Sift together flour, baking soda, salt, cloves, cinnamon, and nutmeg, and add to applesauce mixture. Mix well. Stir in raisins and nuts. Spread in greased 9" × 13" baking pan. Bake at 350°F for 35–40 minutes. Frost while warm. *Makes 2 dozen.*

# Frosting

¼ cup melted butter
¼ cup cream

1¾ cups confectioners' sugar
½ teaspoon vanilla

Beat together butter, cream, sugar, and vanilla.

*Margaret Wister, North Congregational Church, Concord, New Hampshire*

# Thumb Cookies

A dainty and altogether fetching confection. Keep them small.

1 cup butter
½ cup sugar
2 egg yolks, beaten
½ teaspoon vanilla

1½ cups flour
Pinch of salt
¼ cup raspberry or apricot jam

Cream butter and sugar. Add egg yolks and vanilla and beat well. Mix in flour and salt. Form into balls just big enough to hold thumbprint. Place on ungreased cookie sheet 1½" apart. Press thumb into center of each cookie to make indentation. Fill indentation with dab (about ¼ teaspoon) of jam. Bake at 350°F for about 15 minutes. They should still be very pale when baked. *Makes about 40.*

*Diana Boulet, The Oratory Chapel, East Burnham, New Hampshire*

# Date Balls

Easy to make but special enough for holidays.

2 eggs, beaten
1 cup sugar
¼ cup soft butter
1 cup (8 ounces) dates, finely chopped

½ cup chopped walnuts
1 teaspoon vanilla
2 cups crispy rice cereal
1½ cups grated coconut or 2 cups confectioners' sugar (optional)

Combine eggs, sugar, butter, dates, walnuts, and vanilla in bowl and blend well. Turn into heavy skillet and cook over medium heat for 5 minutes, stirring constantly. Remove from heat and add cereal. Mix well. Cool. Shape into small balls by rolling dough in buttered hands. Roll each cookie to coat in coconut or confectioners' sugar, if desired. Let set for 24 hours on wax paper for best flavor. *Makes 24.*

*Edna Foss, Suncook United Methodist Church, Suncook, New Hampshire*

# Frosted Orange Cookies

Passed down through several generations of a Kansas family,
these tender cookies are really good keepers.

3 cups flour
2 teaspoons baking powder
½ teaspoon baking soda
⅛ teaspoon salt
1 orange
3/4 cup solid vegetable shortening
1½ cups light brown sugar

2 eggs, beaten
½ cup buttermilk
1 teaspoon orange extract or
   vanilla
2 cups confectioners' sugar
3 tablespoons butter, softened

On a sheet of waxed paper, combine flour, baking powder, baking soda, and salt; set aside. Grate orange rind; set aside. Squeeze 3 tablespoons of orange juice into small bowl; set aside.

In a mixing bowl, beat shortening and sugar until smooth. Add eggs, buttermilk, orange extract or vanilla, and all but 1 teaspoon orange rind. Beat until smooth. Add dry ingredients, one-third at a time, stirring until blended. Drop by teaspoonfuls on ungreased cookie sheets. Bake at 350°F about 10 minutes or until tops spring back when pressed. Remove to rack. Meanwhile, in mixing bowl, whisk confectioners' sugar, butter, reserved orange juice, and remaining 1 teaspoon orange rind until smooth. Frost cookies. ***Makes 4½ dozen.***

*Angie Johnston, Crossroads Christian Church, Shawnee, Kansas*

# Pies, Pies, and More Pies

$\mathrm{F}$ew homemakers will undertake to bake a pie for public consumption unless they are very sure of its success. For some reason, perhaps stemming from the "Home, Mother, and Apple Pie" ideal, makers of memorable pies are elevated to a high culinary pedestal in America and remembered when other cooks and their creations are forgotten. All the pies in this chapter have been tested by the ultimate critic: time. They have been enjoyed and admired year after year by families and communities across the country.

Classic Apple Pie  253

Apples and Cream Pie  254

Swedish Apple Pie  254

Wild Blueberry Pie  255

Crustless Coconut Pie  255

Blueberry-Yogurt Pie  256

Butterscotch Chiffon Pie  256

Cheesecake Pie  257

Cherry Breeze  258

Coconut Pie  258

Chocolate Angel Pie  259

Cottage Cheese Pie  259

Cranberry Parfait Pie  260

Custard Pie  260

Lemon Meringue Pie  261

Frozen Lemon Pie  262

Lemon Sponge Pie  262

Key Lime Pie  263

Pecan Pie  263

Tiny Pecan Pies  264

Raisin–Sour Cream Pie  264

Glorious Pineapple Pie  265

Kentucky Bourbon Pumpkin Pie  266

Pumpkin Ice Cream Pie  266

Impossible Pumpkin Pie  267

Pink Lady Pie  267

Raspberry Ribbon Pie  268

Pastiera Di Grano (Wheat Pie)  268

Strawberry Crumb Pie  270

Strawberry Parfait Pie  270

Mile-High Strawberry Pie  271

Banana Split Pie  271

# Classic Apple Pie

Need we say more . . .

## Crust

2⅔  **cup flour**

1  **teaspoon salt**

1  **cup shortening**

½  **cup (approximately) cold water**

Mix flour, salt, and shortening (I use margarine) until consistency of cornmeal. Add water until dough sticks together and you can form it into a ball. Divide dough in 2 halves. Roll out 1 half to fit 10" pie plate. Line plate with pastry.

## Filling

12  **cups apples, peeled, cored, and sliced (10–12 large apples)**

¾  **cup sugar**

1  **tablespoon lemon juice**

1  **teaspoon nutmeg**

1  **teaspoon cinnamon**

1  **tablespoon butter**

Slice apples into 10" pie plate until heaping full. Then turn apples into bowl along with sugar, lemon juice, nutmeg, and cinnamon. Mix well. Return apple mixture to pie plate, pressing apples firmly as you do. Dot with butter. Roll out second half of pastry and place on top of pie, sealing edges firmly. Slash the letter *A* in top to let steam out. Bake at 425°F for 20 minutes, reduce heat to 400°F, and bake another 20 minutes. Then reduce heat again to 375°F for 20 minutes more, or until crust is nicely browned and apples feel done when you put knife through slashed *A*. If you use McIntosh apples, this may not take whole hour. ***Serves 12.***

*Moira Burnham, Church of the Epiphany, New York, New York*

# Apples and Cream Pie

Apple pie with an attractive difference.

4 medium apples, peeled, cored, and sliced
1 unbaked 9" pie shell
1 cup whipping cream
3 tablespoons flour
1 teaspoon cinnamon

¼ teaspoon nutmeg
1 cup sugar
1 egg, beaten
1 teaspoon vanilla
⅛ teaspoon salt
¾ cup coarsely chopped walnuts

Arrange apples in pie shell. Mix together cream, flour, cinnamon, nutmeg, sugar, egg, vanilla, and salt until well-blended. Pour over apples. Sprinkle with walnuts. Bake at 450°F for 10 minutes, then reduce heat to 350°F and bake until apples are tender, 35–40 minutes. *Makes one 9" pie.*

*Evelyn H. Chase, Concord Unitarian Church, New Hampshire*

# Swedish Apple Pie

Apples with a crunchy topping instead of a pie crust.

7 medium apples, peeled, cored, and sliced
1 tablespoon + 1 cup sugar
1 tablespoon cinnamon
¾ cup melted butter

1 cup flour
1 egg, beaten
1½ cups chopped nuts (any kind)
Pinch of salt

Fill 9" pie pan two-thirds full of apple slices. Sprinkle with 1 tablespoon sugar and cinnamon. In medium bowl, combine butter, remaining 1 cup sugar, flour, egg, nuts, and salt. Spread over apples in pan to cover. Bake at 350°F for 45 minutes, or until golden brown. *Serves 6–8.*

*Eldora Hager, United Church of Christ, Keene, New Hampshire*

# Wild Blueberry Pie

The lemon and spices make this blueberry pie something really special. Cultivated berries may be substituted for the wild ones.

¾ cup sugar
3½ tablespoons quick-cooking tapioca
¼ teaspoon salt
½ teaspoon cinnamon
¼ teaspoon cloves
1 tablespoon lemon juice

4 cups fresh wild blueberries, or frozen berries, thawed
1 unbaked 9" pastry shell, and pastry for lattice crust
1 tablespoon butter + 2 tablespoons melted butter
2 tablespoons sugar

Combine sugar, tapioca, salt, cinnamon, and cloves. Mix with lemon juice and blueberries. Turn into unbaked pastry shell. Dot with 1 tablespoon butter. Top with lattice crust. Brush with melted butter and sprinkle with sugar. Cover edges with foil to prevent burning and bake at 425°F for 30 minutes. Remove foil and bake 10 more minutes, or until crust is browned. *Serves 8.*

*Carol Jensen, The United Church, Hardwick, Vermont*

# Crustless Coconut Pie

Though there is no crust, the dessert bakes into a pie and cuts like one.

4 eggs
¼ cup butter
1 cup sugar
¼ cup flour
½ teaspoon baking powder

2 cups milk
1 teaspoon vanilla
¼ teaspoon salt
1 cup coconut

In blender, combine eggs, butter, sugar, flour, baking powder, milk, vanilla, salt, and coconut. Blend until smooth. Pour into greased 10" pie pan. Bake at 350°F for 1 hour. *Serves 8.*

*Pauline Hammond, Free Will Baptist Church, Northwood, New Hampshire*

# Blueberry-Yogurt Pie

Creamy and smooth, this dessert is very rich in a graham cracker crust.

1 envelope (1 tablespoon)
   unflavored gelatin
½ cup sugar
½ teaspoon salt
¼ cup water
2 slightly beaten egg yolks
1 cup cottage cheese

1 cup blueberry yogurt
2 egg whites
½ cup fresh (or canned, drained)
   blueberries
1 baked 9" pastry or graham
   cracker shell
Whipped cream

Soak gelatin in a little bit of cold water for 3–5 minutes. In saucepan, combine ¼ cup sugar, gelatin, and salt; add water and egg yolks. Cook and stir over low heat until gelatin is dissolved and mixture begins to thicken. Cool. Sieve cottage cheese; stir in egg-gelatin mixture. Add yogurt and beat until well-blended. Beat egg whites to soft peaks. Gradually add remaining ¼ cup sugar, beating to stiff peaks. Fold yogurt mixture and blueberries into egg whites. Turn into pie shell. Chill 6 hours till firm. Garnish with whipped cream. *Serves 6.*

*Don Wyant, Woodmont United Church of Christ, Milford, Connecticut*

# Butterscotch Chiffon Pie

Tastes good, like butterscotch chiffon should.

1 envelope plain gelatin
¼ cup cold water
3 eggs, separated
1 cup light brown sugar
1 cup scalded milk
2 tablespoons butter

¼ teaspoon salt
½ teaspoon vanilla
¼ cup sugar
1 baked 10" pie shell
Whipped cream

Soak gelatin in cold water 5 minutes. Beat egg yolks. Gradually beat in brown sugar, then beat in milk gradually. Add butter and salt and cook in double boiler, stirring until custardlike, about 10 minutes. Stir in gelatin. Cool, then add vanilla. Beat egg whites with sugar until stiff. Fold into mixture. Pour into pie shell. Cool and top with whipped cream. ***Serves 6–8.***

*Louise Coleman, First Congregational Church, Littleton, New Hampshire*

# Cheesecake Pie

Easy to make, good to eat, and looks great. Serve with thawed frozen strawberries.

| | |
|---|---|
| 2 **packages (8 ounces each) cream cheese** | ⅔ **cup sugar** |
| 3 **eggs** | ½ **teaspoon almond extract** |
| | **Pinch of salt** |

## Topping

| | |
|---|---|
| 2 **cups sour cream** | 1 **teaspoon vanilla** |
| 3 **tablespoons sugar** | **Pinch of salt** |

Beat cream cheese until smooth. Beat in eggs. Add sugar, almond extract, and salt. Pour into greased 9" pie pan. (There is *no* crust in this recipe.) Bake at 325°F for 50 minutes. Cool for 20 minutes. Combine sour cream, sugar, vanilla, and salt. Pour over pie, return to oven, and bake at 325°F for 15 minutes more. ***Serves 8.***

*Marcia Fletcher, St. Anne's Episcopal Church, Calais, Maine*

# Cherry Breeze

No-cook filling. No-bake crust. Just blend and chill.

1 cup crushed cornflakes
⅓ cup butter, melted
1 package (8 ounces) cream
   cheese, softened
1 can (15 ounces) sweetened

condensed milk
½ cup lemon juice
1 teaspoon vanilla
1 can (21 ounces) chilled cherry
   pie filling

Mix cornflake crumbs and butter thoroughly in 9" pan. Press firmly and evenly over bottom and sides of pan to form crust. Chill. Beat cream cheese until light and fluffy. Add condensed milk and blend thoroughly. Stir in lemon juice and vanilla. Turn into crust. Refrigerate 3–4 hours, or until firm. (Do not freeze.) Top with filling just before serving. *Serves 8.*

*Woodmont United Church of Christ, Milford, Connecticut*

# Coconut Pie

The coconut rises to the top over a rich, puddinglike layer.

3 beaten eggs
1½ cups sugar
½ cup melted butter
4 teaspoons lemon juice

1 teaspoon vanilla
1⅓ cups coconut
1 unbaked 9" pie shell
   Whipped cream

Combine eggs, sugar, butter, lemon juice, and vanilla. Stir in coconut and pour mixture into pie shell. Bake at 350°F for 40–45 minutes until coconut is browned and pie has begun to set. Cool thoroughly. Pie will become firmer as it cools. Serve with whipped cream. *Serves 8.*

*Marcia Fletcher, St. Anne's Episcopal Church, Calais, Maine*

# Chocolate Angel Pie

Serve this heavenly food in small portions—a little goes a long way.

2 egg whites
⅛ teaspoon salt
⅛ teaspoon cream of tartar
½ cup sugar
½ cup chopped nuts (any kind)
1½ teaspoons vanilla

1 package (4 ounces) Baker's German Chocolate
3 tablespoons water
1 cup sweetened whipped cream
1 Heath candy bar (1.4 ounces)

Beat egg whites with salt and cream of tartar until foamy. Add sugar gradually, beating until stiff peaks hold. Fold in nuts and ½ teaspoon vanilla. Spread in 8" pan, building up sides. Bake at 300°F for 50 minutes. Cool.

Melt chocolate in water over low heat, stirring constantly. Cool until thickened. Add remaining 1 teaspoon vanilla. Fold in half of whipped cream. Pile into meringue shell. Chill 3 hours. Put rest of whipped cream on top. Grate candy bar on top. *Serves 8.*

*Barbara Lockhart, United Church of Christ, Keene, New Hampshire*

# Cottage Cheese Pie

Use of the blender is necessary to the texture of this superb pie.

4 eggs, separated
16 ounces cottage cheese
1½ cups sugar

Juice and grated rind of 1 lemon
1 baked 10" pie shell

Put yolks, cottage cheese, sugar, and lemon juice and rind into blender and blend at medium speed. Beat egg whites until stiff and fold into blended mixture. Turn into pie shell and bake at 375°F for 35–40 minutes, or until set. *Serves 8.*

*Jeannette M. Miller, Morris Congregational Church, Morris, Connecticut*

# Cranberry Parfait Pie

A festive note for Thanksgiving.

1 package (3 ounces) lemon gelatin
1 cup cranberry juice cocktail
1 pint vanilla ice cream
1 can (16 ounces) whole-berry cranberry sauce
3 tablespoons lemon juice
1 teaspoon grated lemon rind
1 baked 9" pastry shell
Whipped cream
Whole cranberries

Soak gelatin in a little bit of cold water for 3–5 minutes. Heat cranberry juice in 2-quart saucepan. Remove from heat and add gelatin, stirring until dissolved. Stir in ice cream until melted. Chill mixture until it begins to thicken. Fold in cranberry sauce, lemon juice, and rind. Pour into cooled pastry shell. Garnish with whipped cream and whole cranberries. *Serves 6–8.*

# Custard Pie

Baked egg custard in a shell. Be sure pie shell is well-chilled.

4 eggs
½ cup sugar
1 teaspoon vanilla
½ teaspoon + ⅛ teaspoon nutmeg
Pinch of salt
2½ cups warm milk
1 unbaked 9" pie shell, chilled

Beat eggs lightly and add sugar, vanilla, ½ teaspoon nutmeg, and salt. Stir in milk and pour into pie shell. Sprinkle with remaining ⅛ teaspoon nutmeg. Bake at 425°F for 10–15 minutes, or until pie begins to brown. Then reduce heat to 300°F and bake about 30 minutes longer, or until knife inserted in center comes out clean. *Serves 6–8.*

*Barbara Lockhart, United Church of Christ, Keene, New Hampshire*

# Lemon Meringue Pie

Famous among all those lucky enough to have tasted it.

1¼ cups sugar
⅛ teaspoon salt
6 tablespoons cornstarch
2 cups boiling water
    Grated rind of 1 lemon

4 tablespoons butter
3 egg yolks
½ cup lemon juice
1 baked 9" pie shell

Mix sugar, salt, and cornstarch. Add water and lemon rind. Cook gently, stirring until thickened; simmer for 10 minutes. Add butter but do not stir. Mix egg yolks with lemon juice and stir into hot sugar mixture. When thoroughly blended, put into lightly browned pastry shell and bake at 400°F for 10 minutes. Top with Meringue (see below) and continue baking at 350°F until lightly browned. *Serves 6–8.*

## Meringue

3 egg whites
    Pinch of salt

1 teaspoon lemon juice or vanilla
6 tablespoons sugar

Beat egg whites and salt until soft peaks form. Add lemon juice or vanilla and beat in sugar gradually until meringue is stiff.

*Blanche Burnett, Dublin Community Church, Dublin, New Hampshire*

# Frozen Lemon Pie

Icy-cold summer delight to serve during the "dog days."

3 eggs, separated
½ cup sugar
¼ cup lemon juice
Rind of ½ lemon, cut into
strips, with white part removed

1 cup whipped cream
½ cup vanilla-wafer crumbs

Beat egg yolks well in top of double boiler; add all but 1 tablespoon of sugar, along with lemon juice and rind. Cook over rapidly boiling water for 10 minutes, or until thickened, stirring constantly. Remove rind and chill. Beat egg whites until stiff and dry. Add remaining sugar and beat until whites hold peaks. Fold in custard and whipped cream. Butter 9" pie pan; coat thoroughly with wafer crumbs. Pour lemon mixture over crumbs, and sprinkle more crumbs over top. Freeze until firm. *Serves 6.*

# Lemon Sponge Pie

Custardy on the bottom, cakey on top.

1 cup sugar
2 tablespoons flour
1 egg, separated
Juice and grated rind of 1 lemon

1 tablespoon melted butter
1 cup milk
1 baked 8" pie shell

Mix together sugar, flour, egg yolk, lemon juice and rind, butter, and milk. Beat egg white until stiff and fold into lemon mixture. Fill pie crust and bake at 375°F for 30 minutes, or until top is brown. Reduce oven temperature to 350°F and bake for 30 minutes longer, or until firm. *Serves 6.*

# Key Lime Pie

If a pie can be gorgeous, this one is—delicious, too.

2 eggs, separated
1 can (15 ounces) sweetened condensed milk
½ cup lime juice (6–8 limes)

2–3 drops green food coloring (optional)
1 8"–9" graham cracker pie shell
3 tablespoons sugar

Beat egg yolks and mix thoroughly with milk. Fold in lime juice and add food coloring, if desired. Pour into pie crust. Beat egg whites until soft peaks form, and beat in sugar gradually until stiff. Spread over pie and put under broiler until lightly browned. Refrigerate 3–4 hours before serving. *Serves 6.*

*Mary Lewis, Christchurch Cathedral, Nassau, Bahamas*

# Pecan Pie

The whipped cream is a New England touch, but it is just as good without.

3 eggs
½ cup sugar
¼ teaspoon salt
1 cup light corn syrup
½ teaspoon vanilla

1 cup pecans, broken
1 unbaked 9" pie crust
1 cup heavy cream, whipped (optional)
Pecan halves

Beat eggs slightly. Add sugar, salt, corn syrup, vanilla, and pecans. Mix well. Pour into pie shell and bake at 300°F for 50–55 minutes. Top with whipped cream, if desired, and garnish with pecan halves. *Serves 6–8.*

*Barbara Lockhart, United Church of Christ, Keene, New Hampshire*

# Tiny Pecan Pies

Once you make these, there is no escape. You just have to go on making them!

| | |
|---|---|
| 1 package (3 ounces) cream cheese | ¾ cup brown sugar |
| ½ cup + 1 tablespoon butter | 1 teaspoon vanilla |
| 1 cup sifted flour | Pinch of salt |
| 1 egg | ⅔ cup coarsely broken pecans |

Let cream cheese and ½ cup butter soften to room temperature. Then blend. Stir in flour, and chill about 1 hour. Shape dough into twenty-four 1" balls. Press on bottom and sides of small cupcake pans.

Beat together egg, brown sugar, remaining 1 tablespoon butter, vanilla, and salt until smooth. Divide half the pecans among pastry-lined cups. Add egg mixture and top with remaining pecans. Bake at 325°F for 25 minutes, or until filling is set. Remove from pans. ***Makes 24 tarts.***

*Lucille Pineault, First Congregational Church, Littleton, New Hampshire*

# Raisin–Sour Cream Pie

Rich as rich—serve in small portions.

| | |
|---|---|
| Pastry for 2-crust pie | ¼ teaspoon salt |
| 1 cup raisins | 1 egg, beaten |
| ¼ cup sugar | 1 cup sour cream |
| 1 tablespoon flour | Vanilla ice cream |

Line bottom of 9" pie plate with half of pastry. Set aside. Put raisins through food chopper. Add sugar, flour, salt, egg, and sour cream. Heat in top of double boiler. Pour hot filling into pastry-lined pie plate. Cover with top crust, seal, and flute edges. Cut slits in top crust. Cover edge of crust with 2"–3" strip of aluminum foil to prevent excessive browning. Remove foil for last 15 minutes of baking. Bat at 425°F for 30–40 minutes, or until crust is brown and juice begins to bubble through slits. Serve warm, topped with scoop of ice cream. ***Serves 8.***

# Glorious Pineapple Pie

Not only glorious but glamorous and wickedly rich. A real star.
Best served the same day it is made.

3 egg whites
1 cup + 1 tablespoon sugar
1 teaspoon vanilla
21 crushed Ritz or similar crackers
⅔ cup chopped nuts (any kind)
1 package (8 ounces) cream cheese, softened

¾ cup confectioners' sugar
1 cup heavy cream
1 can (8 ounces) crushed unsweetened pineapple, drained
Chopped nuts for garnish

Beat egg whites until stiff, then beat in 1 cup sugar and vanilla gradually. Fold in cracker crumbs and nuts. Spread in nonstick or lightly greased 9" pie pan. Bake at 350°F for 30 minutes, then cool.

Blend cream cheese with confectioners' sugar and spread over baked crust. Beat cream with remaining 1 tablespoon sugar until stiff, and fold in pineapple. Spread over pie and refrigerate 2 hours or more. Decorate top with a few chopped nuts. *Serves 8.*

*Mildred T. Melvin, Concord Unitarian Church, Concord, New Hampshire*

# Kentucky Bourbon Pumpkin Pie

Somehow, this makes one of the best pumpkin pies ever.
Maybe it is the bourbon, but you certainly don't taste it.

| | |
|---|---|
| 1 unbaked 9" pie shell | 1 teaspoon ginger |
| 1 tablespoon melted shortening | 2 teaspoons cinnamon |
| 2 large eggs | ¼ tablespoon cloves |
| ½ cup brown sugar | 2 cups solid-pack canned pumpkin |
| 2 tablespoons molasses | 1½ cups light cream |
| ½ teaspoon salt | 1 tablespoon bourbon whiskey |

Brush pie shell lightly with shortening. Preheat oven to 450°F. Beat eggs with brown sugar, molasses, salt, ginger, cinnamon, and cloves until well-blended. Add pumpkin, cream, and bourbon and mix well. Pour into pie shell and bake on lower shelf of oven for 10 minutes. Lower oven temperature to 400°F and bake about 30 minutes longer, or until knife inserted in center comes out clean. *Serves 6.*

*Elizabeth Bauhan, All Saints Episcopal Church, Peterborough, New Hampshire*

# Pumpkin Ice Cream Pie

A frozen variation of good old pumpkin pie, this is both easy and delicious.

| | |
|---|---|
| 1 pint vanilla ice cream | ½ teaspoon ginger |
| 1 baked 9" pie shell | ¼ teaspoon nutmeg |
| ¾ cup sugar | 1 cup solid-pack canned pumpkin |
| ½ teaspoon salt | 1 cup heavy cream, whipped |
| ½ teaspoon cinnamon | |

Spread softened ice cream in bottom of cooled pie shell. Put in freezer while mixing together sugar, salt, cinnamon, ginger, nutmeg, and pumpkin. Fold pumpkin mixture into whipped cream and spread over ice cream. Freeze. Set out 20–30 minutes before serving. *Serves 8.*

*Martha Fountain, Center Congregational Church, Torrington, Connecticut*

# Impossible Pumpkin Pie

"Impossible" because the biscuit mix somehow
magically gets its act together to form a bottom crust!

2 eggs
1½ cups solid-pack canned pumpkin
¾ cup sugar
2 tablespoons butter, melted
½ cup biscuit mix
1 cup evaporated milk

1 cup water
½ teaspoon salt
1 teaspoon cinnamon
¼ teaspoon cloves
¼ teaspoon nutmeg
½ teaspoon ginger

In blender, combine eggs, pumpkin, sugar, butter, biscuit mix, milk, water, salt, cinnamon, cloves, nutmeg, and ginger. Blend on low for 2 minutes. Grease and flour 10" pie plate. Pour filling in and bake at 350°F for 45–50 minutes. *Serves 6–8.*

*Mary Nichol, First Presbyterian Church, Monroe, New York*

# Pink Lady Pie

Raspberries, orange juice, marshmallows, and whipped cream—
delicate flavor and rich texture.

1½ cups finely crushed vanilla
    wafers
¼ cup softened butter
¼ cup sugar
¾ cup orange juice

12 ounces marshmallows
1½ cups heavy cream, whipped
1 package (10 ounces) frozen
    raspberries, thawed

Blend vanilla wafers, butter, and sugar together and press firmly into 9" pie plate. Bake at 375°F for 5 minutes. Cool and chill.

Heat orange juice in double boiler, add marshmallows, and stir until melted. Cool mixture and chill in refrigerator until partially set. Fold in whipped cream, then raspberries. Pour filling into crust. Top with extra whipped cream, if desired. *Serves 8.*

# Raspberry Ribbon Pie

Light and delicious, with super eye appeal.

1 package (3 ounces) raspberry gelatin
¼ cup sugar
1¼ cups boiling water
1 package (10 ounces) frozen red raspberries
1 tablespoon lemon juice

1 package (3 ounces) cream cheese, softened
⅓ cup sifted confectioners' sugar
1 teaspoon vanilla
Dash of salt
1 cup cream, whipped, no sugar
1 baked 9" pie shell

*Red Layers:* Soak gelatin in a little bit of cold water for 3–5 minutes, dissolve gelatin and sugar in boiling water. Add berries and lemon juice. Stir until berries thaw. Chill until partially set.

*White Layers:* Blend cream cheese, confectioners' sugar, vanilla, and salt. Fold in small amount of whipped cream first, then fold in remainder.

Spread half of white cheese mixture on bottom of pie shell. Cove with half of red gelatin mixture. Repeat layers, ending with red layer on top. Chill until set. Garnish with more whipped cream on top, if desired. *Serves 6–8.*

*Barbara Lockhart, United Church of Christ, Keene, New Hampshire*

# Pastiera Di Grano (Wheat Pie)

The traditional Italian Easter dessert.

## Sweet Pastry

3 cups sifted flour
Pinch of salt
¾ cup sugar

¾ cup butter
4 egg yolks
1½ tablespoons milk

Sift flour, salt, and sugar into bowl. Cut in butter evenly with fingertips, knives, or pastry blender. Stir in egg yolks one at a time, mixing with wooden spoon. Work dough with hands until it is manageable and clears the bowl. Add ½ tablespoon milk at a time as necessary to hold dough together. Form into 3 balls and chill for at least 30 minutes. Roll out 2 pastry balls and line two 9" pie plates, leaving ½" overhang. Roll out remaining ball and cut into strips to use as lattice.

## Filling

1½ cups cooked soaked wheat,* tapioca, or rice
½ cup scalded milk
1 teaspoon salt (not necessary if cereal was cooked in salted water)
1 teaspoon + 1½ cups sugar
¼ cup minced glacé citron†
¼ cup orange peel
24 ounces ricotta cheese

6 egg yolks, beaten
1 teaspoon vanilla
Dash of cinnamon
Grated rind of 1 lemon
1–2 tablespoons orange flower water, or ½ tablespoon orange extract
4 egg whites, beaten stiff
Confectioners' sugar

To hot cooked wheat, tapioca, or rice, add milk, salt (if necessary), and 1 teaspoon sugar. Return to heat and simmer for 5 minutes. Remove from stove, stir in citron and orange peel, and let stand until cool.

Beat ricotta and remaining 1½ cups sugar together. Add beaten egg yolks, vanilla, cinnamon, lemon rind, and orange flower water or extract and blend well. Stir in cooled cereal and fold in egg whites. Turn filling into prepared pie shells. Arrange lattice strips crisscross over fillings to edge and, using overhang, flute heavily. Bake pies at 350°F for 1 hour, or until firm in center and crust is nicely browned. Turn off oven and leave pies in oven to cool. Serve sprinkled with confectioners' sugar. *Serves 16.*

*Margharita Amoroso, St. Mary's Church, Marlboro, New York*

*Wheat, dry or soaked, may be bought in health food stores. To make soaked wheat from dry, cover dry wheat with cold water and boil for 15 minutes, or until husks crack open. Remove husks and let wheat soak in water to cover for 24 hours. Drain soaked wheat and cook in salted boiling water in covered saucepan, stirring frequently to prevent sticking. When wheat thickens (as when making oatmeal), it is cooked.
†Glacé citron is a type of candied citrus. It is available in most supermarkets and in specialty shops.

# Strawberry Crumb Pie

Serve this different sort of strawberry pie either warm or cool, with cream.

3 pints fresh strawberries, hulled
and halved
¼ cup sugar
¼ cup cornstarch
1⅓ cups sifted flour
½ teaspoon salt

½ cup shortening
2–3 tablespoons water
¼ cup brown sugar
½ teaspoon cinnamon
½ cup light cream (optional)

Combine strawberries, sugar, and cornstarch and let stand while you make pastry. Combine flour and salt in bowl. Cut in shortening until uniform but coarse. Set aside about ⅔ cup of mixture. Sprinkle water over remainder, toss with fork, and press into ball. On lightly floured surface, roll out pastry 1½" larger than inverted 9" pie plate. Fit into plate and trim ½" beyond plate edge. Fold under to make double thickness around edge, and flute so that edge is high. Fill pastry shell with strawberry mixture. Blend reserved flour mixture with brown sugar and cinnamon. Sprinkle crumbs over strawberries. Bake at 400°F on sheet of aluminum foil for 45 minutes, or until crust is nicely browned. Pass cream, if desired, with pie. *Serves 6–8.*

# Strawberry Parfait Pie

A dainty strawberry treat that is oh, so easy to make.

1 package (3 ounces) strawberry
gelatin
1 package (16 ounces) frozen
strawberries, thawed
Water

1 pint vanilla ice cream
1 baked 9" pie shell, chilled
1 cup heavy cream, whipped
Few fresh strawberries for
garnish

Soak gelatin in a little bit of cold water for 3–5 minutes. Drain strawberries, reserving the juice, and set aside. Combine strawberry juice with enough water to make 1¼ cups liquid; heat liquid to boiling. Remove from heat and add gelatin, stirring until dissolved. Cut vanilla ice cream into chunks and add to hot mixture, stirring until melted. Fold in strawberries. Chill in refrigerator for 15–30 minutes, stirring occasionally. Spoon into pie shell. Chill for 30 minutes, or until firm. Top with whipped cream and fresh berries. *Serves 6–8.*

*Lynette R. Tuttle, United Methodist Church of the Hamptons, Hampton, New Hampshire*

# Mile-High Strawberry Pie

A celestial way to beat the heat.

1 package (10 ounces) frozen
  strawberries, thawed to mushy
  state
2 egg whites
⅛ teaspoon salt

¾ cup sugar
1 tablespoon lemon juice
½ cup heavy cream
1 teaspoon vanilla
1 baked 9" pie shell

Chill large mixer bowl and beaters in refrigerator. (Make sure they are spotlessly clean, or egg whites will not beat up properly.) Turn strawberries into bowl and add egg whites, salt, sugar, and lemon juice. Beat at top speed of electric mixer until stiff (about 20–25 minutes). Whip cream and flavor with vanilla. Fold gently into strawberry mixture. (Large mixer bowl should be completely filled.) Turn into pie shell. Place pie in freezer. Serve frozen. Do not keep frozen more than 3–4 days. *Serves 6–8.*

# Banana Split Pie

For a pretty garnish, use a vegetable peeler to shave chocolate curls
from a 3½-ounce chocolate bar.

1 prepared 9" deep-dish pie crust,
  baked and cooled or 1 large
  (9-ounce) prepared graham
  cracker or cookie crumb crust
2 medium bananas, sliced
2 packages (3.4 ounces each) French
  Vanilla Pudding and Pie Mix
3 cups cold milk

2 cans (8-ounces each) pineapple
  chunks, drained, patted dry,
  finely chopped
1 pint strawberries, sliced
1 carton (8 ounces) whipped
  non-dairy topping
1 ounce semi-sweet chocolate
  shavings

Cover bottom and sides of prepared crust with bananas. In mixing bowl, beat pudding mix and milk with whisk for 2 minutes, until thickened. Pour one-third over bananas. Top with pineapple and half of remaining pudding. Cover with strawberries and remaining pudding. Refrigerate for at least 1 hour, until pudding is firm. Spread topping over pie, swirling to make peaks. Sprinkle with chocolate. Serve right away or refrigerate for several hours. *Makes 8 servings.*

*Mel Stephenson, Estancia United Methodist Church, Estancia, New Mexico*

# Puddings, Crisps, and Such

Yummy, yummy, yummy may not always be the *best* thing for the tummy, but it is true that "a bit of sweet makes the meal complete"! Years ago, when we all had more time (and got more exercise), dessert was part of every meal. But no matter how time-pressed we are today, a good dessert still puts the seal on a meal. So take a little time to enjoy the pleasure of a well-made dessert. Just keep in mind that age-old maxim, still true today, which says that a rich dessert is best enjoyed with a light meal and vice versa.

Apple Cake  273

Apple Crumb–Crunch  273

Apple Roly-Poly  274

Maple Apple Crunch  275

Cranberry Crunch  275

Pioneer Bread Pudding  276

Steamed Chocolate Pudding  276

Cranberry Goodin'-Puddin'  277

Steamed Cranberry Pudding  278

Cream Puffs  278

Strawberry Cheesecake  280

Aunt Vi's Grape-Nuts Custard  281

Indian Pudding  281

Jewel Dessert  282

Pineapple Delight  283

Judge Peter's Pudding  283

Frosted Strawberry Squares  284

Lemon Bisque  284

Lemon Delicacy  285

Lemon Pie Filling Dessert  286

Lime-Chocolate Delicious  286

Pumpkin Shell Dessert  287

Strawberry Mousse  287

Vacation Pudding  288

# Apple Cake

Despite its name, more strudel than cake.

2½ cups flour
1 tablespoon + 1 cup sugar
1 teaspoon salt
¼ cup shortening
1 egg yolk
   Milk

¾ cup crushed cornflakes
6 cups apples, peeled, cored, and sliced
2 tablespoons quick tapioca
2 teaspoons cinnamon
¾ cup confectioners' sugar

Sift flour, 1 tablespoon sugar, and salt into mixing bowl. Cut in shortening. Drop egg yolk into measuring cup and add milk to make ⅔ cup. Stir well with fork, add to dry ingredients, and mix well. Chill pastry thoroughly. Divide in half on floured board and roll out one half to fit over bottom of jelly-roll pan. Place in pan and sprinkle with cornflakes. Mix apples with remaining 1 cup sugar, tapioca, and cinnamon, and lay on top of cornflakes. Roll out other half of pastry and cover as top crust (slit crust every 2"). Bake at 400°F for 30 minutes, or until golden brown. Glaze with confectioners' sugar thinned with a little water. *Serves 8–10.*

Opal Wilkinson, Killingworth Congregational Church, Killingworth, Connecticut

# Apple Crumb–Crunch

*Everybody* likes apple crisp! Serve with hard sauce; plain, whipped, or ice cream; or as is.

4 cups apple slices
1 teaspoon cinnamon
½ teaspoon salt
¼ cup water

¾ cup flour
¾ cup sugar
⅓ cup butter

Grease 8" × 8" pan. Put apples in pan. Sprinkle cinnamon and salt over apples. Pour on water. Mix flour and sugar and cut in butter until it reaches coarse, crumblike consistency. Sprinkle over apples in pan. Bake at 350°F for 20 minutes. Cut into squares. *Serves 6.*

Lois W. White, First Congregational Church, Newbury, Vermont

# Apple Roly-Poly

Flaky apple-filled pastry roll.

## Pastry

1½ cups flour
1 teaspoon salt

½ cup shortening
5–8 tablespoons water

Sift flour with salt. Cut in shortening. Add enough water to make rollable pastry. Roll pastry into a 12" × 14" rectangle.

## Filling

3 cups diced apples
½ cup brown sugar
1 teaspoon cinnamon or nutmeg

1 tablespoon lemon juice
2 tablespoons butter, melted

Combine apples, brown sugar, cinnamon or nutmeg, lemon juice, and butter, and spread evenly over pastry. Roll up pastry (14" side) like jelly roll. Pinch edges together to seal. Cut 3 slits in top crust, or punch design of small holes with ice pick. Place on greased jelly-roll pan and bake at 425°F for about 40 minutes, or until tender. Serve warm with heavy cream or vanilla ice cream. *Serves 6.*

*Flora C. Hammond, Unitarian Universalist Church, Keene, New Hampshire*

# Maple Apple Crunch

A whole cup of maple syrup makes this a super apple crisp.

8 baking apples (about
   2 pounds), peeled, cored,
   and sliced
2 tablespoons flour
¾ cup sugar
1 cup maple syrup
1 teaspoon cinnamon

1½ cups old-fashioned rolled oats
1½ cups flour
¾ cup brown sugar
¾ cup melted butter
1 teaspoon baking soda
1 teaspoon baking powder
½ cup chopped nuts (any kind)

Mix apples, flour, sugar, ½ cup maple syrup, and cinnamon, and put in ungreased 8" × 12" glass baking dish or 9" pie plate. Combine oats, flour, brown sugar, remaining ½ cup maple syrup, butter, baking soda, baking powder, and nuts. Spread on top of apple mixture. Bake at 350°F for 40 minutes. Good served warm with cream or ice cream. **Serves 12.**

*Evelyn I. Johnson, Our Savior Lutheran Church, Hanover, New Hampshire*

# Cranberry Crunch

Though made in a jiffy, ver-y spiffy!

1 cup uncooked rolled oats
½ cup flour
1 cup brown sugar
½ cup butter

1 can (16 ounces) cranberry
   sauce (either whole-berry
   or jellied)

Mix oats, flour, and brown sugar. Cut in butter until crumbly. Place half the mixture in greased 8" × 8" pan and cover with cranberry sauce. Top with other half of crumb mixture. Bake at 350°F for 45 minutes. Serve hot or cold with whipped cream or ice cream. **Serves 6–8.**

*Cheryl Tutt, Ascutney Union Church, Ascutney, Vermont*

# Pioneer Bread Pudding

Inspired version of an old-time favorite.

2 cups milk
3 tablespoons butter
¼ cup sugar
2 eggs
   Pinch of salt

½ teaspoon vanilla
¼ teaspoon nutmeg
½ cup raisins
2 cups bread cubes

Scald milk with butter and sugar. Beat eggs slightly. Add salt. Stir in warm milk and vanilla gradually. Add nutmeg and raisins and pour over bread cubes placed in greased casserole. Set baking dish in warm water up to level of pudding. Bake at 350°F for 1 hour. *Serves 6.*

*Shirley T. Oladell, Harwinton Congregational Church, Harwinton, Connecticut*

# Steamed Chocolate Pudding

A truly luscious pudding with a cakelike texture.

3 tablespoons butter
⅔ cup sugar
1 egg, beaten
2¼ cups flour
1½ tablespoons baking powder

¼ teaspoon salt
¾ cup milk
2 squares chocolate, melted
1 teaspoon vanilla

Cream butter and sugar and add egg. Sift flour, baking powder, and salt together and add alternately with milk to creamed mixture. Add melted chocolate and vanilla and beat thoroughly. Put in pudding mold.

Bring to boil about 5" of water in pot large enough to hold mold and be covered. Put pudding mold into pot and cover pot tightly. Cook, keeping water at simmer, for 1–1½ hours. Check water level often. Pudding is done when it springs back from touch. This is very easy to make and cooks well on woodstove. Serve with Hard Sauce. *Serves 8–10.*

# Hard Sauce

¼ cup butter, softened
1 cup confectioners' sugar

¼ cup heavy cream, whipped
½ teaspoon vanilla

Cream butter and sugar. Add whipped cream and vanilla. *Makes about 1½ cups.*

*Dianne Johnson, Dublin Community Church, Dublin, New Hampshire*

# Cranberry Goodin'-Puddin'

A baked cranberry pudding cake with a rich, foamy sauce.

1 cup cranberries
¾ cup sugar
¼ cup walnuts
1 egg

½ cup flour
¼ cup butter, melted
2 tablespoons melted shortening

Grease an 8" pie pan *well*. Spread cranberries over bottom. Sprinkle with ¼ cup sugar and walnuts. Beat egg well. Add remaining ½ cup sugar, then flour, butter, and shortening to egg and beat well. Pour batter over cranberries. Bake at 325°F for 45 minutes, or until crust browns. Serve with either vanilla ice cream or Sterling Sauce (see below). *Serves 6.*

## Sterling Sauce

½ cup butter
1 cup brown sugar

1 teaspoon vanilla
¼ cup hot milk

Mix butter and brown sugar until fluffy. Put vanilla in hot milk and dribble into butter mixture while beating in mixing bowl.

*Ruth Howes Oleskey, Concord Unitarian Church, Concord, New Hampshire*

# Steamed Cranberry Pudding

A great-tasting and great-looking holiday pudding. Needs its sauce.

2 cups whole cranberries
1⅓ cups flour
½ teaspoon salt

2 teaspoons baking soda
⅓ cup boiling water
½ cup molasses

Wash and drain cranberries. Sift flour and salt over them and dredge well. Dissolve baking soda in water and add molasses, then stir into cranberry mixture. Mix well and turn into greased and floured 1-quart pudding mold with tight-fitting cover. Place covered mold on rack in pot filled with boiling water halfway up to depth of mold. Cover pot tightly. Cook, keeping water at simmer, for 1–1½ hours. Check water level often. Pudding is done when it springs back from touch. Unmold pudding and serve with Sauce (see below) in separate bowl. *Serves 6.*

## Sauce

1 cup sugar
1 cup butter

1 cup cream
1 teaspoon vanilla

Mix together sugar, butter, cream, and vanilla. Cook until slightly thickened, stirring frequently.

*Laverna E. Murphy, Durham Evangelical Church, Durham, New Hampshire*

# Cream Puffs

Easy to make, but always impressive—a wonderful finishing touch.

1 cup water
½ cup cooking oil
½ teaspoon salt

1 cup flour
4 eggs

Bring water to boil in saucepan. Add oil and salt. Then add flour all at once and beat rapidly over low heat until mixture leaves sides of pan and forms smooth, compact ball. Remove from heat. Add unbeaten eggs, one at a time, beating *hard* after each addition, until mixture is shiny. Drop by tablespoonfuls onto greased baking sheet 2" apart. Bake at 450°F for 20 minutes. Reduce heat to 350°F and bake 20 minutes longer. Let cool. Slice off tops, scoop out filaments, and fill (see below). Top with Chocolate-Roll Icing (page 175) or Confectioners' Sugar Glaze (page 181). ***Makes 12 puffs.***

## Custard Filling

½ cup sugar
⅓ cup flour
½ teaspoon salt
2 cups milk

4 egg yolks, beaten
2 teaspoons vanilla, or
   1 teaspoon almond extract and
   1 teaspoon vanilla

Mix sugar, flour, and salt in saucepan. Stir in milk. Cook over medium heat, stirring until it boils. Boil 1 minute; remove from heat. Stir about one-third of mixture into egg yolks. Blend back into hot mixture in saucepan. Bring just to boil, then remove from heat, cool, and blend in vanilla or almond extract with vanilla. Fill cream puffs.

## Caramel Fluffy Filling

2 cups heavy cream
¾ cup brown sugar

1 teaspoon vanilla

Combine cream, brown sugar, and vanilla. Chill 1 hour. Whip until stiff. Fill cream puffs.

## Fruity Filling

1 cup heavy cream

1 cup fruit cocktail, drained, or
   1 cup mincemeat

Chill deep bowl and beaters. Whip cream until stiff. Blend in fruit cocktail or mincemeat. Fill cream puffs.

*Mary Wakefield, First Congregational Church, Rindge, New Hampshire*

# Strawberry Cheesecake

One of the very best! The tester, whose own cheesecake recipe is famous, discarded hers for this one. Lucky enough to have tasted it, we agree—superlative! If fresh berries are in season, you could skip the topping and decorate the top with fresh strawberries, blueberries, or your favorite berries.

## Crust

16 double graham crackers, crushed (about 2 cups)
½ cup butter, melted

¼ cup sugar
Dash of cinnamon

## Cheesecake

2 packages (8 ounces each) cream cheese
½ cup + ⅓ cup sugar

2 eggs
½ teaspoon vanilla
1 pint sour cream

## Topping

1½ pounds frozen sliced strawberries (about 3 cups)
1½ teaspoons cornstarch

1½ tablespoons sugar
Juice of ½ lemon

Mix graham crackers, butter, sugar, and cinnamon. Line 9" springform pan with mixture, going up 1" along sides. Mix cream cheese, ½ cup sugar, eggs, and vanilla until smooth and pour into pan. Bake at 350°F for 20 minutes. Mix sour cream with remaining ⅓ cup sugar. Pour over baked mixture and return to 350°F oven for 20 minutes. Let cool. For topping, thaw and drain strawberries, reserving liquid. Return berries to refrigerator. Stir together cornstarch, sugar, and lemon juice; add to reserved strawberry juice and bring to boil in 1½-quart saucepan, stirring constantly. Boil and stir until thick and clear. Cool, then add to berries. Spread on top of cheesecake. Refrigerate 3–4 hours. *Serves 10–12.*

*Lyn Matzke, Our Savior Lutheran Church, Hanover, New Hampshire*

# Aunt Vi's Grape-Nuts Custard

A different sort of custard dessert.

1 cup Grape-Nuts cereal
1 quart milk
1 cup sugar

2 beaten eggs
1 teaspoon vanilla

Combine cereal, milk, sugar, eggs, and vanilla, and pour into greased 2-quart casserole dish. Set dish in another pan of hot water and bake at 350°F for 1 hour, or until custard is set and silver knife inserted into center comes out clean. Stir twice during first half-hour of baking time. *Serves 8.*

*Mark Jeffreys, Elmwood Community Church, West Hartford, Connecticut*

# Indian Pudding

A recipe that has been brought to church suppers by
three generations of Mrs. Slipp's family, especially in fall and winter.

½ cup yellow cornmeal
5 cups milk
½ teaspoon salt
2 tablespoons butter
2 eggs, beaten

½ cup brown sugar
¾ cup molasses
1 teaspoon cinnamon
½ teaspoon ginger
1 cup raisins

In 2-quart saucepan, combine cornmeal, 3 cups milk, salt, and 1 tablespoon butter. Heat slowly to boil, stirring constantly. Remove from heat. Combine eggs, brown sugar, molasses, remaining 1 tablespoon butter, cinnamon, and ginger. Add to cornmeal mixture with raisins and 1 cup milk. Pour into greased 2-quart baking dish. Bake at 300°F, stirring every 20 minutes, for 2 hours. Stir in 1 more cup milk halfway through baking time.

At end of 2 hours, stop stirring, turn off oven, and let pudding set for about 30 minutes. Serve warm, topped with whipped cream or ice cream. *Serves 6–8.*

*Leeda H. Slipp, Killingworth Congregational Church, Killingworth, Connecticut*

# Jewel Dessert

Takes time to make, but a tasty and very decorative holiday dessert. Use red and green gelatins for Christmastime, orange and yellow for Thanksgiving or Halloween.

4 packages (3 ounces each)
   gelatin dessert, of which one
   must be lemon
3 cups boiling water

1½ cups cold water
2 cups whipping cream
¼ cup sugar
1 cup pineapple juice

Soak each package of gelatin separately in a little bit of cold water for 3–5 minutes. Reserving lemon gelatin, dissolve each of the other 3 in separate bowls each containing 1 cup boiling water. Then add ½ cup cold water to each bowl and stir. Pour into separate shallow pans (cake pans are fine) and refrigerate to set. Meanwhile, whip cream. Combine sugar with pineapple juice in saucepan and bring to boil. Then add lemon gelatin and cool to syrupy stage. Cut 3 cake pans of gelatin into cubes. Fold lemon-pineapple mixture into whipped cream, then gelatin cubes. Pour over Graham Cracker Crust (see below) and refrigerate at least 4 hours. *Serves 15–18.*

# Graham Cracker Crust

20 double graham crackers
¼ pound butter, softened

¼ cup sugar

Roll crackers to fine crumbs. Mix with butter and sugar and press firmly into 9" × 13" pan to form crust.

*Vera MacLeay, Plainfield Community Church, Plainfield, New Hampshire*

# Pineapple Delight

Unusual and delightful whether served as a dessert or as a side dish with baked ham.

½ cup butter
¾ cup sugar
3 eggs

1 can (16 ounces) crushed pineapple
5 slices white bread, cubed and crusts removed

Cream butter and sugar. Add eggs and beat well. Stir in pineapple (with juice) and bread cubes. Bake in 8" × 8" greased pan at 325°F for 40–50 minutes. *Serves 6.*

*Doree McCauley, Seventh Day Adventist Church, Concord, New Hampshire*

# Judge Peter's Pudding

Fruited gelatin made from scratch, this well-traveled recipe originated in New Hampshire during the 19th century but was picked up by its Vermont contributor on Cape Cod. Dried fruits should not be cut up too fine.

3 tablespoons plain gelatin
1 cup cold water
2 cups boiling water
¼ cup lemon juice
Juice of 2 oranges
⅛–¼ teaspoon food coloring (optional)

1¾ cups sugar
6 dried figs, cut up
9 dates, cut up
2 bananas, sliced
2 oranges, sectioned
½ cup walnut meats, broken up

In 3- or 4-quart bowl, dissolve gelatin in cold water, then add boiling water. Add lemon and orange juices, food coloring, if using, and sugar. Refrigerate until thickened to syrupy stage. Add cut-up figs, dates, bananas, oranges, and walnuts. Stir only enough to mix through gelatin. Return to refrigerator until set. *Serves 12.*

*Elizabeth Hughes, Old Brick Church, Clarendon, Vermont*

# Frosted Strawberry Squares

Light-'n'-easy summer dessert. Serve with a dollop of whipped cream atop each square.
Count on 6-hour freezing time.

| | |
|---|---|
| 1 cup flour | 2 cups sliced fresh strawberries |
| ½ cup chopped nuts (any kind) | or 1 package (10 ounces) |
| ¼ cup brown sugar | frozen strawberries, thawed |
| ½ cup butter, melted | 2 tablespoons lemon juice |
| 2 egg whites | 1 cup heavy cream, whipped |
| ⅔ cup sugar | |

Mix together flour, nuts, brown sugar, and butter, and spread evenly over bottom of jelly-roll pan or cookie sheet. Bake at 350°F for 20 minutes. Stir occasionally. Sprinkle two-thirds of these crumbs in 9" × 13" pan.

Combine egg whites, sugar, strawberries, and lemon juice in large bowl. Beat at high speed until stiff peaks form. Fold in whipped cream. Spoon over crumbs. Sprinkle remaining crumbs over top. Freeze 6 hours or overnight. Cut into squares. *Serves 15–20.*

*Do Buffington, First Congregational Church, Littleton, New Hampshire*

# Lemon Bisque

Make this church supper favorite with honey—you'll love it.

| | |
|---|---|
| 1 package (3 ounces) lemon gelatin | 3 tablespoons lemon juice |
| | Grated rind of 1 lemon |
| 1¼ cups boiling water | 1 can (13 ounces) evaporated |
| ⅓ cup honey or sugar | milk, chilled overnight |
| ⅛ teaspoon salt | 2 cups crushed vanilla wafers |

Soak gelatin in a little bit of cold water for 3–5 minutes, then dissolve gelatin in boiling water and add honey or sugar, salt, lemon juice, and lemon rind. Put in freezer for about 15 minutes until partly congealed. Whip evaporated milk until thick, and whip in gelatin mixture. Sprinkle 1 cup vanilla wafer crumbs evenly over bottom of 9" × 13" glass dish. Pour bisque mixture over crumbs and top with remaining 1 cup crumbs. Refrigerate. **Serves 12–15.**

*Mildred Dimock, Ellington Congregational Church, Ellington, Connecticut*

# Lemon Delicacy

Somewhat like a pudding cake, this dessert comes out of the oven
a lemon jelly topped with a nicely browned crust.

| | |
|---|---|
| 1 **cup sugar** | **Grated rind and juice of** |
| 2 **tablespoons flour** | **1 lemon** |
| **Pinch of salt** | 2 **tablespoons butter, melted** |
| 2 **egg yolks, beaten** | 2 **egg whites, stiffly beaten** |
| 1 **cup milk** | |

Sift together sugar, flour, and salt. Stir in egg yolks. Beat in milk, lemon rind and juice, and butter. Fold in egg whites. Pour into greased 8" pie plate or 1-quart baking dish. Set pie plate or baking dish in pan of hot water (about halfway up sides of pie plate) and bake at 350°F for 30–40 minutes. Serve cold. **Serves 6.**

*Mildred Lakeway, First Congregational Church, Littleton, New Hampshire*

# Lemon Pie Filling Dessert

Very rich and sweet; disappears fast. Double for 9" × 13" pan.

| | |
|---|---|
| 1 package (3 ounces) lemon pie filling (not instant) | 2 eggs, separated |
| ¾ cup sugar | 2 tablespoons lemon juice |
| 2¼ cups water | 16 ladyfingers, split |
| | 1½ cups whipped cream |

Combine lemon pie filling and ½ cup sugar in saucepan. Gradually blend in water, slightly beaten egg yolks, and lemon juice. Cook, stirring, until mixture thickens. Remove from heat. Beat egg whites until soft peaks form. Add remaining ¼ cup sugar and continue to beat until stiff peaks form. Fold into lemon mixture. Arrange ladyfingers in bowl or serving dish and pour lemon mixture on top. Chill. Just before serving, spread with whipped cream. **Serves 9.**

*Evelyn Shaw, Pilgrim Congregational Church, New Haven, Connecticut*

# Lime-Chocolate Delicious

Really elegant in both taste and appearance. Good make-ahead hot-weather dessert.

| | |
|---|---|
| 1 package (3 ounces) lime gelatin | ¼ cup lime juice |
| 2 cups chocolate wafer crumbs | 1 can (13 ounces) evaporated milk, chilled overnight in refrigerator |
| ½ cup melted butter | |
| 1½ cups hot water | 3 cups whipped cream |
| 1 cup sugar | Chocolate syrup |
| 2 teaspoons lemon juice | |

Soak gelatin in a little bit of cold water for 3–5 minutes. Combine crumbs and butter; press into 9" × 13" pan. Chill. Mix gelatin and hot water. Cool in refrigerator until consistency of unbeaten egg white. Whip, adding sugar and lemon and lime juices. Whip evaporated milk into peaks and fold into gelatin. Pour into pan and chill. Cover with whipped cream and drizzle with chocolate syrup. **Serves 24.**

*Arlene Foulds, Center Congregational Church, Torrington, Connecticut*

# Pumpkin Shell Dessert

Put it in a pumpkin shell, and there you'll keep it very well!
Combine leftovers with a package of mincemeat and make pies or tarts.

1 small (7" diameter) pumpkin or
hard-skinned squash
2 cups peeled, chopped apple
⅓ cup sugar (dash more if brown
is used)

1 teaspoon lemon juice
1 cup raisins
1 cup chopped pecans
¼ teaspoon cinnamon
¼ teaspoon nutmeg

Wash and dry pumpkin or squash. Slice off top for lid. Scrape out fibers and seeds. Mix together apple, sugar, lemon juice, raisins, pecans, cinnamon, and nutmeg. Fill pumpkin with mixture. Top with pumpkin or squash lid. Place on large pie dish. Bake at 350°F until apples are tender. Begin checking after 40 minutes—it may take as long as 1 hour and 45 minutes. Serve from shell, spooning some pumpkin with each portion. Top with sour cream or ice cream, if desired. **Serves 6.**

*Evelyn H. Chase, Concord Unitarian Church, Concord, New Hampshire*

# Strawberry Mousse

Scrumptious substitute for ice cream, this is good without macaroon crumbs, but even better with the slight hint of almond donated by the macaroons (see page 196).

½ tablespoon gelatin
1 pint fresh strawberries
⅓ cup sugar
3 tablespoons cold water

3 tablespoons corn syrup
Pinch of salt
½ pint heavy cream, whipped
½ cup macaroon crumbs (optional)

Soak gelatin in a little bit of cold water for 3–5 minutes. Wash and hull berries and sprinkle with sugar. Let stand for 1 hour, mash, and rub through sieve. In top of double boiler or in metal bowl, dissolve gelatin in cold water. Place over pan of simmering water and stir until gelatin thickens. Pour into berry puree with corn syrup and salt. Chill, and fold in cream and macaroon crumbs, if using. Freeze. **Serves 6.**

# Vacation Pudding

By its very nature, could also be called Holiday Pudding.

## Pudding

1 cup chopped walnuts
1 cup chopped dates
3 tablespoons flour
1 teaspoon baking powder

½ cup sugar
2 eggs, separated
1 teaspoon vanilla

Combine walnuts, dates, flour, and baking powder. Mix sugar with egg yolks and vanilla and add to walnut mixture. Beat egg whites until stiff and fold in. Pour into 1-quart casserole dish set in pan of hot water. Bake at 300°F for 1 hour. *Serves 6.*

## Sauce

½ cup butter
1 cup confectioners' sugar

¼ cup milk
1 teaspoon vanilla

Cream butter and sugar. Blend with milk and vanilla and warm over pan of boiling water. Serve pudding either hot or cold, with warm sauce.

*Katheryn Blood, Harwinton Congregational Church, Harwinton, Connecticut*

# Recipes to Feed a Big Crowd

$W$hether it is a wedding, church supper, scout banquet, high school reunion, block party, or teenage invasion, most everyone has to feed a big crowd at least once in a lifetime. It won't be difficult with these recipes, including everything from soup to salad, contributed by experts in the art.

Corn Chowder  290

Gazpacho  290

Old-Fashioned Biscuits  291

Sauerbraten  292

Shipwreck  292

Quick Beet Relish  293

Chicken for 16  294

Southwestern Chicken Stew  295

Three-Step Sweet and Sour Pork for 24  296

South Texas Pork Shoulder  297

Larry's Spaghetti and Meatballs  298

Chili con Carne for 25–30 People  300

Baked Beans for 25  300

Cheese Strata  301

Macaroni and Cheese for 20–25  302

Baked Onions  302

Turkey Salad for 50  304

Manchu Garden Salad for 50  304

Quick Bread  305

The More or Less Tuna and Macaroni Salad  306

Refrigerator Rolls  307

Cole Slaw for 24  307

Blueberry Muffins  308

Aunt Lois's Bran Muffins  308

Double-Chocolate Chip Pecan Cookies  309

# Corn Chowder

With cold sliced ham (or hot dogs), rolls, and salad, an excellent supper.

½ pound salt pork, cut into ¼" dice
1 pound onions, finely chopped
5 pounds potatoes, peeled and sliced
4–5 quarts water
2 gallons milk

8 cans (16 ounces each) cream-style corn
Salt
2 teaspoons pepper
¾ cup butter

Fry out salt pork, remove browned bits, and reserve. Add onions to fat, and sauté until transparent. Add potatoes and cover with water. Boil gently until potatoes are tender, and pour off cooking water. Add milk, corn, salt pork bits, salt to taste, and pepper. Heat but do not boil. Add butter at serving time. *Serves 50.*

*Mildred A. Dimock, Ellington Congregational Church, Ellington, Connecticut*

# Gazpacho

Brenda McKay relishes this recipe from her mother-in-law in Louisiana. The refreshing soup, topped with crispy croutons, is particularly welcome at summertime gatherings.

2 bottles (46 ounces each) V-8 juice
4 cups finely chopped fresh or canned tomatoes
2 cups celery, finely chopped
2 cups cucumber, seeded and finely chopped
2 cups green bell pepper, finely chopped
2 cups green onions, white and light green parts, finely chopped

½ cup red wine vinegar
¼ cup olive oil
2 tablespoons fresh parsley, finely chopped
2 tablespoons minced garlic
2 teaspoons chili powder
2 teaspoons Worcestershire sauce
1 teaspoon salt
1 teaspoon celery salt
1 teaspoon pepper
1 teaspoon Tabasco sauce (optional)

In large bowl, combine V-8 Juice, tomatoes, celery, cucumber, green bell peppers, onions, vinegar, oil, parsley, garlic, chili powder, Worcestershire sauce, salt, celery salt, pepper, and Tabasco sauce, if using. Cover and refrigerate at least 8 hours. Taste and add more seasonings, if needed. ***Makes 5 quarts. Serves 26 (³⁄₄ cup per serving)***

*Brenda McKay, Trinity Presbyterian Church, Claymont, Delaware*

# Old-Fashioned Biscuits

These freeze well. Put uncooked biscuits on cookie sheet, freeze, then put in bags to store. Bake frozen biscuits about 30 minutes at 400°F.

| | |
|---|---|
| 6 cups flour | 2 teaspoons salt |
| ½ cup dry milk | 2 teaspoons cream of tartar |
| ¼ cup baking powder | 2 cups shortening |
| ¼ cup sugar | 1¾ cups water |

Mix flour, dry milk, baking powder, sugar, salt, and cream of tartar together with fork. Cut in shortening with pastry blender. Stir in about 1½ cups water. If dry, add ¼ cup more. Turn onto floured surface, and knead 8 to 10 times. Roll dough ¾" thick. Cut with biscuit cutter. Bake at 400°F for 20–25 minutes. ***Makes 45 2" biscuits.***

*Rosamond Emerson Leland, Community Church of Durham, Durham, New Hampshire*

# Sauerbraten

In the bowl used by our test cook, this recipe used a lot of wine vinegar (1½ quarts!),
but the tenderness of the end product was well worth it.

5 pounds pot roast
  Enough liquid made up of half
  wine vinegar and half water to
  cover meat
2 teaspoons salt

1 large onion, sliced
2 bay leaves
¼ teaspoon peppercorns
3½ tablespoons cornstarch mixed
  with ½ cup cold water

Place meat in glass (or other nonmetal) bowl, and combine vinegar and water, salt, onion, bay leaves, and peppercorns. Pour over meat to cover. Put bowl in refrigerator and let stand 3–4 days, turning meat daily. At end of this time, take meat from bowl and dry off. Strain and reserve brine, removing and discarding bay leaves. Brown on all sides and cook like pot roast with about 3 cups of reserved brine. Simmer, covered, for about 4 hours, adding more liquid if necessary. Remove meat from pot. Add cornstarch and water to liquid in pot. Add reserved brine if necessary to bring up volume to 3½ cups. Simmer, stirring, until gravy thickens. *Serves 15.*

*Edith Moritz, Woodmont United Church of Christ, Milford, Connecticut*

# Shipwreck

Members of the Mission Committee at Grace United Church of Christ voted unanimously
to share this popular casserole.

3 pounds lean ground beef
12 cups diced potatoes
6 cups diced onion
3 cups diced celery
1 can (40½ ounces) kidney beans,
  undrained

5½ cups tomato juice
¾ cup uncooked rice
1 teaspoon salt
1 teaspoon pepper
2 packages (12 ounces each)
  shredded Cheddar cheese

Crumble beef evenly into two greased 5-quart rectangular baking dishes. Evenly scatter half the potatoes, onion, celery, beans with liquid, tomato juice, rice, salt, and pepper into each dish. Stir with fork to combine. Cover dishes with aluminum foil. Bake at 350°F for 1 hour. Carefully remove foil and stir. Re-cover and bake about 30 minutes or until potatoes are tender when pierced with knife. Remove foil. Sprinkle with cheese. Bake 10 minutes or until cheese is bubbly and golden. *Serves 24.*

*Marilyn Miller, Grace United Church of Christ, Lancaster, Pennsylvania*

# Quick Beet Relish

A favorite at Pilgrim Church dinners.

| | |
|---|---|
| 2 cups sugar | 1 cup water |
| 1 teaspoon salt | 1 quart finely chopped cooked beets |
| ⅛ teaspoon pepper | 1 quart finely chopped cabbage |
| 1 cup cider vinegar | ½ cup horseradish |

Combine sugar, salt, pepper, vinegar, and water. Bring to boil and pour over beets, cabbage, and horseradish. Refrigerate at least 24 hours to let season. Serve as a condiment. *Makes 25 half-cup servings.*

*Mrs. W. H. Kellogg, Jr., Pilgrim Congregational Church, New Haven, Connecticut*

# Chicken for 16

This thrifty but elegant dish can be doubled or tripled and frozen ahead for a large party.

| | | | |
|---|---|---|---|
| 4 | whole small chickens (2½–3½ pounds each, with necks and gizzards for stock) | 1 | teaspoon Italian seasoning |
| 12 | stalks celery, diced (use leaves for stock) | ½ | teaspoon salt |
| 8 | peppercorns | 2 | bay leaves |
| 4 | quarts water | 3 | cups dry white wine or vermouth |
| 8 | medium carrots, scraped and sliced | 1 | cup butter (2 sticks) |
| 8 | medium onions, sliced | 1 | cup flour |
| | | 1½ | cups heavy cream |
| | | 4 | ounces Swiss cheese, grated |
| | | 4 | tablespoons butter |

Cut up chickens as follows: Remove fat and livers (do not use in this recipe); cut out backs and put in large pot with necks and gizzards,* celery leaves, and peppercorns. Add water and simmer uncovered for about 2½ hours, or until liquid is reduced by one-half (2 quarts). Skim and strain.

Meanwhile, divide chickens into quarters (2 leg and thigh sections, 2 half-breast and wing sections), and slice celery, carrots, and onions. In 2 pots—one for leg sections, one for breast sections—place a layer of chicken, then vegetables, some Italian seasoning, and some salt. Repeat until chicken and vegetables are used up. Poke a bay leaf in each pot. Pour half of wine or vermouth into each pot and then pour in chicken stock—about 1 quart per pot. Cook on top of stove or bake at 375°F until chicken is tender—½ hour or longer. Leg meat takes longer than breast.

When chicken is cooked, strain off liquid and boil over high heat until liquid is reduced to 2 quarts. Remove and discard bay leaves. Meanwhile, melt butter, add flour, stir, and cook, bubbling, for 2 minutes (do not burn). Remove from heat and slowly add reduced stock, continuing to stir. Return to heat, stir, and cook until thickened. Remove from heat, cool slightly, and gradually add cream. Pour some of this mixture into bottom of 2 buttered baking dishes. Place leg sections in one dish, breast sections in other. Stir cooked vegetables into sauce and divide between 2 dishes. Cool uncovered. Sprinkle with grated cheese and bits of butter (2 tablespoons per container). Bake uncovered at 375°F for at least ½ hour until top is browned. Or, store covered in refrigerator or freezer. Allow longer cooking time from cold or frozen state.

*R. M. Eldredge, All Saints Church, Peterborough, New Hampshire*

*Fat and livers can be made into a nice pâté for a first course. Gizzards and neck meat may be ground up with onion and mixed with mayonnaise and seasoning for sandwiches.

# Southwestern Chicken Stew

Like most stews, this one comes together quickly and then slowly simmers itself to perfection. Be sure to make it ahead so the flavors can mellow.

7 pounds bone-in chicken pieces, skin and fat removed
Flour
½ cup olive oil
4 tablespoons minced garlic
2 cans (48 ounces each) chicken broth
1 can (28 ounces) whole tomatoes, with juice
1 can (12 ounces) tomato paste
1 tablespoon seasoned salt
1 tablespoon cumin
2 teaspoons oregano
2 teaspoons thyme
2 bay leaves

1½–2 teaspoons crushed red pepper
1½ pounds smoked kielbasa or other smoked sausage, cut into 1" chunks
2 cups 1" cubed new potatoes
2 cups 1" cubed carrots
2 cups 1" cubed zucchini
2 cups 1" cubed yellow squash
2 cups loose-pack frozen pearl onions or 1 jar (15 ounces) pearl onions, drained
1 can (15¼ ounces) whole kernel corn, drained or 1½ cups frozen whole kernel corn
1 cup chopped fresh cilantro

Coat chicken pieces with flour. Divide oil between two large pots set over high heat. Fry chicken, turning as needed, about 8 minutes, until browned on all sides. Remove and set aside. Drain all but 2 tablespoons oil from each pot. Place pots over medium heat. Into each pot, whisk 3 tablespoons flour and 2 tablespoons garlic. Sauté 30 seconds, until fragrant. To each pot, add 2 cups broth; whisk until thickened. Scrape bottoms of pots to remove browned bits. Divide the following ingredients equally between the pots: tomatoes with juice, tomato paste, seasoned salt, cumin, oregano, thyme, bay leaves, 1½ teaspoons cayenne, and remaining broth. Stir, breaking up tomatoes with back of spoon. Bring almost to boiling then reduce heat and simmer 20 minutes. Add chicken, kielbasa, potatoes, and carrots to both pots. Cover pots with lids slightly askew. Simmer 20 minutes. Skim and discard excess fat. Add zucchini and yellow squash to both pots. Cover partially and simmer 30 minutes or until potatoes are tender. Add onions and corn to both pots. Simmer about 5 minutes. Remove and discard bay leaves. Taste and add ½ teaspoon crushed red pepper, if needed. Sprinkle with cilantro. *Serves 18–20.*

*Jo Gannon, St. Daniel the Prophet Catholic Community, Scottsdale, Arizona*

# Three-Step Sweet and Sour Pork for 24

One-two-three and there's your supper!

## Step 1

5 pounds pork
4 teaspoons salt or garlic salt

Several grinds of pepper
1 cup shortening

Cut pork into 1" cubes and season with salt and pepper. Divide between two 9" × 13" pans. Add ½ cup shortening to each pan. Bake in preheated 400°F oven for 1 hour, stirring often. Remove from oven and pour off fat from pans.

## Step 2

4 large green peppers

2 cans (20 ounces each) pineapple chunks

While meat is browning, cut peppers into strips. Drain pineapple and reserve juice. Set aside.

## Step 3

1 cup cornstarch, mixed with 1 cup reserved pineapple juice (above)
3 cups sugar

8 cups (2 quarts) chicken stock
3 cups cider vinegar
½ cup soy sauce

Combine cornstarch mixture, sugar, stock, vinegar, and soy sauce. Mix in green peppers and pineapple chunks. Divide entire mixture evenly between 2 pans of cooked, drained meat and return to 400°F oven for 45 minutes, stirring often. Serve over rice.

*R. M. Eldredge, All Saints Church, Peterborough, New Hampshire*

# South Texas Pork Shoulder

An American adaptation of pit barbecue from Mexico's Yucatan region, this spicy pork is so tender you can shred it with a fork. Serve with steaming corn tortillas to soak up the fragrant gravy.

| | |
|---|---|
| 7 pounds pork shoulder roast | 2 teaspoons pepper |
| 2 large red onions, each cut into 8 wedges | 1½ teaspoons cumin |
| 6 banana peppers, seeded and cut into thin strips | 1½ teaspoons cinnamon |
| ½ cup coarsely chopped garlic | 1½ teaspoons coriander |
| ½ cup flour | 1½ teaspoons paprika |
| 2 teaspoons salt | ⅓ cup red wine vinegar |
| | ¼ cup water |

Cut roast into 8 chunks, cutting around shoulder blade if necessary. Place pork, onions, peppers, and garlic in 8-quart slow-cooker.

In bowl, combine flour, salt, pepper, cumin, cinnamon, coriander, and paprika. Whisk in vinegar and water. Pour into pot. Toss ingredients to coat thoroughly with seasonings. Set cooker to high. Cook for 30 minutes. Reduce setting to low and cook for 7 hours. Uncover; allow to sit for 30 minutes. Skim off and discard fat that rises to surface. *Serves 14–16.*

# Larry's Spaghetti and Meatballs

By using the different quantities furnished by Mr. Barnes in this unusual recipe,
you can feed 8, 16, 24, or 32 people his zesty and authentically Italian dinner.
The pork cutlets that are in the sauce, by the way, cook down
to nothing but a taste, but an important one.

| Sauce | To Serve 8 | 16 | 24 | 32 |
|---|---|---|---|---|
| Peeled tomatoes, 28-ounce cans | 1 | 2 | 3 | 4 |
| Ground beef, pound(s) | ½ | 1 | 1½ | 2 |
| Large onions, chopped | 1 | 2 | 3 | 4 |
| Cloves garlic | 7 | 14 | 21 | 28 |
| Tomato paste, 6-ounce cans | 2 | 4 | 6 | 8 |
| Water (use 28-ounce tomato cans) | 1 | 2 | 3 | 4 |
| Water (use 6-ounce tomato paste cans) | 2 | 4 | 6 | 8 |
| Boneless pork cutlets, pound(s) | ½ | 1 | 1½ | 2 |
| Mushrooms, 4-ounce cans, drained | 1 | 2 | 3 | 4 |
| Sugar, tablespoons(s) | 1 | 2 | 3 | 4 |
| Oregano, basil, marjoram, rosemary, salt, and pepper, teaspoon(s) of each | ½ | 1 | 1½ | 2 |
| Red wine, cup(s) | ½ | 1 | 1½ | 2 |

Heat tomatoes and crush with potato masher. Brown ground beef and add to tomatoes. Sauté onions and garlic and add to sauce. Add tomato paste. Fill tomato and tomato paste cans with water and add water to sauce. Blend well and bring to a boil. Brown pork cutlets and add to sauce, along with mushrooms, sugar, oregano, basil, marjoram, rosemary, salt, pepper, and wine. Add meatballs and simmer 3 hours or longer until thick.

| Meatballs | To Serve | | | |
|---|---|---|---|---|
| | 8 | 16 | 24 | 32 |
| **Ground beef, pounds** | 1½ | 3 | 4½ | 6 |
| **Medium onions, chopped** | 1 | 2 | 3 | 4 |
| **Seasoned bread crumbs, cup(s)** | ½ | 1 | 1½ | 2 |
| **Parsley, teaspoon(s)** | ½ | 1 | 1½ | 2 |
| **Grated cheese, teaspoon(s)** | 1 | 2 | 3 | 4 |
| **Eggs** | 1 | 2 | 3 | 4 |
| **Salt and pepper** | | —to taste— | | |

Mix ground beef, onions, bread crumbs, parsley, cheese, eggs, salt, and pepper well together (a dough hook is helpful) and roll into balls. Brown meatballs on all sides and add to sauce.

# Spaghetti

One 16-ounce package spaghetti will serve 8.

# Sloppy Joes

A variation of this recipe is to omit the meatballs, but brown the amount of ground beef you would have used for the meatballs and add to the sauce to make a superb Sloppy Joe to serve on buns.

*Larry Barnes, The Unitarian Church, Peterborough, New Hampshire*

# Chili con Carne for 25–30 People

This recipe can be extended with cooked rice to feed up to 40.

| | |
|---|---|
| 10 medium onions, sliced | 1½ teaspoons Tabasco Sauce |
| ⅔ cup cooking oil | ½ teaspoon oregano |
| 6 pounds ground beef | 4 cans (28 ounces each) tomatoes |
| 6–8 tablespoons chili powder | 2 cans (6 ounces each) tomato paste |
| 2 teaspoons salt | |
| 2 teaspoons paprika | 6 cans (12 ounces each) red |
| 2 teaspoons ground red pepper | kidney beans |

Cook onions in hot oil until tender but not brown. Add meat sprinkled with chili powder, salt, paprika, red pepper, Tabasco Sauce, and oregano. Break up meat with fork and brown. Add tomatoes (with juice) and tomato paste. Cover and simmer 45 minutes or longer, adding water as needed to maintain original level of liquid. Add beans and simmer for another 15–20 minutes. You can make this ahead (with or without beans) and reheat. Freezes well, too. Two aluminum-foil roasting pans will conveniently hold the chili (without beans) for freezing. Total volume of recipe—42 cups.

*Marion S. Chaffee, First Congregational Church, Newfane, Vermont*

# Baked Beans for 25

A baked bean supper is both thrifty and popular.
Serve with hot bread, green salad or cole slaw, and dessert.

| | |
|---|---|
| 8 cups dry beans | 2½ tablespoons salt |
| Soaking water to cover | 1 tablespoon dry mustard |
| ¾ pounds salt pork | ¾ teaspoon pepper |
| 1 medium onion, finely chopped | 1 cup boiling water + boiling |
| ½ cup sugar | water to cover |
| 1 cup molasses | |

Soak beans in water to cover overnight. Next morning, add water as necessary to cover, and simmer in soaking water until bean skins wrinkle and part when blown on. Drain. Cut salt pork into 1" cubes and place about a third of the cubes on bottom of baking dish or dishes (large roasting pan or pans covered with aluminum foil are fine) along with onion. Add beans mixed with rest of salt pork cubes. Combine sugar, molasses, salt, dry mustard, and pepper with boiling water until well-mixed and pour over beans. Add more boiling water to cover. Bake, covered, in 275°F oven for about 12 hours, adding more boiling water as necessary. Remove cover for last hour of baking.

*Mrs. E. M. Charlton, Saint Matthew's Church, Bedford, New York*

# Cheese Strata

Contributor Nancy M. Alward tells us that Christ Church of Exeter, New Hampshire, served this puffy egg-and-cheese dish at a brunch for about 200 people (the recipe is easily multiplied), accompanied by sliced ham, orange juice, rolls, and coffee. "Everyone loved it, and it couldn't be easier."

| | |
|---|---|
| 48 slices day-old bread, trimmed of all crusts | 10 cups milk |
| | 2 teaspoons prepared mustard |
| 2 pounds Cheddar cheese, thinly sliced | ¼ cup minced onion |
| | 4 teaspoons salt |
| 16 eggs | ½ teaspoon pepper |

Arrange half the bread slices in greased baking dishes 2" deep. Cover with cheese slices. Top with remaining bread. Beat eggs. Add milk, mustard, onion, salt, and pepper, and blend in. Pour over bread and cheese. Refrigerate 1 hour or overnight. Bake uncovered at 325°F for about 50 minutes, or until puffy and brown. *Serves 24.*

*Nancy M. Alward, Christ Church, Exeter, New Hampshire*

# Macaroni and Cheese for 20–25

This recipe may be made all at once to be served immediately, refrigerated, or frozen. The sauce may be made ahead and frozen, defrosted, and mixed with freshly cooked macaroni.

¾ **cup butter (1½ sticks)**
¼ **cup minced onion**
1 **cup flour**
1 **tablespoon salt**
1½ **teaspoons dry mustard**
2 **teaspoons powdered ginger**
2 **quarts milk**

2 **teaspoons Worcestershire sauce**
2 **pounds sharp Cheddar cheese, cut into small pieces, finely sliced, coarsely shredded, or grated**
2 **pounds elbow macaroni**

Melt butter in 3-quart (or larger) kettle. Cook onion in butter until soft. Add flour mixed with salt, mustard, and ginger, and cook, stirring constantly, until bubbly. Turn off heat, and add milk, stirring or whisking continuously. Put back on heat and continue stirring until sauce thickens. Turn off heat, and stir in Worcestershire sauce and cheese. Stir until cheese is melted. Mix with elbow macaroni cooked according to package directions. Bake in 400°F oven in 2 buttered 11" × 15" shallow pans, or 3 buttered 2-quart casseroles, or 2 buttered 3-quart casseroles. Bake uncovered for 20 minutes, then covered for an additional 15–20 minutes. (Use aluminum foil to cover if you don't have lids.) If baked frozen, bake an additional 20 minutes.

*R. M. Eldredge, All Saints Church, Peterborough, New Hampshire*

# Baked Onions

A different way to serve onions for any size group. The number of onions depends on the number of people. Plan on 2 slices per person.

Skin Spanish onions and cut them crosswise into three slices. Place slices side by side in greased pan and season with salt, pepper, and paprika. Dot generously with butter. Add boiling stock of onion soup or canned consommé to depth of ¼" in pan. Bake at 325°F, basting for at least an hour until stock is absorbed and onions are tender and brown.

*Moira Burnham, Church of the Epiphany, New York, New York*

# Amounts to Serve 100

This chart is from the Lempster, New Hampshire, Cookbook, published in 1890.

Soup . . . . . . . . . . . . . . . . . . . . . . . . . . . . . . . . 5 gallons
Chowder . . . . . . . . . . . . . . . . . . . . . . . . . . . . . 8 gallons
Oysters (to be scalloped) . . . . . . . . . . . . . . . . . . 12 quarts
Fish . . . . . . . . . . . . . . . . . . . . . . . . . . 40–50 pounds
Meat for loaf or stew . . . . . . . . . . . . . . . . . . . . 20 pounds
Roast beef . . . . . . . . . . . . . . . . . . . . . . . . . . . . 40 pounds
Roast lamb . . . . . . . . . . . . . . . . . . . . . . . . . . . . 50 pounds
Baked ham . . . . . . . . . . . . . . . . . . . . . 3 12-pound hams
Chicken . . . . . . . . . . . . . . . . . . . . . . . . . . . . 50 pounds
Chicken salad . . . . . . . . . . . . . . . . . . . . . 15–20 pounds
Potato salad . . . . . . . . . . . . . . . . . . . . . . . . 24 quarts
Vegetable salad . . . . . . . . . . . . . . . . . . . . . . . 20 quarts
Fruit salad . . . . . . . . . . . . . . . . . . . . . . . . . . . 30 quarts
Mayonnaise . . . . . . . . . . . . . . . . . . . . . . . . . . . 2 quarts
Beets . . . . . . . . . . . . . . . . . . . . . . . . . . . . . . . 30 quarts
Cabbage (slaw) . . . . . . . . . . . . . . . . . . . . . . 12 pounds
Celery . . . . . . . . . . . . . . . . . . . . . . . . . . . . . 8 bunches
Lettuce . . . . . . . . . . . . . . . . . . . . . . . . . . . . . 12 heads
Ice cream . . . . . . . . . . . . . . . . . . . . . . . 16–20 quarts
Coffee . . . . . . . . . . . . . . . . . . 2½ pounds, 5 gallons water
Whipping cream . . . . . 1 quart cream makes 2 quarts whipped
Rolls . . . . . . . . . . . . . . . . . . . . . . . . . . . . . . . 18 dozen
Butter . . . . . . . . . . . . . . . . . . . . . . . . . . . . . 4 pounds
Layer cakes . . . . . . . . . . . . . . . . . . . . . . . . . . . . . 12
Pies . . . . . . . . . . . . . . . . . . . . . . . . . . . . . . . . . . 18

*Courtesy of Louise T. Mac Veagh*

# Turkey Salad for 50

Unmold onto a bed of lettuce or fresh spinach, and garnish.

4 quarts cooked turkey meat, diced
4 cups diced celery
1 cup finely chopped scallions
2½ cups blanched almonds, toasted
½ cup red wine vinegar
1 cup olive oil
  Juice of 1 lemon

¼ cup finely chopped parsley
  Salt and pepper
6 hard-boiled eggs, chopped
3¼ cups mayonnaise
¼ cup capers, drained
  Parsley, watercress, olives
  (black or green), and pimientos
  for garnishing

Combine turkey, celery, scallions, and almonds with ¼ cup vinegar and chill in refrigerator. Beat together olive oil, remaining ¼ cup vinegar, lemon juice, parsley, and salt and pepper to taste until well-blended. Add to chilled turkey mixture and mix well. Then add eggs, mayonnaise, and capers. Taste and add additional seasonings as required. Pack into 1 oiled 4-quart mold or 2 oiled 2-quart molds and chill for several hours

*R. M. Eldredge, All Saints Church, Peterborough, New Hampshire*

# Manchu Garden Salad for 50

A green salad with attractive touches of color and interesting textures.

## Salad

4 heads lettuce, washed and torn
6 apples, cored and diced
3 cans (11 ounces each)
  mandarin oranges, drained

½ head cabbage, shredded
½–1 cup shredded raw carrot
1 can (5 ounces) sliced water
  chestnuts, drained, or walnuts

Toss together lettuce, apples, oranges, cabbage, carrot, and water chestnuts or walnuts.

# Dressing

1 teaspoon salt
2 tablespoons wine vinegar
1 tablespoon prepared mustard
¾ cup salad oil

⅓ cup honey
1 tablespoon finely chopped
   onion
1 tablespoon poppy seeds

Combine salt, vinegar, and mustard; gradually add oil and honey until well-blended. Add onion and poppy seeds. Cover and chill. Toss salad with dressing.

*Evelyn H. Chase, Concord Unitarian Church, Concord, New Hampshire*

# Quick Bread

A crunchy slice of this biscuit-y bread can be buttered
within an hour and fifteen minutes of sifting the flour.

12 cups flour
½ cup baking powder
1 tablespoon salt
¾ cup sugar
1 cup melted shortening

2 eggs (optional)
1 quart (approximately) milk
½ cup chopped dates (optional)
2 tablespoons honey (optional)

Sift flour, baking powder, salt, and sugar. Add shortening and eggs, if using. Pour milk, and stir promptly. Add more milk if necessary until batter will pour into greased pans. Mix dates and honey and stir into batter, if using. Fill six 8" × 4" loaf pans about half-full. Bake at 425°F for 40 minutes. ***Makes 6 loaves.***

*Walter Clement, United Methodist Church, Plymouth, New Hampshire*

# The More or Less Tuna
# and Macaroni Salad

Designed for a flexible number, 50–75, without unwieldy leftovers.
With tuna, a one-dish meal; without it, an excellent salad for a bean supper.

6 pounds elbow macaroni
¼ cup salad oil
8 heads leaf lettuce
2 whole unblemished lemons
1 quart chopped green peppers
2 quarts sliced celery
2 cups chopped scallions or mild onions

2 quarts mayonnaise
1 cup lemon juice
1 cup plain yogurt
10 cups tuna (one 6½-ounce can equals 1 cup)
Salt and pepper
Garnish: whatever is handy—such as tomatoes, parsley, watercress

*DO AHEAD:* Cook macaroni as package directs in two 3-pound lots—a canning pot works well. Add 2 tablespoons oil to each pot of cooking water to prevent macaroni from sticking together. Because pot is usually too heavy to drain safely all at once, use a small sieve to remove most of macaroni from pot when done. Cool as quickly as possible and refrigerate.

*WASH LETTUCE:* Fill 2 sinks or large bowls, one with very warm water and one with very cold water. Dip each whole head upside down in warm water; leaves will open up so dirt will fall out. Quickly dip head into cold water to revive. Shake off excess water, take head apart, and put in spinner if you have one or can borrow one. Store damp lettuce divided between 2 plastic bags with a whole lemon in each one (the lemon acts as a crisping agent). Close bags securely and refrigerate.

*VEGETABLES:* Cut up green peppers, celery, and scallions or onions and store in separate containers in refrigerator.

*TO SERVE:* The above ingredients used all at once in amounts specified will make about 75 cups of salad. Mix up only the amount you think you will need. (All leftover ingredients can be used in future dishes.) Thin mayonnaise with lemon juice and yogurt. Combine macaroni, green peppers, celery, scallions or onions, and tuna. The large canning pot works well here, too. Add salt and pepper to taste. Put in serving bowl or platter and garnish. Serve lettuce separately.

*LEFTOVER INGREDIENTS:* Use macaroni in macaroni and cheese or other favorite casserole. Eat now or freeze for later consumption. Onions and green pepper can be either frozen or stored a few days in refrigerator. Use celery in casseroles, store a few days in refrigerator for salads, or freeze as creamed celery. Keep lettuce stored with the lemon in refrigerator for use in salads—a happy few days ahead with no lettuce to wash!

*R. M. Eldredge, All Saints Church, Peterborough, New Hampshire*

# Refrigerator Rolls

A soft and very light potato roll.

| | |
|---|---|
| 1 package dry yeast | 1 cup hot sieved mashed |
| 1 cup lukewarm water | potatoes |
| ½ cup butter | 1 cup cold water |
| ½ cup vegetable shortening | 1 teaspoon salt |
| ¾ cup sugar | 6–6½ cups sifted flour |

Dissolve yeast in lukewarm water. Combine butter, shortening, sugar, and potatoes. Stir in yeast and let stand 2 hours in warm room. Add cold water, salt, and flour. Cover tightly and refrigerate 24 hours. (Dough may be kept in refrigerator as long as 2 weeks.) Punch down. Shape as desired and place on greased baking sheet. Let rise 2 hours and bake at 425°F for 12 minutes. ***Makes 7 dozen rolls.***

*Helen T. Dwelley, Portland, Maine*

# Cole Slaw for 24

As a general rule, use ½ cup dressing for every 2 cups cabbage,
and allow ½ cup cabbage per person.

| | |
|---|---|
| 4 cups mayonnaise | ¼ teaspoon pepper |
| 1 cup sugar | 8 teaspoons prepared mustard |
| 1 cup vinegar | 2 teaspoons celery seed |
| 4 teaspoons salt | 12 cups shredded cabbage |

With electric mixer or blender, combine mayonnaise, sugar, vinegar, salt, pepper, mustard, and celery seed. Toss with cabbage and chill.

*Edith Downing, Killingworth Congregational Church, Killingworth, Connecticut*

# Blueberry Muffins

A good recipe to use when you need lots—makes 18 muffins as is and can be multiplied.

| | |
|---|---|
| 2 eggs | 1 teaspoon salt |
| ⅔ cup sugar | 4 teaspoons baking powder |
| ½ cup cooking oil | 1 cup milk |
| 3 cups flour | 2 cups blueberries |

Beat together eggs, sugar, and oil. Sift flour with salt and baking powder. Add to egg mixture with milk and blueberries, stirring just enough to blend. Fill greased muffin tins three-quarters full and bake at 400°F for 20–25 minutes.

*Frances Harding, Harwinton Congregational Church, Harwinton, Connecticut*

# Aunt Lois's Bran Muffins

This batter may be kept in the refrigerator for up to 2 weeks
and used in whatever portions may suit your particular needs.
Do not stir the batter after it has been refrigerated.

| | |
|---|---|
| 5 cups flour (½ cup more if you use molasses) | 1 box (15 ounces) raisin-bran cereal |
| 3 cups sugar, or 1½ cups sugar and 1½ cups molasses | 1 quart buttermilk |
| 5 teaspoons baking soda | 4 eggs |
| 2 teaspoons salt | 1 cup oil |

Mix together flour, sugar or sugar and molasses, baking soda, salt, and cereal. In a separate bowl, mix together buttermilk, eggs, and oil. Combine with dry ingredients. Bake in greased muffin tins at 375°F for 15 minutes (a little longer if batter is cold). ***Makes 6 dozen.***

*Jeananne Farrar, United Church of Christ, Keene, New Hampshire*

# Double-Chocolate Chip Pecan Cookies

This Southern take on the classic American cookie features pecans
and a double dose of chocolate—chocolate chips *and* milk chocolate. True chocoholics
may want to replace the milk chocolate with dark bittersweet chocolate.

5 cups uncooked rolled oats
4 cups flour
2 teaspoons baking powder
2 teaspoons baking soda
1 teaspoon salt
2 cups butter, softened
2 cups granulated sugar

2 cups dark brown sugar
4 eggs, beaten
2 teaspoons vanilla
1 bag (24 ounces) semisweet chocolate chips
3 cups chopped pecans
1 bar (8 ounces) milk chocolate, coarsely chopped

In blender or food processor fitted with a steel blade, grind oats into powder (in batches if necessary). Remove to large bowl. Add flour, baking powder, baking soda, and salt. Stir with fork; set aside.

In bowl of a large heavy-duty stand mixer with flat beater on high speed or by hand in large bowl, beat butter until creamy. In two additions, add granulated and brown sugars; beat until creamy. On medium speed, beat in 2 eggs until smooth. Add remaining eggs and vanilla. Beat until smooth. On low speed or stirring slowly, add one quarter of dry ingredients, blending well before adding more. Continue until all dry ingredients are mixed in. Stir in chocolate chips, pecans, and chopped chocolate. Roll dough into 1" balls and place 2" apart on greased cookie sheet. Bake at 375°F for 10 minutes (for chewy cookies) to 12 minutes (for crisp cookies). Continue baking in batches. Remove to cooling rack. ***Makes about 14 dozen.***

*D'Idra T. Plain, Second Baptist Church, Baton Rouge, Louisiana*

# Index

Note: **Boldfaced** page references indicate photographs.

Almonds
  Almond Butter Balls, 235
  Almond Spice Cookies, 235
  Far East Celery, 125
  Guisado de Pollo, 72
  Hot Chicken Salad, 60
  Manicotti with Creamed Chicken and Almonds, 56
  Nutty Chicken Pie, 65
  Real Almond Macaroons, 236
  Scripture Cake, 212
  Turkey Salad for 50, 304
Appetizers
  Chili Dip, 156
  Crispy Tuna Balls with Spicy Cheddar Dip, 100
  Dill Dip, 155
  Sesame Scallops and Salmon with Cucumber, 98
  Spicy Shrimp with Mango-Fennel Salsa, 96
  Three-Cheese Deviled Eggs, 83, **110**
Apples
  Apple Bread, 167
  Apple Cake, 273
  Apple Coffee Cake, 175
  Apple Crumb-Crunch, 273
  Apple Meat Loaf, 7
  Apple Muffins, 165
  Apple Roly-Poly, 274
  Apples and Cream Pie, 254
  Apple Upside-Down Cake, 192
  Astoria Salad, 157, **218**
  Babootie, 23
  Baked Apple and Carrot Casserole, 118
  Cabbage Slaw, 155
  Classic Apple Pie, 253
  Fruit Torte, 202
  Ham Pancake Pie, 40
  Manchu Garden Salad for 50, 304–5
  Maple Apple Crunch, 275
  Pork Tenderloin with Granny Smith Apples, 45
  Pumpkin Shell Dessert, 287

  Swedish Apple Pie, 254
  Turkey Curry, 76
Applesauce
  Saucy Bars, 249
  Special Applesauce Cake, 192
Apricots
  Apricot-Coconut Squares, **223**, 236–37
  Apricot Pound Cake, 193
  Babootie, 23
Asian-style dishes
  Asian-Style Beef Strips, 4
  Asian-Style Chicken, 58
  Asian Wilted Greens Salad, 147
  Beef Chop Suey, 30–31
  Beef or Pork Chow Mein, 16
  Chinese Pepper Steak, 5
  Far East Celery, 125
  Sesame Scallops and Salmon with Cucumber, 98
  Teriyaki Pork Loin, 46–47
  Three-Step Sweet and Sour Pork for 24, 296

Bacon
  Chicken Sour Cream Bake, 61
  Green Pea Salad, 149
  Hot German Potato Salad, 153
  Magnificent Meatballs, 11
  Mixed Salad, 148
  Pennsylvania Dutch Green Beans, **114**, 121
  Quiche Lorraine, 86–87
  Salad Excelsior, 150, **216**
  Spaghetti Carbonara, 86
  Spinach Salad, 150–51
  24-Hour Layered Salad, 146, **215**
Bananas
  Babootie, 23
  Banana Split Pie, 271
  Judge Peter's Pudding, 283
  Strawberry Nut Salad, 161
Beans
  Baked Beans, **113**, 118
  Baked Beans for 25, 300–301
  Bean Salad, 143
  Beef 'n' Bean Roll-Ups, 22

  Black Beans and Rice, 119
  Cassoulet, 51
  Chili con Carne for 25-30 People, 300
  Cowboy Bob Beans, 48
  Grace Manney's Baked Beans, 119
  Marinated Vegetable Salad, 147
  Mixed Vegetable Casserole, 135
  Pennsylvania Dutch Green Beans, **114**, 121
  Sausage Chowder, 143
  Shipwreck, 292–93
  Stewed Green Beans, 120
  Swedish Lamb and Lentil Stew, 53
  Thick Spiced Lentil Soup, 142
  T.L.C. Vegetable Casserole, 138
  Vegetable Cobbler, 136
  Wagon-Wheel Sausage-Bean Casserole, 48
Bean sprouts
  Asian-Style Chicken, 58
  Beef Chop Suey, 30–31
  Beef or Pork Chow Mein, 16
Beef
  Apple Meat Loaf, 7
  Arcadian Shepherd's Pie, 22–23, **103**
  Asian-Style Beef Strips, 4
  Babootie, 23
  Barbecue Meat Loaf, 8
  Beef Chop Suey, 30–31
  Beef/Ham Loaf with Mustard Sauce, 6–7
  Beef 'n' Bean Roll-Ups, 22
  Beef or Pork Chow Mein, 16
  Beefsteak Pie, 4–5
  Beef Stroganoff, 2
  Boeuf Abdullah (Lebanese Meatballs), 9
  Boeuf Bourguignonne, 29
  Boeuf Flamande, 32
  Burger Bundles, 16–17
  Calorie Counter's Moussaka, 18–19
  Cannelloni, 26–27, **104**
  Carry-Out Casserole, 20
  Cheesy Meat Loaf, 9
  Chicken Sour Cream Bake, 61

Chili con Carne, 33
Chili con Carne for 25-30 People, 300
Chinese Pepper Steak, 5
Classic Lasagna Plus 2, 19
Classic Meatballs, 12, **101**
Company Beef Ragout, 28
French Pork Pie (Tourtière), 44
Glorified Hash, 6
Italian Delight, 15
Jackpot Pie, 15
Larry's Spaghetti and Meatballs, 298–99
Lazy Man's Beef Stew, 30
Louisiana Beef Stew, 31
Magnificent Meatballs, 11
Meatballs and Green Noodles, 10
Old-Fashioned Boiled Dinner, 3
One-Dish Ground Beef, 21
Pastitsio (Greek Macaroni Pie), 25
Quick Hamburger and Potato Casserole, 20–21
Red Flannel Hash, 3
Roast "Lion," 2
Sauerbraten, 292
Shipwreck, 292–93
Sloppy Joes, 299
Snowtime Beef Casserole, 17, **102**
Spaghetti Pie, 24
Mouthwatering Mouthwatering Tamale Pie, 18
Beets
Harvard Beets, 120
Molded Beet Salad, 144, **214**
Old-Fashioned Boiled Dinner, 3
Orangey Beets, 121
Quick Beet Relish, 293
Red Flannel Hash, 3
Bell peppers
Brunch Eggs, 83
Chinese Pepper Steak, 5
Gazpacho, 290–91
Ham and Eggs Brunch Casserole, 84–85
Marinated Vegetable Salad, 147
Mixed Vegetables Italienne, 136–37
The More or Less Tuna and Macaroni Salad, 306
Pork Chop Roast with Honeyed Sweet Potatoes, 46
Sweet and Sour Sauce, 14, **101**
Three-Step Sweet and Sour Pork for 24, 296

Berries
Banana Split Pie, 271
Blueberry Bread, 169
Blueberry Muffins, 167, 308
Blueberry-Pineapple Loaf, 169
Blueberry Salad, 158
Blueberry-Yogurt Pie, 256
Cranberry Crunch, 275
Cranberry Goodin'-Puddin', 277
Cranberry Parfait Pie, 260
Cranberry Salad, 157
Cranberry Sauce, 42
Frosted Strawberry Squares, 284
Mile-High Strawberry Pie, **227**, 271
Oatmeal-Cranberry Bar Cookies, 241
Pink Lady Pie, 267
Raspberry Ribbon Pie, 268
Steamed Cranberry Pudding, 278
Strawberry Cheesecake, 280
Strawberry Crumb Pie, 270
Strawberry Mousse, 287
Strawberry Nut Salad, 161
Strawberry Parfait Pie, 270
Wild Blueberry Pie, 255
Biscuits
Baking Powder Biscuits, 64
Old-Fashioned Biscuits, **228**, 291
Squash Biscuits, 189
Blueberries
Blueberry Bread, 169
Blueberry Muffins, 167, 308
Blueberry-Pineapple Loaf, 169
Blueberry Salad, 158
Blueberry-Yogurt Pie, 256
Wild Blueberry Pie, 255
Blue Cheese
Shrimp and Blue Cheese Casserole, 97
Special Stuffing, 78
Bran
Aunt Lois's Bran Muffins, 308
Five-Grain Pancakes, 164
Molasses-Bran Bread, 183
Bread puddings
Cheese Strata, 301
Chicken Soufflé, 69
Ham and Cheese Almost Soufflé, 36
Mushroom Business, 85
Pineapple Delight, 283
Pioneer Bread Pudding, 276
Breads. See also Bread puddings
Apple Bread, 167
Apple Coffee Cake, 175
Apple Muffins, 165

Aunt Lois's Bran Muffins, 308
Baking Powder Biscuits, 64
Beer Bread, 168
Blueberry Bread, 169
Blueberry Muffins, 167, 308
Blueberry-Pineapple Loaf, 169
Bohemian Coffee Cake, 200
Bread Crumb Pancakes, 163
Butter Dips, 185
Cherry Coffee Cake, 175
Cinnamon Rolls, 186–87
Cinnamon Roll-Ups, 190
Cornbread, 170
Corn Muffins, 166
Crumb Cake, 177
Danish Kringle, 176–77
Danish Puff, 178
Date Nut Bread, 171
Dill Bread, 182, **219**
Feather-Light Dinner Rolls, 184
Flora's Doughnuts, 164
Irish Oatmeal Bread, 170
Julekage (Scandinavian Christmas Bread), 174
Maple Oatmeal Bread, 182–83
Milk Chocolate Doughnuts, 165
Molasses-Bran Bread, 183
Oatmeal Bread, 184
Old-Fashioned Biscuits, **228**, 291
Orange Bow Knots, 188, **221**
Parsley-Lemon Stuffing, 79
Patty's Pumpkin Muffins, 168
Pineapple-Raisin Tea Ring, 173
Potato Doughnuts, 166
Quick Bread, 305
Quick Graham Bread, 172
Raised Rolls, 189
Refrigerator Rolls, 187, 307
Rhubarb Coffee Cake, 179
Rindge Rye Bread, 185
Sausage Cake, 171
Sour Cream Coffee Cake, 178–79
Special Stuffing, 78
Squash Biscuits, 189
Swedish Coffee Ring, 180
Toast Cups, 69
Turkey Dressing, 79
Walnut-Raisin Coffee Cake, 181
White Bread, 186
Zucchini Bread, 172
Breakfast and brunch
Bread Crumb Pancakes, 163
Deli-Cakes, 163, **220**
Five-Grain Pancakes, 164

Breakfast and brunch dishes. *See also* Breads
Baked Omelet, 81
Brunch Eggs, 83
Cheese Strata, 301
Corn Flan, 88
Deviled Egg and Spinach Casserole, 84
Deviled Eggs, Shrimp, and Mushrooms in Cheese Sauce, 96–97
Easy Eggs and Tomato Benedict, 81
Glorified Hash, 6
Ham and Eggs Brunch Casserole, 84–85
Ham in Cream Sauce, 35
Kedgeree, 90–91, **111**
Mushroom Business, 85
Mushroom Quiche, 87
Quiche Lorraine, 86–87
Scrambled Eggs in Mushroom and Cheese Sauce, 82
Spaghetti Carbonara, 86
Spinach Quiche, 87
Broccoli
Broccoli and Cheese Casserole, 123
Broccoli Casserole, 122
Governor's Casserole, 37
Stuffed Broccoli, 123
The Sultan's Favorite Chicken, 57
Brownies
Brownies, 238
Chocolate Brownies, **224**, 237
Ever-So-Good Golden Brownies, 238

Cabbage
Asian-Style Chicken, 58
Cabbage Slaw, 155
Cole Slaw for 24, 307
Everlasting Cole Slaw, 154
Greek Cabbage Salad, 145
Jellied Vegetable Salad, 161
Manchu Garden Salad for 50, 304–5
Old-Fashioned Boiled Dinner, 3
Quick Beet Relish, 293
Red Flannel Hash, 3
Sauerkraut Salad, 148
Sauerkraut Surprise Cake, 206
3 Weeks Cole Slaw, 156

Cakes
Apple Cake, 273
Apple Coffee Cake, 175
Apple Upside-Down Cake, 192
Apricot Pound Cake, 193
Birthday Cake, 194
Tempting Bishop's Cake, 193, **222**
Bohemian Coffee Cake, 200
Broiler Cake, 195
Cherry Coffee Cake, 175
Chocolate Roll, 199
Cottage Pudding, 201
Crumb Cake, 177
Danish Kringle, 176–77
Danish Puff, 178
Extra-Rich Chocolate Cake, 197
Fresh Pear Cake, 205
Fruit Cocktail Cake, 197
Fruit Torte, 202
Key Lime Cake, 202–3
Mayonnaise Cake, 203
Molasses Cake, 204
Mother's Hot Weather Cake, 204–5
Oatmeal Cake, 211
Pineapple Nut Cake, 207
Pineapple-Raisin Tea Ring, 173
Pineapple Upside-Down Cake, 208
Poppy Seed Cake, 208–9
Pound Cake, 209
Pumpkin Cake, 210
Red Velvet Cake, 196
Rhubarb Coffee Cake, 179
Satin's Velvet Robe Cake, 198
Sauerkraut Surprise Cake, 206
Sausage Cake, 171
Scripture Cake, 212
Sour Cream Coffee Cake, 178–79
Special Applesauce Cake, 192
Sponge Cake with Orange Sauce, 229
Strawberry Cheesecake, 280
Swedish Coffee Ring, 180
Upside-Down Gingerbread, 232
Wacky Cake, 232–33
Walnut Cake, 233
Walnut-Raisin Coffee Cake, 181
White Cake, 230
Yogurt Cake Dessert, 230–31
Carrots
Baked Apple and Carrot Casserole, 118
Carrot Casserole, **115**, 124

Carrots Excelsior, 124
Chicken Pie with Biscuit Topping, 64
Chicken Pie with Crust, 63, **107**
Company Beef Ragout, 28
Copper Pennies, 144–45
Everlasting Cole Slaw, 154
Jellied Vegetable Salad, 161
Lazy Man's Beef Stew, 30
Louisiana Beef Stew, 31
Marinated Vegetable Salad, 147
Mixed Vegetable Casserole, 135
Mixed Vegetables Italienne, 136–37
Old-Fashioned Boiled Dinner, 3
Red Flannel Hash, 3
Roasted Herbed Vegetables, 137
Southwestern Chicken Stew, 295
Summer Delight, 132–33
Vegetable Cobbler, 136
Cauliflower
Governor's Casserole, 37
24-Hour Layered Salad, 146, **215**
Celery
Asian-Style Beef Strips, 4
Beef or Pork Chow Mein, 16
Chicken Rice Casserole, 66–67
Chinese Pepper Steak, 5
Cranberry Salad, 157
Far East Celery, 125
Gazpacho, 290–91
Green Pea Salad, 149
Ham and Rice Dinner, 36–37
Hot Chicken Salad, 60
Marinated Vegetable Salad, 147
Mixed Vegetable Casserole, 135
Molded Beet Salad, 144, **214**
The More or Less Tuna and Macaroni Salad, 306
One-Dish Ground Beef, 21
T.L.C. Vegetable Casserole, 138
Turkey Salad for 50, 304
Cheddar cheese
Broccoli and Cheese Casserole, 123
Cheese Strata, 301
Cheesy Meat Loaf, 9
Chicken Enchiladas, 71
Chicken Soufflé, 69
Corn Flan, 88
Governor's Casserole, 37
Ham and Cheese Almost Soufflé, 36
Italian Delight, 15
Lemon-Spinach Rice, 139

Macaroni and Cheese for 20-25, 302
Mushroom Business, 85
Shipwreck, 292–93
Shrimp and Rice Casserole, 95
Spicy Cheddar Dip, 100
Spinach Squares, 132
Super Salad Sandwich, 149
Mouthwatering Mouthwatering
  Tamale Pie, 18
Tomato-Cheese Crunch, 135
Turkey Florentine, 78
24-Hour Layered Salad, 146, **215**
Cheese. *See* also Cheddar cheese
Astoria Salad, 157, **218**
Baked Omelet, 81
Blueberry-Yogurt Pie, 256
Broccoli and Cheese Casserole,
  123
Broccoli Casserole, 122
Brunch Eggs, 83
Calorie Counter's Moussaka,
  18–19
Carry-Out Casserole, 20
Cheesecake Pie, 257
Cheese Sauce, 97
Cherry Breeze, 258
Cinnamon Roll-Ups, 190
Classic Lasagna Plus 2, 19
Corn-Zucchini Bake, 126
Cottage Cheese Pie, 259
Cream Cheese Frosting, 200
Deviled Egg and Spinach
  Casserole, 84
Dill Bread, 182, **220**
Eggplant Casserole, 125
Eggplant Italiano, 127
Fabulous Flounder Fillets, 94
French Onion Soup, 142, **213**
Glorified Hash, 6
Glorious Pineapple Pie, 265
Governor's Casserole, 37
Greek Cabbage Salad, 145
Italian Turkey Casserole, 76–77
Italian Zucchini Casserole, 139
Jackpot Pie, 15
Lemon-Spinach Rice, 139
Manicotti with Creamed Chicken
  and Almonds, 56
Marit's Fish Casserole, 91
Mushroom Quiche, 87
Pastiera Di Grano (Wheat Pie),
  268–69
Pastitsio (Greek Macaroni Pie), 25
Quiche Lorraine, 86–87

Rich Chicken Noodle Casserole, 67
Scalloped Sweet Spanish Onions,
  128
Scrambled Eggs in Mushroom and
  Cheese Sauce, 82
Shrimp and Blue Cheese
  Casserole, 97
Snowtime Beef Casserole, 17, **102**
Soft Clouds, 131
Spaghetti Carbonara, 86
Spaghetti Pie, 24
Spanish Rice, 140
Special Stuffing, 78
Spinach Quiche, 87
Squash and Hominy Dish, 134
Strawberry Cheesecake, 280
Super Salad Sandwich, 149
Three-Cheese Deviled Eggs, 83,
  **110**
Tiny Pecan Pies, 264
Tomato-Corn Rarebit, 134
Turkish Eggplant Salad, 146
Cherries
Tempting Bishop's Cake, 193, **222**
Cherry Breeze, 258
Cherry Coffee Cake, 175
Chicken
Asian-Style Chicken, 58
California Oven-Fried Chicken,
  61, **106**
Chicken à la King, 68–69
Chicken and Corn Pudding, 70
Never-fail Chicken Delicious,
  72–73
Chicken Enchiladas, 71
Chicken for 16, 294
Chicken Loaf or Ring, 64
Chicken Marengo, 73, **108**
Chicken Pie with Biscuit Topping,
  64
Chicken Pie with Crust, 63, **107**
Chicken Piquant, 59
Chicken Potato Casserole, 70
Chicken Rice Casserole, 66–67
Chicken Soufflé, 69
Chicken Sour Cream Bake, 61
Chicken Spaghetti Dinner, 66
Coq au Vin, 74
Crêpes Fasnacloich, 38
Easy Chicken Cacciatore, 74
Guisado de Pollo, 72
Ham and Chicken Luncheon Dish,
  35, **105**
Hot Chicken Salad, 60

Layered Chicken, 58–59
Lazy Chicken in Herbed Sauce, 60
Manicotti with Creamed Chicken
  and Almonds, 56
Mixed Salad, 148
Nutty Chicken Pie, 65
Paella Valenciana, 75, **109**
Peachy Chicken, 68
Rich Chicken Noodle Casserole, 67
Southwestern Chicken Stew, 295
Spring Chicken Maryland, 62
stuffings for, 78–79
The Sultan's Favorite Chicken, 57
Chile peppers
South Texas Pork Shoulder, 297
Spanish Rice, 140
Squash and Hominy Dish, 134
Chili
Chili con Carne, 33
Chili con Carne for 25-30 People,
  300
Chocolate
Tempting Bishop's Cake, 193, **222**
Brownies, 238
Chocolate Angel Pie, 259
Chocolate Brownies, **224**, 237
Chocolate Layer Bars, **223**, 239
Chocolate Roll, 199
Cocoa Frosting, 198
Double–Chocolate Chip Pecan
  Cookies, **223**, 309
Extra-Rich Chocolate Cake, 197
Forgotten Cookies, 243
Lime-Chocolate Delicious, 286
Mayonnaise Cake, 203
Milk Chocolate Doughnuts, 165
No-Bake Oatmeal Fudgies, 240
Satin's Velvet Robe Cake, 198
Sauerkraut Surprise Cake, 206
Sour Cream Chocolate Frosting,
  206
Steamed Chocolate Pudding,
  276–77
Wacky Cake, 232–33
Chowders
Corn Chowder, 290
Sausage Chowder, 143
Cinnamon
Cinnamon Rolls, 186–87
Cinnamon Roll-Ups, 190
Clams
Clam Casserole, 88
Paella Valenciana, 75, **109**
Scalloped Clams, 89

Coconut
    Apricot-Coconut Squares, **223**, 236–37
    Bohemian Coffee Cake, 200
    Broiler Cake, 195
    Coconut Pie, 258
    Crustless Coconut Pie, 255
    5-Cup Salad, 160
    Macadamia Rum Balls, 242
    Oatmeal Cake, 211
    Swedish Coffee Ring, 180
Coffee cakes
    Apple Coffee Cake, 175
    Bohemian Coffee Cake, 200
    Cherry Coffee Cake, 175
    Crumb Cake, 177
    Danish Kringle, 176–77
    Danish Puff, 178
    Pineapple-Raisin Tea Ring, 173
    Rhubarb Coffee Cake, 179
    Sausage Cake, 171
    Sour Cream Coffee Cake, 178–79
    Swedish Coffee Ring, 180
    Walnut-Raisin Coffee Cake, 181
Coleslaws
    Cabbage Slaw, 155
    Cole Slaw for 24, 307
    Everlasting Cole Slaw, 154
    3 Weeks Cole Slaw, 156
Cookies and bars
    Almond Butter Balls, 235
    Almond Spice Cookies, 235
    Apricot-Coconut Squares, **223**, 236–37
    Brownies, 238
    Chocolate Brownies, **224**, 237
    Chocolate Layer Bars, **223**, 239
    Date Balls, 250
    Double–Chocolate Chip Pecan Cookies, **223**, 309
    Easiest Peanut Butter Cookies Ever, **223**, 244
    Easy Filled Drops, 242–43
    Ever-So-Good Golden Brownies, 238
    Forgotten Cookies, 243
    Foxon Ginger Cookies, 245
    Frosted Orange Cookies, 251
    Great-Great-Grandma's Old-Fashioned Gingersnaps, 244
    Macadamia Rum Balls, 242
    Molasses Cookies, 246
    No-Bake Carob Oatmeal Bars, 240
    No-Bake Oatmeal Fudgies, 240

Oatmeal-Cranberry Bar Cookies, 241
    Pineapple Cookies, 246
    Potato Chip Cookies, 247
    Real Almond Macaroons, 236
    Rich Cookies, 247
    Saucy Bars, 249
    Sour Cream Cookies, 248
    Thumb Cookies, 250
    Vermont Ginger Cookies, 245
Corn
    Chicken and Corn Pudding, 70
    Chicken Enchiladas, 71
    Corn Chowder, 290
    Corn Flan, 88
    Corn-Zucchini Bake, 126
    Crab and Corn Bake, 89
    Jackpot Pie, 15
    Quick Hamburger and Potato Casserole, 20–21
    Shrimp and Blue Cheese Casserole, 97
    Southwestern Chicken Stew, 295
    Mouthwatering Tamale Pie, 18
    Tomato-Corn Rarebit, 134
    Vegetable Cobbler, 136
Cornmeal
    Cornbread, 170
    Corn Muffins, 166
    Five-Grain Pancakes, 164
    Indian Pudding, 281
    Italian Turkey Casserole, 76–77
    Quick Graham Bread, 172
    Mouthwatering Tamale Pie, 18
    Vegetable Cobbler, 136
Cottage cheese
    Blueberry-Yogurt Pie, 256
    Broccoli and Cheese Casserole, 123
    Carry-Out Casserole, 20
    Classic Lasagna Plus 2, 19
    Cottage Cheese Pie, 259
    Dill Bread, 182, **220**
    Rich Chicken Noodle Casserole, 67
    Snowtime Beef Casserole, 17, **102**
    Spaghetti Pie, 24
    Spanish Rice, 140
    Super Salad Sandwich, 149
Crabmeat
    Crab and Corn Bake, 89
Cranberries
    Cranberry Crunch, 275
    Cranberry Goodin'-Puddin', 277
    Cranberry Parfait Pie, 260
    Cranberry Salad, 157

Cranberry Sauce, 42
    Oatmeal-Cranberry Bar Cookies, 241
    Steamed Cranberry Pudding, 278
Cream cheese
    Calorie Counter's Moussaka, 18–19
    Cheesecake Pie, 257
    Cherry Breeze, 258
    Cinnamon Roll-Ups, 190
    Cream Cheese Frosting, 200
    Glorious Pineapple Pie, 265
    Strawberry Cheesecake, 280
    Tiny Pecan Pies, 264
Crêpes
    Crêpes Fasnacloich, 38
Crowd-feeding recipes
    Aunt Lois's Bran Muffins, 308
    Baked Beans for 25, 300–301
    Baked Onions, 302
    Blueberry Muffins, 308
    Cheese Strata, 301
    Chicken for 16, 294
    Chili con Carne for 25-30 People, 300
    Cole Slaw for 24, 307
    Corn Chowder, 290
    Double–Chocolate Chip Pecan Cookies, **223**, 309
    Gazpacho, 290–91
    Larry's Spaghetti and Meatballs, 298–99
    Macaroni and Cheese for 20-25, 302
    Manchu Garden Salad for 50, 304–5
    The More or Less Tuna and Macaroni Salad, 306
    Old-Fashioned Biscuits, **228**, 291
    Quick Beet Relish, 293
    Quick Bread, 305
    Refrigerator Rolls, 307
    Sauerbraten, 292
    Shipwreck, 292–93
    Sloppy Joes, 299
    South Texas Pork Shoulder, 297
    Southwestern Chicken Stew, 295
    Three-Step Sweet and Sour Pork for 24, 296
    Turkey Salad for 50, 304
Cucumbers
    Cucumber Sauce, 99
    Gazpacho, 290–91
    Sesame Scallops and Salmon with Cucumber, 98

Curried dishes
  Babootie, 23
  Turkey Curry, 76
Custards and flans
  Aunt Vi's Grape-Nuts Custard,
    281
  Corn Flan, 88
  Custard Pie, 260

D<sub>ates</sub>
  Tempting Bishop's Cake, 193, **222**
  Date Balls, 250
  Date Nut Bread, 171
  Easy Filled Drops, 242–43
  Judge Peter's Pudding, 283
  Vacation Pudding, 288
Desserts. *See also* Cakes; Cookies and
    bars; Pies, dessert; Puddings,
    dessert
  Apple Crumb-Crunch, 273
  Apple Roly-Poly, 274
  Cranberry Crunch, 275
  Cream Puffs, 278–79
  Frosted Strawberry Squares, 284
  Jewel Dessert, 282
  Lemon Bisque, 284–85
  Lemon Delicacy, 285
  Lemon Pie Filling Dessert, 286
  Lime-Chocolate Delicious, 286
  Maple Apple Crunch, 275
  Pumpkin Shell Dessert, 287
  Strawberry Mousse, 287
Dill
  Dill Bread, 182, **220**
  Dill Dip, 155
Dips
  Chili Dip, 156
  Dill Dip, 155
  Spicy Cheddar Dip, 100
Doughnuts
  Flora's Doughnuts, 164
  Milk Chocolate Doughnuts, 165
  Potato Doughnuts, 166

E<sub>ggplant</sub>
  Calorie Counter's Moussaka,
    18–19
  Eggplant Casserole, 125
  Eggplant Italiano, 127
  Mediterranean Lamb and
    Eggplant Bake, 52
  Turkish Eggplant Salad, 146

Eggs
  Baked Omelet, 81
  Brunch Eggs, 83
  Cheese Strata, 301
  Deviled Egg and Spinach
    Casserole, 84
  Deviled Eggs, Shrimp, and
    Mushrooms in Cheese Sauce,
    96–97
  *See also*
  Ham and Eggs Brunch Casserole,
    84–85
  Mushroom Quiche, 87
  Quiche Lorraine, 86–87
  Scrambled Eggs in Mushroom and
    Cheese Sauce, 82
  Spaghetti Carbonara, 86
  Spinach Quiche, 87
  Three-Cheese Deviled Eggs, 83,
    **110**

F<sub>ennel</sub>
  Spicy Shrimp with Mango-Fennel
    Salsa, 96
Feta cheese
  Greek Cabbage Salad, 145
  Turkish Eggplant Salad, 146
Figs
  Judge Peter's Pudding, 283
  Scripture Cake, 212
Fish. *See also* Shellfish
  Crispy Tuna Balls with Spicy
    Cheddar Dip, 100
  Fabulous Flounder Fillets, 94
  Fish Casserole, 93
  Flounder Crowns with Florentine
    Stuffing, 92–93, **112**
  Kedgeree, 90–91, **111**
  Marit's Fish Casserole, 91
  Mixed Salad, 148
  Mock Lobster Casserole, 90
  The More or Less Tuna and
    Macaroni Salad, 306
  Salmon Mousse with Cucumber
    Sauce, 99
  Salmon Pudding, 92
  Sesame Scallops and Salmon with
    Cucumber, 98
  Super Salad Sandwich, 149
Flounder
  Fabulous Flounder Fillets, 94
  Flounder Crowns with Florentine
    Stuffing, 92–93, **112**

Frankfurters
  Cowboy Bob Beans, 48
French-style dishes
  Baked Omelet, 81
  Boeuf Bourguignonne, 29
  Cassoulet, 51
  Coq au Vin, 74
  Crêpes Fasnacloich, 38
  French Onion Soup, 142, **213**
  French Pork Pie (Tourtière), 44
  Mushroom Quiche, 87
  Quiche Lorraine, 86–87
  Spinach Quiche, 87
Frostings
  Butter Cream Frosting, 233
  Cocoa Frosting, 198
  Cream Cheese Frosting, 200
  Orange Frosting, 210
  Sour Cream Chocolate Frosting,
    206
  Vanilla Filling and Frosting, 196
  Vanilla Frosting, 207
  White Frosting, 194
Fruit. *See also* specific fruits
  Fruit Cocktail Cake, 197
  Fruit Torte, 202
  Julekage (Scandinavian Christmas
    Bread), 174
Fruit salads
  Astoria Salad, 157, **218**
  Blueberry Salad, 158
  Christmas Fruit Salad, 158
  Cranberry Salad, 157
  5-Cup Salad, 160
  Foam Over the Sea, 159
  Manchu Garden Salad for 50,
    304–5
  Spicy Peach Salad, 160
  Strawberry Nut Salad, 161

G<sub>erman-style dishes</sub>
  Hot German Potato Salad, 153
  Sauerbraten, 292
  Sauerkraut Salad, 148
Ginger
  Almond Spice Cookies, 235
  Foxon Ginger Cookies, 245
  Great-Great-Grandma's Old-
    Fashioned Gingersnaps, 244
  Molasses Cake, 204
  Molasses Cookies, 246
  Upside-Down Gingerbread, 232
  Vermont Ginger Cookies, 245

Grains. *See also* Cornmeal; Oats; Rice
    Aunt Lois's Bran Muffins, 308
    Five-Grain Pancakes, 164
    Molasses-Bran Bread, 183
    Pastiera Di Grano (Wheat Pie),
        268–69
Grape-Nuts
    Aunt Vi's Grape-Nuts Custard,
        281
Grapes
    Christmas Fruit Salad, 158
Gravy
    Cream Gravy, 13
Greek-style dishes
    Calorie Counter's Moussaka,
        18–19
    Greek Cabbage Salad, 145
    Pastitsio (Greek Macaroni Pie), 25
Green Beans
    Bean Salad, 143
    Marinated Vegetable Salad, 147
    Pennsylvania Dutch Green Beans,
        **114**, 121
    Stewed Green Beans, 120
    Vegetable Cobbler, 136
Greens. *See* Cabbage; Lettuce;
    Spinach

Haddock
    Fish Casserole, 93
    Mock Lobster Casserole, 90
Ham
    Beef/Ham Loaf with Mustard
        Sauce, 6–7
    Crêpes Fasnacloich, 38
    Governor's Casserole, 37
    Guisado de Pollo, 72
    Ham and Cheese Almost Soufflé,
        36
    Ham and Chicken Luncheon Dish,
        35, **105**
    Ham and Eggs Brunch Casserole,
        84–85
    Ham and Rice Dinner, 36–37
    Ham in Cream Sauce, 35
    Ham Loaf with Cranberry Sauce,
        42
    Ham Pancake Pie, 40
    Mushroom Quiche, 87
    Pineapple Upside-Down Ham
        Loaf, 39
    Spinach Quiche, 87
    Sweet Ham and Pork Loaf, 41

Hash
    Glorified Hash, 6
    Red Flannel Hash, 3
Hominy
    Squash and Hominy Dish, 134

Icings and glazes
    Chocolate-Roll Icing, 199
    Confectioners' Sugar Glaze, 205
Italian-style dishes
    Cannelloni, 26–27, **104**
    Classic Lasagna Plus 2, 19
    Easy Chicken Cacciatore, 74
    Eggplant Italiano, 127
    Italian Delight, 15
    Italian Turkey Casserole, 76–77
    Italian Zucchini Casserole, 139
    Larry's Spaghetti and Meatballs,
        298–99
    Manicotti with Creamed Chicken
        and Almonds, 56
    Mixed Vegetables Italienne,
        136–37
    Pastiera Di Grano (Wheat Pie),
        268–69
    Spaghetti Carbonara, 86

Lamb
    Cassoulet, 51
    Lamb Poulette, 54
    Lamb-Rice Casserole, 49
    Mediterranean Lamb and
        Eggplant Bake, 52
    Rosemary Lamb Stew, 53
    Slow-Cooker Middle-Eastern
        Lamb Shanks, 50
    Swedish Lamb and Lentil Stew, 53
Lasagna
    Classic Lasagna Plus 2, 19
Lemons
    Frozen Lemon Pie, 262
    Lemon Bisque, 284–85
    Lemon Delicacy, 285
    Lemon Meringue Pie, 261
    Lemon Nutmeg Sauce, 201
    Lemon Pie Filling Dessert, 286
    Lemon-Spinach Rice, 139
    Lemon Sponge Pie, 262
    Parsley-Lemon Stuffing, 79
Lentils
    Swedish Lamb and Lentil Stew, 53
    Thick Spiced Lentil Soup, 142

Lettuce
    Asian Wilted Greens Salad, 147
    Main Dish Potato Salad, 152
    Manchu Garden Salad for 50,
        304–5
    Mixed Salad, 148
    The More or Less Tuna and
        Macaroni Salad, 306
    Salad Excelsior, 150, **216**
    24-Hour Layered Salad, 146, **215**
Lima Beans
    Mixed Vegetable Casserole, 135
    T.L.C. Vegetable Casserole, 138
    Vegetable Cobbler, 136
    Wagon-Wheel Sausage-Bean
        Casserole, 48
Limes
    Key Lime Cake, 202–3
    Key Lime Pie, **225**, 263
    Lime-Chocolate Delicious, 286

Macaroni
    Macaroni and Cheese for 20-25, 302
    Marit's Fish Casserole, 91
    The More or Less Tuna and
        Macaroni Salad, 306
    Pastitsio (Greek Macaroni Pie), 25
Main dishes, beef
    Apple Meat Loaf, 7
    Arcadian Shepherd's Pie, 22–23,
        **103**
    Asian-Style Beef Strips, 4
    Babootie, 23
    Barbecue Meat Loaf, 8
    Beef Chop Suey, 30–31
    Beef/Ham Loaf with Mustard
        Sauce, 6–7
    Beef 'n' Bean Roll-Ups, 22
    Beef or Pork Chow Mein, 16
    Beefsteak Pie, 4–5
    Beef Stroganoff, 2
    Boeuf Abdullah (Lebanese
        Meatballs), 9
    Boeuf Bourguignonne, 29
    Boeuf Flamande, 32
    Burger Bundles, 16–17
    Calorie Counter's Moussaka, 18–19
    Cannelloni, 26–27, **104**
    Carry-Out Casserole, 20
    Cheesy Meat Loaf, 9
    Chili con Carne, 33
    Chili con Carne for 25-30 People,
        300

Chinese Pepper Steak, 5
Classic Lasagna Plus 2, 19
Classic Meatballs, 12, **101**
Company Beef Ragout, 28
Glorified Hash, 6
Italian Delight, 15
Jackpot Pie, 15
Larry's Spaghetti and Meatballs, 298–99
Lazy Man's Beef Stew, 30
Louisiana Beef Stew, 31
Magnificent Meatballs, 11
Meatballs and Green Noodles, 10
Old-Fashioned Boiled Dinner, 3
One-Dish Ground Beef, 21
Pastitsio (Greek Macaroni Pie), 25
Quick Hamburger and Potato Casserole, 20–21
Red Flannel Hash, 3
Roast "Lion," 2
Sauerbraten, 292
Shipwreck, 292–93
Sloppy Joes, 299
Snowtime Beef Casserole, 17, **102**
Spaghetti Pie, 24
Mouthwatering Tamale Pie, 18
Main dishes, chicken
Asian-Style Chicken, 58
California Oven-Fried Chicken, 61, **106**
Chicken à la King, 68–69
Chicken and Corn Pudding, 70
Never-fail Never-fail Chicken Delicious, 72–73
Chicken Enchiladas, 71
Chicken for 16, 294
Chicken Loaf or Ring, 64
Chicken Marengo, 73, **108**
Chicken Pie with Biscuit Topping, 64
Chicken Pie with Crust, 63, **107**
Chicken Piquant, 59
Chicken Potato Casserole, 70
Chicken Rice Casserole, 66–67
Chicken Soufflé, 69
Chicken Sour Cream Bake, 61
Chicken Spaghetti Dinner, 66
Coq au Vin, 74
Crêpes Fasnacloich, 38
Easy Chicken Cacciatore, 74
Guisado de Pollo, 72
Ham and Chicken Luncheon Dish, 35, **105**
Hot Chicken Salad, 60

Layered Chicken, 58–59
Lazy Chicken in Herbed Sauce, 60
Manicotti with Creamed Chicken and Almonds, 56
Mixed Salad, 148
Nutty Chicken Pie, 65
Paella Valenciana, 75, **109**
Peachy Chicken, 68
Rich Chicken Noodle Casserole, 67
Southwestern Chicken Stew, 295
Spring Chicken Maryland, 62
The Sultan's Favorite Chicken, 57
Main dishes, fish
Fabulous Flounder Fillets, 94
Fish Casserole, 93
Flounder Crowns with Florentine Stuffing, 92–93, **112**
Kedgeree, 90–91, **111**
Marit's Fish Casserole, 91
Mixed Salad, 148
Mock Lobster Casserole, 90
The More or Less Tuna and Macaroni Salad, 306
Salmon Mousse with Cucumber Sauce, 99
Salmon Pudding, 92
Super Salad Sandwich, 149
Main dishes, ham
Beef/Ham Loaf with Mustard Sauce, 6–7
Crêpes Fasnacloich, 38
Governor's Casserole, 37
Ham and Cheese Almost Soufflé, 36
Ham and Chicken Luncheon Dish, 35, **105**
Ham and Rice Dinner, 36–37
Ham in Cream Sauce, 35
Ham Loaf with Cranberry Sauce, 42
Ham Pancake Pie, 40
Pineapple Upside-Down Ham Loaf, 39
Sweet Ham and Pork Loaf, 41
Main dishes, lamb
Cassoulet, 51
Lamb Poulette, 54
Lamb-Rice Casserole, 49
Mediterranean Lamb and Eggplant Bake, 52
Rosemary Lamb Stew, 53
Slow-Cooker Middle-Eastern Lamb Shanks, 50
Swedish Lamb and Lentil Stew, 53

Main dishes, pasta
Cannelloni, 26–27, **104**
Chicken Spaghetti Dinner, 66
Classic Lasagna Plus 2, 19
Larry's Spaghetti and Meatballs, 298–99
Manicotti with Creamed Chicken and Almonds, 56
The More or Less Tuna and Macaroni Salad, 306
Pastitsio (Greek Macaroni Pie), 25
Spaghetti Carbonara, 86
Spaghetti Pie, 24
Main dishes, pork
Babootie, 23
Beef or Pork Chow Mein, 16
Cajun Pork Meatloaf, 43
Cassoulet, 51
Cowboy Bob Beans, 48
French Pork Pie (Tourtière), 44
Main Dish Potato Salad, 152
Pork Chop Roast with Honeyed Sweet Potatoes, 46
Pork Tenderloin with Granny Smith Apples, 45
Roast "Lion," 2
Sausage and Rice Casserole, 41
Sausages Cooked in White Wine, 47
South Texas Pork Shoulder, 297
Teriyaki Pork Loin, 46–47
Three-Step Sweet and Sour Pork for 24, 296
Wagon-Wheel Sausage-Bean Casserole, 48
Main dishes, salad
Main Dish Potato Salad, 152
Mixed Salad, 148
The More or Less Tuna and Macaroni Salad, 306
Salad Excelsior, 150, **216**
Super Salad Sandwich, 149
Turkey Salad for 50, 304
Main dishes, shellfish
Clam Casserole, 88
Crab and Corn Bake, 89
Deviled Eggs, Shrimp, and Mushrooms in Cheese Sauce, 96–97
Gourmet Shrimp, 95
Salad Excelsior, 150, **216**
Scalloped Clams, 89
Shrimp and Blue Cheese Casserole, 97
Shrimp and Rice Casserole, 95

Main dishes, turkey
    Italian Turkey Casserole, 76–77
    Turkey Curry, 76
    Turkey Florentine, 78
    Turkey Salad for 50, 304
    Turkey Terrapin, 77
Main dishes, veal
    Main Dish Potato Salad, 152
Mangoes
    Spicy Shrimp with Mango-Fennel
        Salsa, 96
Manicotti
    Manicotti with Creamed Chicken
        and Almonds, 56
Maple syrup
    Maple Apple Crunch, 275
    Maple Oatmeal Bread, 182–83
Marshmallows
    5-Cup Salad, 160
    Pink Lady Pie, 267
Meat. See Bacon; Beef; Ham; Lamb;
    Pork; Sausages; Veal
Meatballs
    Boeuf Abdullah (Lebanese
        Meatballs), 9
    Classic Meatballs, 12, **101**
    Larry's Spaghetti and Meatballs,
        298–99
    Magnificent Meatballs, 11
    Meatballs and Green Noodles, 10
    sauces for, 13–14
Meat loaf
    Apple Meat Loaf, 7
    Barbecue Meat Loaf, 8
    Beef/Ham Loaf with Mustard
        Sauce, 6–7
    Cajun Pork Meatloaf, 43
    Cheesy Meat Loaf, 9
    Chicken Loaf or Ring, 64
    Ham Loaf with Cranberry Sauce,
        42
    Pineapple Upside-Down Ham
        Loaf, 39
    Sweet Ham and Pork Loaf, 41
Middle Eastern–style dishes
    Boeuf Abdullah (Lebanese
        Meatballs), 9
    Slow-Cooker Middle-Eastern
        Lamb Shanks, 50
    Turkish Eggplant Salad, 146
Molasses
    Almond Spice Cookies, 235
    Aunt Lois's Bran Muffins, 308
    Baked Beans, **113**, 118

Baked Beans for 25, 300–301
Beef 'n' Bean Roll-Ups, 22
Blueberry Bread, 169
Foxon Ginger Cookies, 245
Great-Great-Grandma's Old-
    Fashioned Gingersnaps, 244
Indian Pudding, 281
Louisiana Beef Stew, 31
Molasses-Bran Bread, 183
Molasses Cake, 204
Molasses Cookies, 246
Oatmeal Bread, 184
Quick Graham Bread, 172
Steamed Cranberry Pudding, 278
Upside-Down Gingerbread, 232
Vermont Ginger Cookies, 245
Mousse
    Salmon Mousse with Cucumber
        Sauce, 99
    Strawberry Mousse, 287
Mozzarella cheese
    Brunch Eggs, 83
    Classic Lasagna Plus 2, 19
    Eggplant Italiano, 127
    Italian Zucchini Casserole, 139
    Snowtime Beef Casserole, 17, **102**
    Spaghetti Pie, 24
Muffins
    Apple Muffins, 165
    Aunt Lois's Bran Muffins, 308
    Blueberry Muffins, 167, 308
    Corn Muffins, 166
    Patty's Pumpkin Muffins, 168
Mushrooms
    Asian-Style Beef Strips, 4
    Beefsteak Pie, 4–5
    Boeuf Bourguignonne, 29
    Calorie Counter's Moussaka,
        18–19
    Chicken à la King, 68–69
    Chicken Marengo, 73, **108**
    Coq au Vin, 74
    Deviled Eggs, Shrimp, and
        Mushrooms in Cheese Sauce,
        96–97
    Ham and Chicken Luncheon Dish,
        35, **105**
    Italian Turkey Casserole, 76–77
    John Russell's Mushroom-Rice
        Casserole, 122
    Layered Chicken, 58–59
    Lazy Man's Beef Stew, 30
    Meatballs and Green Noodles, 10
    Mushroom Business, 85

Mushroom Quiche, 87
Mushroom Sauce, 14
Nutty Chicken Pie, 65
One-Dish Ground Beef, 21
Scrambled Eggs in Mushroom and
    Cheese Sauce, 82
7-Minute Zucchini, 138
Special Stuffing, 78
Turkey Curry, 76
Turkey Dressing, 79
Turkey Florentine, 78
Turkey Terrapin, 77
Mustard
    Mustard Sauce, 7

Noodles
    Cannelloni, 26–27, **104**
    Carry-Out Casserole, 20
    Classic Lasagna Plus 2, 19
    Italian Delight, 15
    Jackpot Pie, 15
    Meatballs and Green Noodles, 10
    Rich Chicken Noodle Casserole,
        67
Nuts. See also Almonds; Walnuts
    Apple Bread, 167
    Tempting Bishop's Cake, 193,
        **222**
    Blueberry-Pineapple Loaf, 169
    Bohemian Coffee Cake, 200
    Broiler Cake, 195
    Chocolate Angel Pie, 259
    Cranberry Salad, 157
    Danish Puff, 178
    Double–Chocolate Chip Pecan
        Cookies, **223**, 309
    Easy Filled Drops, 242–43
    Ever-So-Good Golden Brownies,
        238
    Frosted Strawberry Squares, 284
    Fruit Cocktail Cake, 197
    Glorious Pineapple Pie, 265
    Macadamia Rum Balls, 242
    Maple Apple Crunch, 275
    Oatmeal Cake, 211
    Pecan Pie, 263
    Pumpkin Cake, 210
    Pumpkin Shell Dessert, 287
    Saucy Bars, 249
    Strawberry Nut Salad, 161
    Swedish Apple Pie, 254
    Swedish Coffee Ring, 180
    Tiny Pecan Pies, 264

Oats
    Cranberry Crunch, 275
    Double–Chocolate Chip Pecan
        Cookies, **223**, 309
    Irish Oatmeal Bread, 170
    Maple Apple Crunch, 275
    Maple Oatmeal Bread, 182–83
    No-Bake Carob Oatmeal Bars, 240
    No-Bake Oatmeal Fudgies, 240
    Oatmeal Bread, 184
    Oatmeal Cake, 211
    Oatmeal-Cranberry Bar Cookies,
        241
Omelets
    Baked Omelet, 81
Onions
    Baked Onions, 302
    Boeuf Bourguignonne, 29
    Boeuf Flamande, 32
    French Onion Soup, 142, **213**
    Onion Pie, 128–29
    Savory Onion Kuchen, 129
    Scalloped Sweet Spanish Onions,
        128
Oranges
    Christmas Fruit Salad, 158
    5-Cup Salad, 160
    Frosted Orange Cookies, 251
    Judge Peter's Pudding, 283
    Manchu Garden Salad for 50,
        304–5
    Orange Bow Knots, 188, **221**
    Orange Frosting, 210
    Orange Sauce, 229
    Orangey Beets, 121

Pancakes
    Bread Crumb Pancakes, 163
    Deli-Cakes, 163, **219**
    Five-Grain Pancakes, 164
Parmesan cheese
    Classic Lasagna Plus 2, 19
    Eggplant Italiano, 127
    Governor's Casserole, 37
    Italian Turkey Casserole, 76–77
    Lemon-Spinach Rice, 139
    Pastitsio (Greek Macaroni Pie), 25
    Scrambled Eggs in Mushroom and
        Cheese Sauce, 82
    Spaghetti Carbonara, 86
Parsley
    Parsley-Lemon Stuffing, 79

Pasta and noodles
    Cannelloni, 26–27, **104**
    Carry-Out Casserole, 20
    Chicken Spaghetti Dinner, 66
    Classic Lasagna Plus 2, 19
    Italian Delight, 15
    Jackpot Pie, 15
    Larry's Spaghetti and Meatballs,
        298–99
    Macaroni and Cheese for 20-25,
        302
    Manicotti with Creamed Chicken
        and Almonds, 56
    Marit's Fish Casserole, 91
    Meatballs and Green Noodles, 10
    The More or Less Tuna and
        Macaroni Salad, 306
    Pastitsio (Greek Macaroni Pie), 25
    Rich Chicken Noodle Casserole, 67
    Spaghetti Carbonara, 86
    Spaghetti Pie, 24
    Spaghetti Salad, 153
Peaches
    Peachy Chicken, 68
    Spicy Peach Salad, 160
Peanut butter
    Easiest Peanut Butter Cookies
        Ever, **223**, 244
    No-Bake Carob Oatmeal Bars,
        240
    No-Bake Oatmeal Fudgies, 240
Pears
    Foam Over the Sea, 159
    Fresh Pear Cake, 205
Peas
    Asian-Style Chicken, 58
    Chicken à la King, 68–69
    Chicken Pie with Biscuit Topping,
        64
    Chicken Pie with Crust, 63, **107**
    Company Beef Ragout, 28
    Green Pea Salad, 149
    Lazy Man's Beef Stew, 30
    Mixed Vegetable Casserole, 135
    Mixed Vegetables Italienne,
        136–37
    Paella Valenciana, 75, **109**
    24-Hour Layered Salad, 146, **215**
    Vegetable Cobbler, 136
Pecans
    Broiler Cake, 195
    Double–Chocolate Chip Pecan
        Cookies, **223**, 309
    Pecan Pie, 263

Pumpkin Shell Dessert, 287
    Strawberry Nut Salad, 161
    Tiny Pecan Pies, 264
Peppers. *See* Bell peppers; Chile
    peppers
Pies, dessert
    Apples and Cream Pie, 254
    Banana Split Pie, 271
    Blueberry-Yogurt Pie, 256
    Butterscotch Chiffon Pie, 256–57
    Cheesecake Pie, 257
    Cherry Breeze, 258
    Chocolate Angel Pie, 259
    Classic Apple Pie, 253
    Coconut Pie, 258
    Cottage Cheese Pie, 259
    Cranberry Parfait Pie, 260
    Crustless Coconut Pie, 255
    Custard Pie, 260
    Frozen Lemon Pie, 262
    Glorious Pineapple Pie, 265
    Impossible Pumpkin Pie, 267
    Kentucky Bourbon Pumpkin Pie,
        **226**, 266
    Key Lime Pie, **225**, 263
    Lemon Meringue Pie, 261
    Lemon Sponge Pie, 262
    Mile-High Strawberry Pie, **227**,
        271
    Pastiera Di Grano (Wheat Pie),
        268–69
    Pecan Pie, 263
    Pink Lady Pie, 267
    Pumpkin Ice Cream Pie, 266
    Raisin–Sour Cream Pie, 264
    Raspberry Ribbon Pie, 268
    Strawberry Crumb Pie, 270
    Strawberry Parfait Pie, 270
    Swedish Apple Pie, 254
    Tiny Pecan Pies, 264
    Wild Blueberry Pie, 255
Pies, meat or poultry
    Arcadian Shepherd's Pie, 22–23,
        **103**
    Beefsteak Pie, 4–5
    Chicken Pie with Biscuit Topping,
        64
    Chicken Pie with Crust, 63, **107**
    French Pork Pie (Tourtière), 44
    Ham Pancake Pie, 40
    Nutty Chicken Pie, 65
    Pastitsio (Greek Macaroni Pie), 25
    Spaghetti Pie, 24
    Mouthwatering Tamale Pie, 18

Pies, vegetable
    Mushroom Quiche, 87
    Onion Pie, 128–29
    Quiche Lorraine, 86–87
    Savory Onion Kuchen, 129
    Spinach Quiche, 87
Pineapple
    Banana Split Pie, 271
    Beef or Pork Chow Mein, 16
    Blueberry-Pineapple Loaf, 169
    Blueberry Salad, 158
    Broiler Cake, 195
    Cabbage Slaw, 155
    Christmas Fruit Salad, 158
    Cowboy Bob Beans, 48
    Cranberry Salad, 157
    5-Cup Salad, 160
    Fruit Torte, 202
    Glorious Pineapple Pie, 265
    Pineapple Cookies, 246
    Pineapple Delight, 283
    Pineapple Nut Cake, 207
    Pineapple-Raisin Tea Ring, 173
    Pineapple Upside-Down Cake, 208
    Pineapple Upside-Down Ham
        Loaf, 39
    Pork Chop Roast with Honeyed
        Sweet Potatoes, 46
    Strawberry Nut Salad, 161
    Sweet and Sour Sauce, 14, **101**
    Three-Step Sweet and Sour Pork
        for 24, 296
    Upside-Down Gingerbread, 232
Poppy seeds
    Poppy Seed Cake, 208–9
Pork. *See also* Bacon; Ham
    Babootie, 23
    Beef or Pork Chow Mein, 16
    Cajun Pork Meatloaf, 43
    Cassoulet, 51
    Never-fail Chicken Delicious,
        72–73
    Cowboy Bob Beans, 48
    French Pork Pie (Tourtière), 44
    Guisado de Pollo, 72
    Ham Loaf with Cranberry Sauce,
        42
    Italian Delight, 15
    Larry's Spaghetti and Meatballs,
        298–99
    Main Dish Potato Salad, 152
    Paella Valenciana, 75, **109**
    Pineapple Upside-Down Ham
        Loaf, 39

Pork Chop Roast with Honeyed
    Sweet Potatoes, 46
Pork Tenderloin with Granny
    Smith Apples, 45
Roast "Lion," 2
Sausage and Rice Casserole, 41
Sausage Cake, 171
Sausage Chowder, 143
Sausages Cooked in White Wine,
    47
South Texas Pork Shoulder, 297
Southwestern Chicken Stew, 295
Sweet Ham and Pork Loaf, 41
Teriyaki Pork Loin, 46–47
Three-Step Sweet and Sour Pork
    for 24, 296
Turkey Dressing, 79
Wagon-Wheel Sausage-Bean
    Casserole, 48
Potatoes
    Arcadian Shepherd's Pie, 22–23,
        **103**
    Baked Potatoes Élégant, 130
    Never-fail Chicken Delicious,
        72–73
    Chicken Potato Casserole, 70
    Company Beef Ragout, 28
    Corn Chowder, 290
    Danish Potato Salad, 154, **217**
    Golden Potato Salad, 151
    Ham and Eggs Brunch Casserole,
        84–85
    Ham Pancake Pie, 40
    Hot German Potato Salad, 153
    Hot Potato Salad, 152
    Lazy Man's Beef Stew, 30
    Main Dish Potato Salad, 152
    Mixed Vegetables Italienne,
        136–37
    Old-Fashioned Boiled Dinner, 3
    Pork Chop Roast with Honeyed
        Sweet Potatoes, 46
    Potato Chip Cookies, 247
    Potato Doughnuts, 166
    Quick Hamburger and Potato
        Casserole, 20–21
    Red Flannel Hash, 3
    Refrigerator Rolls, 307
    Roasted Herbed Vegetables, 137
    Shipwreck, 292–93
    Soft Clouds, 131
    Southwestern Chicken Stew,
        295
Poultry. *See* Chicken; Turkey

Puddings, dessert
    Aunt Vi's Grape-Nuts Custard,
        281
    Cranberry Goodin'-Puddin', 277
    Indian Pudding, 281
    Judge Peter's Pudding, 283
    Pineapple Delight, 283
    Pioneer Bread Pudding, 276
    Steamed Chocolate Pudding,
        276–77
    Steamed Cranberry Pudding, 278
    Vacation Pudding, 288
Puddings, savory
    Carrots Excelsior, 124
    Cheese Strata, 301
    Chicken and Corn Pudding, 70
    Chicken Soufflé, 69
    Corn Flan, 88
    Ham and Cheese Almost Soufflé,
        36
    Mushroom Business, 85
    Salmon Pudding, 92
Pumpkin
    Impossible Pumpkin Pie, 267
    Patty's Pumpkin Muffins, 168
    Pumpkin Cake, 210
    Pumpkin Ice Cream Pie, 266
    Kentucky Bourbon Pumpkin Pie,
        **226**, 266
    Pumpkin Shell Dessert, 287

Quiche
    Mushroom Quiche, 87
    Quiche Lorraine, 86–87
    Spinach Quiche, 87

Raisins
    Astoria Salad, 157, **218**
    Cabbage Slaw, 155
    Indian Pudding, 281
    Julekage (Scandinavian Christmas
        Bread), 174
    Louisiana Beef Stew, 31
    Patty's Pumpkin Muffins, 168
    Pineapple-Raisin Tea Ring, 173
    Pioneer Bread Pudding, 276
    Pumpkin Shell Dessert, 287
    Raisin–Sour Cream Pie, 264
    Saucy Bars, 249
    Sausage Cake, 171
    Scripture Cake, 212
    Sour Cream Cookies, 248

Special Applesauce Cake, 192
Walnut-Raisin Coffee Cake, 181
Raspberries
 Pink Lady Pie, 267
 Raspberry Ribbon Pie, 268
Relish
 Quick Beet Relish, 293
Rhubarb
 Rhubarb Coffee Cake, 179
Rice
 Autumn Leaves, **116**, 133
 Black Beans and Rice, 119
 Chicken Rice Casserole, 66–67
 Fabulous Flounder Fillets, 94
 Ham and Rice Dinner, 36–37
 John Russell's Mushroom-Rice
  Casserole, 122
 Kedgeree, 90–91, **111**
 Lamb-Rice Casserole, 49
 Layered Chicken, 58–59
 Lemon-Spinach Rice, 139
 One-Dish Ground Beef, 21
 Paella Valenciana, 75, **109**
 Sausage and Rice Casserole, 41
 Shipwreck, 292–93
 Shrimp and Rice Casserole, 95
 Spanish Rice, 140
 Spanish Rice II, 140
Ricotta cheese
 Classic Lasagna Plus 2, 19
 Eggplant Italiano, 127
 Manicotti with Creamed Chicken
  and Almonds, 56
 Pastiera Di Grano (Wheat Pie),
  268–69
Rolls and biscuits
 Baking Powder Biscuits, 64
 Cinnamon Rolls, 186–87
 Feather-Light Dinner Rolls,
  184
 Old-Fashioned Biscuits, **228**,
  291
 Orange Bow Knots, 188, **221**
 Raised Rolls, 189
 Refrigerator Rolls, 187, 307
 Squash Biscuits, 189

Salads, fruit
 Astoria Salad, 157, **218**
 Blueberry Salad, 158
 Christmas Fruit Salad, 158
 Cranberry Salad, 157
 5-Cup Salad, 160

Foam Over the Sea, 159
Manchu Garden Salad for 50,
 304–5
Spicy Peach Salad, 160
Strawberry Nut Salad, 161
Salads, main dish
 Main Dish Potato Salad, 152
 Mixed Salad, 148
 The More or Less Tuna and
  Macaroni Salad, 306
 Salad Excelsior, 150, **216**
 Super Salad Sandwich, 149
 Turkey Salad for 50, 304
Salads, vegetable
 Asian Wilted Greens Salad,
  147
 Bean Salad, 143
 Cabbage Slaw, 155
 Cole Slaw for 24, 307
 Copper Pennies, 144–45
 Danish Potato Salad, 154, **217**
 Everlasting Cole Slaw, 154
 Golden Potato Salad, 151
 Greek Cabbage Salad, 145
 Green Pea Salad, 149
 Hot German Potato Salad, 153
 Hot Potato Salad, 152
 Jellied Vegetable Salad, 161
 Manchu Garden Salad for 50,
  304–5
 Marinated Vegetable Salad, 147
 Molded Beet Salad, 144, **214**
 Sauerkraut Salad, 148
 Spaghetti Salad, 153
 Spinach Salad, 150–51
 3 Weeks Cole Slaw, 156
 Turkish Eggplant Salad, 146
 24-Hour Layered Salad, 146,
  **215**
Salmon
 Salmon Mousse with Cucumber
  Sauce, 99
 Salmon Pudding, 92
 Sesame Scallops and Salmon with
  Cucumber, 98
Sandwiches
 Sloppy Joes, 299
 Super Salad Sandwich, 149
Sauces
 Barbecue Sauce, 8
 Besciamella (Cream) Sauce, 27
 Brown Sauce, 13
 Cheese Sauce, 97
 Cranberry Sauce, 42

Cream Gravy, 13
Cucumber Sauce, 99
Hard Sauce, 277
Lemon Nutmeg Sauce, 201
Mushroom Sauce, 14
Mustard Sauce, 7
Orange Sauce, 229
Sour Cream Sauce, 13
Sterling Sauce, 277
Sweet and Sour Sauce, 14, **101**
Sauerkraut
 Sauerkraut Salad, 148
 Sauerkraut Surprise Cake, 206
Sausages
 Cassoulet, 51
 Never-fail Chicken Delicious,
  72–73
 Guisado de Pollo, 72
 Italian Delight, 15
 Paella Valenciana, 75, **109**
 Sausage and Rice Casserole, 41
 Sausage Cake, 171
 Sausage Chowder, 143
 Sausages Cooked in White Wine,
  47
 Southwestern Chicken Stew,
  295
 Turkey Dressing, 79
 Wagon-Wheel Sausage-Bean
  Casserole, 48
Scallops
 Sesame Scallops and Salmon with
  Cucumber, 98
Seafood. See Fish; Shellfish
Shellfish
 Clam Casserole, 88
 Crab and Corn Bake, 89
 Deviled Eggs, Shrimp, and
  Mushrooms in Cheese Sauce,
  96–97
 Flounder Crowns with Florentine
  Stuffing, 92–93, **112**
 Gourmet Shrimp, 95
 Paella Valenciana, 75, **109**
 Salad Excelsior, 150, **216**
 Scalloped Clams, 89
 Sesame Scallops and Salmon with
  Cucumber, 98
 Shrimp and Blue Cheese
  Casserole, 97
 Shrimp and Rice Casserole,
  95
 Spicy Shrimp with Mango-Fennel
  Salsa, 96

Shrimp
    Deviled Eggs, Shrimp, and
        Mushrooms in Cheese Sauce,
        96–97
    Flounder Crowns with Florentine
        Stuffing, 92–93, **112**
    Gourmet Shrimp, 95
    Paella Valenciana, 75, **109**
    Salad Excelsior, 150, **216**
    Shrimp and Blue Cheese
        Casserole, 97
    Shrimp and Rice Casserole, 95
    Spicy Shrimp with Mango-Fennel
        Salsa, 96
Side dishes. *See also* Salads, fruit;
    Salads, vegetable
    Autumn Leaves, **116**, 133
    Baked Apple and Carrot Casserole,
        118
    Baked Beans, **113**, 118
    Baked Beans for 25, 300–301
    Baked Onions, 302
    Baked Potatoes Élégant, 130
    Black Beans and Rice, 119
    Broccoli and Cheese Casserole,
        123
    Broccoli Casserole, 122
    Carrot Casserole, **115**, 124
    Carrots Excelsior, 124
    Corn-Zucchini Bake, 126
    Eggplant Casserole, 125
    Eggplant Italiano, 127
    Far East Celery, 125
    Grace Manney's Baked Beans, 119
    Harvard Beets, 120
    Italian Zucchini Casserole, 139
    John Russell's Mushroom-Rice
        Casserole, 122
    Lemon-Spinach Rice, 139
    Macaroni and Cheese for 20-25,
        302
    Mixed Vegetable Casserole, 135
    Mixed Vegetables Italienne,
        136–37
    Onion Pie, 128–29
    Orangey Beets, 121
    Parsley-Lemon Stuffing, 79
    Pennsylvania Dutch Green Beans,
        **114**, 121
    Roasted Herbed Vegetables, 137
    Savory Onion Kuchen, 129
    Scalloped Sweet Spanish Onions,
        128
    7-Minute Zucchini, 138

Soft Clouds, 131
Spanish Rice, 140
Spanish Rice II, 140
Special Stuffing, 78
Spinach Rockefeller, 130–31
Spinach Squares, 132
Squash and Hominy Dish, 134
Stewed Green Beans, 120
Stuffed Broccoli, 123
Summer Delight, 132–33
T.L.C. Vegetable Casserole, 138
Tomato-Cheese Crunch, 135
Tomato-Corn Rarebit, 134
Turkey Dressing, 79
Vegetable Cobbler, 136
Slaws
    Cabbage Slaw, 155
    Cole Slaw for 24, 307
    Everlasting Cole Slaw, 154
    3 Weeks Cole Slaw, 156
Soups. *See also* Stews
    Corn Chowder, 290
    French Onion Soup, 142, **213**
    Gazpacho, 290–91
    Sausage Chowder, 143
    Thick Spiced Lentil Soup, 142
Southwestern-style dishes
    Chicken Enchiladas, 71
    Chili con Carne, 33
    Chili con Carne for 25-30 People,
        300
    Cowboy Bob Beans, 48
    Guisado de Pollo, 72
    South Texas Pork Shoulder, 297
    Southwestern Chicken Stew, 295
    Mouthwatering Tamale Pie, 18
    Wagon-Wheel Sausage-Bean
        Casserole, 48
Spaghetti
    Chicken Spaghetti Dinner, 66
    Larry's Spaghetti and Meatballs,
        298–99
    Spaghetti Carbonara, 86
    Spaghetti Pie, 24
    Spaghetti Salad, 153
Spanish-style dishes
    Paella Valenciana, 75, **109**
    Spanish Rice, 140
    Spanish Rice II, 140
Spinach
    Asian Wilted Greens Salad, 147
    Cannelloni, 26–27, **104**
    Deviled Egg and Spinach
        Casserole, 84

Flounder Crowns with Florentine
    Stuffing, 92–93, **112**
Lemon-Spinach Rice, 139
Salad Excelsior, 150, **216**
Snowtime Beef Casserole, 17, **102**
Spinach Quiche, 87
Spinach Rockefeller, 130–31
Spinach Salad, 150–51
Spinach Squares, 132
Turkey Florentine, 78
Squash
    Autumn Leaves, **116**, 133
    Classic Lasagna Plus 2, 19
    Corn-Zucchini Bake, 126
    Impossible Pumpkin Pie, 267
    Italian Zucchini Casserole, 139
    Mixed Vegetables Italienne,
        136–37
    Patty's Pumpkin Muffins, 168
    Pumpkin Cake, 210
    Pumpkin Ice Cream Pie, 266
    Pumpkin Pie, **226**, 266
    Pumpkin Shell Dessert, 287
    7-Minute Zucchini, 138
    Southwestern Chicken Stew, 295
    Squash and Hominy Dish, 134
    Squash Biscuits, 189
    Summer Delight, 132–33
    Zucchini Bread, 172
Stews
    Beef Chop Suey, 30–31
    Boeuf Bourguignonne, 29
    Boeuf Flamande, 32
    Chili con Carne, 33
    Chili con Carne for 25-30 People,
        300
    Company Beef Ragout, 28
    Coq au Vin, 74
    Guisado de Pollo, 72
    Lamb Poulette, 54
    Lazy Man's Beef Stew, 30
    Louisiana Beef Stew, 31
    Rosemary Lamb Stew, 53
    Southwestern Chicken Stew, 295
    Swedish Lamb and Lentil Stew, 53
Strawberries
    Banana Split Pie, 271
    Frosted Strawberry Squares, 284
    Mile-High Strawberry Pie, **227**, 271
    Strawberry Cheesecake, 280
    Strawberry Crumb Pie, 270
    Strawberry Mousse, 287
    Strawberry Nut Salad, 161
    Strawberry Parfait Pie, 270

Stuffings
  Parsley-Lemon Stuffing, 79
  Special Stuffing, 78
  Turkey Dressing, 79
Sweet potatoes
  Ham Pancake Pie, 40
  Pork Chop Roast with Honeyed
    Sweet Potatoes, 46
Swiss cheese
  Corn-Zucchini Bake, 126
  Fabulous Flounder Fillets, 94
  French Onion Soup, 142, **213**
  Manicotti with Creamed Chicken
    and Almonds, 56
  Mushroom Quiche, 87
  Quiche Lorraine, 86–87
  Scalloped Sweet Spanish Onions,
    128
  Spinach Quiche, 87

Tomatoes and tomato sauce
  Autumn Leaves, **116**, 133
  Babootie, 23
  Barbecue Sauce, 8
  Brunch Eggs, 83
  Cannelloni, 26–27, **104**
  Chicken Spaghetti Dinner, 66
  Chili con Carne, 33
  Chili con Carne for 25-30 People,
    300
  Classic Lasagna Plus 2, 19
  Easy Chicken Cacciatore, 74
  Easy Eggs and Tomato Benedict, 81
  Eggplant Italiano, 127
  Fabulous Flounder Fillets, 94
  Gazpacho, 290–91
  Italian Delight, 15
  Italian Turkey Casserole, 76–77
  Larry's Spaghetti and Meatballs,
    298–99
  Magnificent Meatballs, 11
  Mediterranean Lamb and
    Eggplant Bake, 52
  Mixed Salad, 148
  Mixed Vegetables Italienne,
    136–37
  Salad Excelsior, 150, **216**
  Sloppy Joes, 299
  Spanish Rice II, 140
  Spicy Shrimp with Mango-Fennel
    Salsa, 96
  Stewed Green Beans, 120
  Mouthwatering Tamale Pie, 18

T.L.C. Vegetable Casserole, 138
Tomato-Cheese Crunch, 135
Tomato-Corn Rarebit, 134
Tuna
  Crispy Tuna Balls with Spicy
    Cheddar Dip, 100
  Mixed Salad, 148
  The More or Less Tuna and
    Macaroni Salad, 306
  Super Salad Sandwich, 149
Turkey
  Italian Turkey Casserole, 76–77
  stuffings for, 78–79
  Turkey Curry, 76
  Turkey Florentine, 78
  Turkey Salad for 50, 304
  Turkey Terrapin, 77
Turnips
  Old-Fashioned Boiled Dinner, 3
  Red Flannel Hash, 3
  Roasted Herbed Vegetables, 137

Veal
  Classic Meatballs, 12, **101**
  Main Dish Potato Salad, 152
Vegetables. *See also* specific vegetables
  Asian-Style Chicken, 58
  Beef or Pork Chow Mein, 16
  Mixed Vegetable Casserole, 135
  Mixed Vegetables Italienne,
    136–37
  Roasted Herbed Vegetables, 137
  T.L.C. Vegetable Casserole, 138
  Vegetable Cobbler, 136
Vegetable salads
  Asian Wilted Greens Salad, 147
  Bean Salad, 143
  Cabbage Slaw, 155
  Cole Slaw for 24, 307
  Copper Pennies, 144–45
  Danish Potato Salad, 154, **217**
  Everlasting Cole Slaw, 154
  Golden Potato Salad, 151
  Greek Cabbage Salad, 145
  Green Pea Salad, 149
  Hot German Potato Salad, 153
  Hot Potato Salad, 152
  Jellied Vegetable Salad, 161
  Manchu Garden Salad for 50,
    304–5
  Marinated Vegetable Salad, 147
  Molded Beet Salad, 144, **214**
  Sauerkraut Salad, 148

Spaghetti Salad, 153
Spinach Salad, 150–51
3 Weeks Cole Slaw, 156
Turkish Eggplant Salad, 146
24-Hour Layered Salad, 146, **215**

Walnuts
  Apples and Cream Pie, 254
  Astoria Salad, 157, **218**
  Blueberry Salad, 158
  Chicken Rice Casserole, 66–67
  Chocolate Layer Bars, **223**, 239
  Cranberry Goodin'-Puddin', 277
  Date Balls, 250
  Date Nut Bread, 171
  Forgotten Cookies, 243
  Judge Peter's Pudding, 283
  Oatmeal-Cranberry Bar Cookies,
    241
  Pineapple Nut Cake, 207
  Poppy Seed Cake, 208–9
  Sausage Cake, 171
  Sour Cream Coffee Cake, 178–79
  Special Applesauce Cake, 192
  Stuffed Broccoli, 123
  Vacation Pudding, 288
  Walnut Cake, 233
  Walnut-Raisin Coffee Cake, 181
Water chestnuts
  Asian-Style Beef Strips, 4
  Asian-Style Chicken, 58
  Far East Celery, 125
  Manchu Garden Salad for 50,
    304–5
  Spinach Salad, 150–51

Yogurt
  Blueberry-Yogurt Pie, 256
  Yogurt Cake Dessert, 230–31

Zucchini
  Classic Lasagna Plus 2, 19
  Corn-Zucchini Bake, 126
  Italian Zucchini Casserole, 139
  Mixed Vegetables Italienne, 136–37
  7-Minute Zucchini, 138
  Southwestern Chicken Stew, 295
  Squash and Hominy Dish, 134
  Zucchini Bread, 172

# Conversion Chart

These equivalents have been slightly rounded to make measuring easier.

### VOLUME MEASUREMENTS

| U.S. | Imperial | Metric |
|---|---|---|
| ¼ tsp | – | 1 ml |
| ½ tsp | – | 2 ml |
| 1 tsp | – | 5 ml |
| 1 Tbsp | – | 15 ml |
| 2 Tbsp (1 oz) | 1 fl oz | 30 ml |
| ¼ cup (2 oz) | 2 fl oz | 60 ml |
| ⅓ cup (3 oz) | 3 fl oz | 80 ml |
| ½ cup (4 oz) | 4 fl oz | 120 ml |
| ⅔ cup (5 oz) | 5 fl oz | 160 ml |
| ¾ cup (6 oz) | 6 fl oz | 180 ml |
| 1 cup (8 oz) | 8 fl oz | 240 ml |

### WEIGHT MEASUREMENTS

| U.S. | Metric |
|---|---|
| 1 oz | 30 g |
| 2 oz | 60 g |
| 4 oz (¼ lb) | 115 g |
| 5 oz (⅓ lb) | 145 g |
| 6 oz | 170 g |
| 7 oz | 200 g |
| 8 oz (½ lb) | 230 g |
| 10 oz | 285 g |
| 12 oz (¾ lb) | 340 g |
| 14 oz | 400 g |
| 16 oz (1 lb) | 455 g |
| 2.2 lb | 1 kg |

### LENGTH MEASUREMENTS

| U.S. | Metric |
|---|---|
| ¼" | 0.6 cm |
| ½" | 1.25 cm |
| 1" | 2.5 cm |
| 2" | 5 cm |
| 4" | 11 cm |
| 6" | 15 cm |
| 8" | 20 cm |
| 10" | 25 cm |
| 12" (1') | 30 cm |

### PAN SIZES

| U.S. | Metric |
|---|---|
| 8" cake pan | 20 × 4 cm sandwich or cake tin |
| 9" cake pan | 23 × 3.5 cm sandwich or cake tin |
| 11" × 7" baking pan | 28 × 18 cm baking tin |
| 13" × 9" baking pan | 32.5 × 23 cm baking tin |
| 15" × 10" baking pan | 38 × 25.5 cm baking tin (Swiss roll tin) |
| 1½ qt baking dish | 1.5 liter baking dish |
| 2 qt baking dish | 2 liter baking dish |
| 2 qt rectangular baking dish | 30 × 19 cm baking dish |
| 9" pie plate | 22 × 4 or 23 × 4 cm pie plate |
| 7" or 8" springform pan | 18 or 20 cm springform or loose-bottom cake tin |
| 9" × 5" loaf pan | 23 × 13 cm or 2 lb narrow loaf tin or pâté tin |

### TEMPERATURES

| Fahrenheit | Centigrade | Gas |
|---|---|---|
| 140° | 60° | – |
| 160° | 70° | – |
| 180° | 80° | – |
| 225° | 110° | – |
| 250° | 120° | ½ |
| 300° | 150° | 2 |
| 325° | 160° | 3 |
| 350° | 180° | 4 |
| 375° | 190° | 5 |
| 400° | 200° | 6 |
| 450° | 230° | 8 |
| 500° | 260° | – |